T0305612

BUSINESS MODEL TRANSFORMATION

A large opportunity exists for Australian organisations to use new and powerful technologies (Artificial intelligence [AI] and Cloud technologies) to transform their businesses to keep pace with or ahead of the leading edge of competitiveness.

This book showcases inspirational Australian case studies in order to inspire Australian (and non-Australian) organisations to undertake the challenge. This book synthesises the key learnings and contrasts those with the conventional wisdom on this topic. The book also defines what AI- and Cloud-based business transformations are and what they can do for businesses. Furthermore, it explains why it is imperative that businesses should address the business opportunities of these technological advancements, without going into the technical details any more than the 'literacy' that is necessary for business leaders. Finally, it also includes international best practice case studies beyond the usual suspects.

This book provides guidance and motivation for business executives, managers and students interested in innovating and transforming their businesses through the use of the two critical new technologies.

Danny Samson (BE Hons, PhD) has been Professor of Management at the University of Melbourne for over three decades, teaching and researching in decision sciences and operations/supply chain management. He has published over a dozen books and 150 research papers. He started his career as a chemical engineer in the petrochemical sector, from which he has strong interests in manufacturing, technology development and innovation management. He has worked extensively in five continents as a board member, adviser to senior executives, executive educator and consultant in a variety of industries including banking and insurance, automotive, oil and gas, building, engineering, and health/hospitals, as well as providing high level advice to governments. His most recent publications have been in the areas of strategic leadership, innovation and entrepreneurship, and implementing strategic change.

Alon Ellis (BE Elec., BSc Comp. Sci) is a Senior Partner in Deloitte's Strategy Consulting business (Monitor Deloitte) and primarily focusses on up-front enterprise strategy design, as organisations look to transform themselves. He began his career in a start-up, focussed on bringing analytical advancements in price optimisation and lifetime value modelling to the insurance industry. He has since transitioned to a variety of other areas of management consulting including innovation and operations, and has worked in transformation and line roles in industry. He has also gained experience across a range of additional industries including banking, telecommunications, logistics and transport, and worked extensively in the US, the UK and Australia.

Stuart Black (BSEE, BA (Economics), MBA) is an Enterprise Fellow at the University of Melbourne. Stuart is also finalising his PhD at the University of Melbourne. Stuart's research interest is in business model disruption and data, with a particular focus on governance and application of the secondary use of data. Prior to returning to academia, Stuart spent 30 years in professional services (Andersen Consulting, A.T. Kearney and Deloitte) and industry, retiring as a Senior Partner of Deloitte Australia. Over that time, Stuart worked with clients across Asia, Australasia, Europe and North America, on strategy, operations and strategic IT issues for clients in industries such as automotive, financial services, oil and gas, and telecommunications.

"AI is hardly a new concept, yet the widespread application thereof is still very limited – especially in the redesign of business models and the reconfiguration of value propositions. It is not the knowledge that is holding us back – it is the leadership resolve to do something meaningful. This book is both a wakeup call and a guide on how to apply this known technology in a meaningful way. It is not something to be afraid of, it is the value language of today".

Gerhard Vorster, *Board Member, Managing Director of Quidni Advisory and Patron Emeritus of Good Design Australia*

"Cloud and Artificial Intelligence are the two major disruptive technology forces of today. Samson, Ellis and Black avoid the temptation of a simple model and instead have sought insight from a wide range of well written case studies. Pleasingly, for an Australian audience, many of these are home-grown! Finding some surprises and much evidence for the need to innovate, everyone from board members through to line managers has much to gain by learning through the experiences of organisations large and small that have already taken the leap".

Rob Hillard, *Deloitte Asia Pacific Consulting Leader and Chairman, Australian Information Industry Association*

"This book offers insights on the best practices of business transformations through new technologies. The book draws on the authors' wealth of experience and makes a compelling case for firms to implement Cloud-based and AI solutions to gain a competitive edge. It would be a useful guide for anyone interested in integrating AI or related technologies in business to improve processes".

Eric Knight, *Executive Dean and Professor of Strategic Management, Macquarie University, Australia*

"The change in perspective needed for companies to transform with AI or Cloud technologies is something challenging, but highly rewarding. I find that this book provides a good understanding of how this could be done in practice, by combining new insights and explanations with relevant real-life cases. That would help readers to have a better understanding of how to transform companies to a new business landscape".

Joakim Wincent, *Professor of Entrepreneurship, Management and Organization at Hanken School of Economics, Finland and at the University of St Gallen, Switzerland*

"This book contributes to a much-needed conversation. I agree with one part of the book which talks about the gap between business and technology competency in firms. This gap is especially evident in many business schools where teaching typically concerns traditional disciplines, ignoring the crucial link between business and modern technology. This book should therefore be studied by contemporary business students so that they learn to act in a digitalised business world".

Thommie Burström, *Assistant Professor, Entrepreneurship Institution, Hanken School of Economics, Helsinki / Finland*

BUSINESS MODEL TRANSFORMATION

The AI & Cloud Technology Revolution

Danny Samson, Alon Ellis and Stuart Black

Routledge
Taylor & Francis Group

LONDON AND NEW YORK

Cover image: © Getty Images | shulz

First published 2023
by Routledge
4 Park Square, Milton Park, Abingdon, Oxon OX14 4RN

and by Routledge
605 Third Avenue, New York, NY 10158

Routledge is an imprint of the Taylor & Francis Group, an informa business

British Library Cataloguing-in-Publication Data
A catalogue record for this book is available from the British Library

Library of Congress Cataloging-in-Publication Data
Names: Samson, Danny, author. | Ellis, Alon, author. |
Black, Stuart (Business consultant), author.
Title: Business model transformation: the AI & Cloud technology revolution/
Danny Samson, Alon Ellis and Stuart Black.
Description: Abingdon, Oxon; New York, NY: Routledge, 2023. |
Includes bibliographical references and index. |
Identifiers: LCCN 2022015248 | ISBN 9781032186412 (hardback) |
ISBN 9781032186405 (paperback) | ISBN 9781003255529 (ebook)
Subjects: LCSH: Information technology–Management. |
Strategic planning–Australia. | Organizational change–Australia.
Classification: LCC HD30.2 .S259 2023 |
DDC 658.4/038–dc23/eng/20220405
LC record available at https://lccn.loc.gov/2022015248

ISBN: 9781032186412 (hbk)
ISBN: 9781032186405 (pbk)
ISBN: 9781003255529 (ebk)

DOI: 10.4324/9781003255529

Typeset in Bembo
by Newgen Publishing UK

CONTENTS

FIGURES

TABLES

PREFACE

We wrote this book to highlight the large opportunity that exists for Australian organisations to use new and powerful technologies, to transform their businesses to keep pace with or ahead of the leading edge of competitiveness. Of course, the other side of that coin is the threat of what will likely occur to laggards who are doing little or nothing about technology-enabled transformations when their competitors are.

We are not the first to reflect on this challenge, either locally or globally. We believe that a certain 'conventional wisdom' has developed about how Australian organisations should respond to the challenge. Whilst we agree with much of this conventional wisdom, we want to challenge this across five specific elements, as shown in Figure 0.1. We will expand on this concept throughout this book.

We believe the time to act on this change in perspective is now. In much of the rest of the developed world, such transformations are moving apace, and since much of competition is global these days, local laggards have only a limited time until their lack of *global* competitiveness is found out. To illustrate international developments, we have compiled case studies of well-known incumbent businesses that have seized the opportunity to remake themselves, including their business model, customer offerings and cost structures, enabled by these technologies: including Rolls Royce, Samsung, Netflix, Bank of America and Asia's DBS bank.

We have interviewed executives and compiled 14 Australian case studies of companies that have proactively transformed on the back of AI and/or Cloud technologies. These case studies come from highly varying sized organisations, across many sectors and industries, and are each quite unique in terms of the context and opportunity set that was involved. Some focussed on new products/services, others on process transformation, and yet others on whole of business model renewal.

These case studies were selected because they demonstrate what was and hence what can be achieved, along with the positive outcomes for customers, presenting

	Conventional Wisdom	Our View
Pathway to Transform	Start with proof points to raise confidence	Anchor in the ambition of the transformation, then determine tech
Need for Scale	Only large organisations have sufficient resources	All organisations can start using appropriate technologies
Tech Debt Constraints	Significant inhibitor of change	Yes, but treat as a issue to work through, not an inhibitor
Boardroom Skills	'Digital NEDs' essential	Whilst beneficial, exploration and future business model skills more important
Actions vs Ideas	Focus on execution _or_ strategy	Seek a balance of actions and ideas as you work towards a 'north star'

FIGURE 0.1 Areas where our research differed from the conventional wisdom

primarily through a combination of improvements in cost, quality/service, delivery, availability, innovation and flexibility/agility. These operational and market-oriented improvements translate into an improved bottom-line outcome for stakeholders.

In principle, we acknowledge in Chapter 1 that there is nothing new about incorporating new technologies to achieve radical innovation, which is what AI and Cloud can bring, as indeed these are the key technologies at the heart of the _fourth_ industrial revolution, not the first! It is worth recalling what happened to organisations that did not embrace previous waves of new technology, with relatively recent examples being Kodak and Blockbuster, who were run over by new technology adopters with more attractive consumer offerings and superior cost structures.

Once boards of directors and executives, even those in local oligopolies, can clearly see the compelling motivational reasons for acting on AI- and/or Cloud-enabled business transformation, critical next questions are how much to do, what to do, and how to do it. In terms of how much, we have deliberately used the term 'transformation' because the opportunity/threat does not warrant incremental efforts and only minor shifts, but rather presents itself for significant and radical innovations.

For example, Bank of America radically altered its service offerings, its cost structures, its workforce skill sets and how it transacts business with tens of millions of customers. Rolls Royce fully transformed from selling machinery (jet engines) to servitised 'power by the hour' using Cloud and AI to offer a radically different and indeed extended service that transformed both its revenue and cost structures, with AI and Cloud being the underlying engine of that growth. Our local case studies, mostly Australian businesses but also including two public sector and one not-for-profit, also transformed their business models through AI- and/or Cloud-enabled innovations.

We identified a number of 'antecedent capability' factors that were generally common to those organisations that successfully transformed, that provided insights and indeed should be used to challenge board directors and executives about their 'transformation readiness'. From these, leaders can assess which capabilities they should be addressing and ramping up as they prepare their transformation strategies.

We note that in our fast-changing world and business environment, technological change is only one of the macro-forces acting on entities, with others being dramatically shifting work and consuming patterns brought on by the COVID-19 pandemic, climate change impacts and geopolitical forces. In such highly dynamic times, it is more than ever the case that standing still in terms of business models and business strategies is actually 'going backwards' in relative terms.

Many Australian businesses, including our case studied organisations have already grasped the nettle and are making effective use of AI and/or Cloud to significantly transform. These businesses recognise that such new technologies are not just what start-ups (e.g. fintechs) do, but that there is an imperative for incumbents to progress them in innovative ways. Further, we observe that for those organisations that have not yet started or done much technology-enabled transformation, it is never too late to start – until it actually and literally is too late, and one experiences a Kodak moment of the worst kind!

We note in our innovation chapter that Scotiabank in Canada was the last of the major Canadian banks to undertake a Digital/Cloud/AI transformation, yet in recent years has substantially closed what was a significant gap in its offering and processes. That chapter on innovation connects, in concept and practice, the important nexus of transformation, innovation, and the technology enablers that produce the sweet spot that constitutes 'best practice'.

On a positive human and personal note, we observed that for those organisational leaders who have embraced and accomplished AI- and/or Cloud-enabled transformations, there is great satisfaction that comes from such achievements[1]. Providing new services, or reducing wasteful use of resources, or reaching customers in a new way that provides them with new or added elements of utility is a matter of great executive and managerial satisfaction, on top of the business performance parameters!

These executives and their organisations took some well-considered risks in exploring and changing, requiring courage and proactivity, knowing that not everything that they tried was going to work, such that when it does, the satisfaction of achievement is high. The lessons to be learned from those organisations such as SEEK, Kogan, Scope, Services NSW, Canningvale, and our other case studies, are presented to stimulate and guide executives in their forward business journey. We wish to inspire Australian business leaders (current and emerging) to act on the opportunity, and we wish to use positive case studies articulating how local companies have successfully made such a transformation as a means to provide comfort and motivation to other business leaders that it can be done.

Naturally, such a journey is not successful without the support of a wide range of individuals. First, we would like to thank our Australian case study participants for their time and their candid statements about their journeys. In each case, the participants were very positive about our cause, and we thank them for their support.

There are also a number of other individuals involved in the development of the book. We would like to thank: Jack Rejtman for making a couple of critical introductions; Jeremy Smith and Andrew Dick for managing that thankless task of trying to keep us on track; Adnan Rajkotwala for his support in the initial literature review; Aakash Madnani, Daniel Manolios Reichert and Ari Sikavitsas for support during the interview gathering process; Cath Thompson for co-authoring the international best practice chapter; Jo McCallum and Cori Stewart for the UAP and Verton case studies; Rachael Akhidenor and Lillian Myer for copy proofing and editing and finally Nigel Adams, Jeremy Drumm, Giselle Hodgson, and Rob Hillard for reviewing the consolidated manuscript and providing their invaluable perspectives.

Note

1 Danny was a board member 20 years ago of the public insurance company Transport Accident Commission (TAC), in Victoria, that transformed as a matter of the third industrial revolution, from largely paper-based to digitalised, that significantly improved cost, speed and services.

1

INTRODUCTION TO AI/CLOUD-ENABLED BUSINESS TRANSFORMATION

The opportunity

The invention and deployment of new technologies have been providing organisations with competitive advantages, when they are successful, for many hundreds of years, and some would argue for many thousands of years. Early technologies seem very unexciting in today's context, yet the same principles of technology-based advantages have existed for a long time. A very simple early example is the wheelbarrow, that gave its originators, some 2,000 years ago, significant productivity advantages, whether for commercial or military purposes, for efficiently distributing goods with higher productivity rather than simply carrying them. The ancient Egyptians developed paper and writing, levers and pullies, and core sciences including mathematics, geometry, medicines and astronomy, that spurred all sorts of new technologies and products. The ancient Greeks developed and deployed numerous types of technologies including machines with gears, bronze casting, and the use of steam. More recently, the agricultural 'combine harvester' increased farm productivity manyfold, releasing large proportions of workforces to engage in other forms of industrial production. To think of harvesting wheat or similar grain at scale without such mechanisation in a modern economy is nonsensical, because of the advantages that such technologies bring. More recently, low–cost robots, 3D printing and a raft of information and communication technologies (ICT) have led to both evolution and transformative revolution of manufacturing industries, supply chains and their participants.

Similarly in service sectors, that now comprise the bulk of our economy, new technologies related to ICT have bloomed in the past 50 years, and particularly in the past 20. In organisations that process a lot of information at their operating core, Robotic Process Automation (RPA) has developed in recent years as a set of software automations that can act as 'bots to replace human effort in routine

DOI: 10.4324/9781003255529-1

process steps'. *CIO* magazine reports on a bank that deployed 300 bots to handle 1.5 million requests per year, being the equivalent of 200 employees, at 30% of the cost.[1] Such instances are from a business perspective, not unlike the advantages that came from mechanical harvesting in fields that replaced human workforces, or containerisation that improved logistics productivity in transport sectors. Intelligent automation, that can go much further than RPA, has much to contribute to the future of service sectors, through adding cognitive reasoning power to RPA or other processing capabilities, using machine learning and other approaches that bring value creating and competitive advantage.

The rise of the modern business organisation in the past 200 years has led to tremendous breakthroughs in ever advancing technologies that serve markets and consumers, hopefully at a profit. Many of these developments were deployed as products and service innovations. They needed quite sophisticated organisations to resource their scaling up and deployment. Millions of lives have been saved by penicillin, not just because it was invented, but also because it was able to be mass produced and distributed to where it could be effective. The COVID-19 vaccines are a very modern example of significant innovations that aim to solve a global problem.

Innovation brings advantages when inventions are effectively harnessed, find a market and are deployed at scale, and the other side of the coin is that in competitive markets, where there is relative advantage, there is also relative disadvantage. An extreme example was of a world-leading, well-branded photographic equipment company called Kodak. From cameras to photographic paper to chemicals and processing centres, Kodak was a global player in manufacturing and services, yet was run over by its failure to embrace the technological shift to fully digital photography. This, meaning going out of business completely, was indeed transformational for Kodak and all its stakeholders!

The rise of information technologies (and the capabilities they bring)

Prior to 1970, most innovation was considered to be related to new products, and some attention was given to new processes of manufacturing. Examples abound such as the steam engine, the internal combustion petrol engine, electricity, the jet engine, and genius process innovations such as line flow manufacturing and assembly and standardised shipping containers: these famous examples all are characterised by their high degree of tangibility; they are physical products or the means of producing them.

We note that as factories and distribution systems became ever more efficient, during the past 200 years, consumers have been increasingly able to exert demand for pure services, being intangible consumption items. Major growing service industries include tourism, health and education, yet there are now a myriad of services available and new ones gaining popularity all the time, such as in the past decades, personal coaches for executives, personal trainers, information and media services, online entertainment and gaming, and a host of pure services from accounting to home food delivery, cleaning and gardening, that households and business now outsource. Many of these services are partly or substantially enabled by information systems. Business outsourcing has grown a great deal this century, also enabled by information systems.

Computing and information systems that became useful on a broad scale around 50 years ago have helped to facilitate such services growth. A bank CEO once told us that if not for computers we would need every person in the workforce, just to process the volume of transactions that underpins our exchange economy. Indeed, over the past 30 years, much of the gain in productivity in OECD economies, that is occurring very much now in developing economies, is the result of information-systems-based improvements within and between organisations. The early breakthroughs were of fast calculation at scale, efficient storage and retrieval of data, and then from 1980, computers and information systems (IS) became themselves transformed into ICT systems, through electronic networking and then the internet. We are now in the age where certain decisions, such as in particular types of bank lending and insurance underwriting, can be more effectively made by computers (software algorithms) than humans. Furthermore, many of the applications that make such decisions have developed over time, with the applications continuing on well past the time that their original programmers retired.

With the platform technologies that are rapidly developing, new services that made effective use of computing power developed fast. Outsourcing became a big 'thing' and it can be argued that just as containerisation in shipping facilitated global product outsourcing and trade growth, the internet led to global services outsourcing. Australian banks, telcos and indeed anyone were able to move their back office to anywhere in the world and achieve significantly lower costs (and sometimes better service). Architects and engineers could specify and design structures in Australia, then get the necessary detailed work done overnight on the other side of the globe at low cost. Many services providers found that if they did not engage in such activities, they were at significant relative disadvantage. Global outsourcing became efficient and as widespread as global product sourcing, thanks to ICT capabilities.

Business model innovation

Technologies and business/market forces that seek ever more advantage move fast and are highly dynamic. Whereas innovation was mostly about products a century ago, and significantly about services more recently, to this we must now add business models themselves. By business model, we mean the very structure of a business and how it survives and prospers, including its assets, processes and products/services, its competitive positioning, and its means for attracting customers, generating revenues and incurring costs, its distribution channels, as well as its relationships with suppliers and ecosystem partners. In the international best practice chapter of this book, we describe how Rolls Royce 'servitised' its jet engine business, moving from selling engines and hardware to selling and servicing/maintaining engine propulsion 'by the hour'. Similarly, we trace Netflix's evolution, or perhaps more correctly revolution, from DVD distribution (using 'snail mail') to Cloud-enabled streaming service and content producer. These and other transformations could not have happened effectively without modern technologies, especially AI and Cloud. They give powerful evidence, as do our other international case studies (see Chapter 4), of DBS Bank, Samsung and Bank of America of how Cloud and AI can enable highly valuable transformations.

Many highly innovative new business models have been created this century, notably Amazon, Uber, Airbnb, Facebook, Google, and a host of others. It is instructive to briefly examine what they did that was innovative, and what was kept the same as in conventional offerings.

1. Amazon began selling books online, needing to draw on and enabled by the internet, electronic payment systems and postal physical distribution systems. It could profit from a superior cost structure, offer a wider range and convenient delivery and extend its services. For example, it provided book reviews and data-informed customised purchasing recommendations, such that traditional companies such as Borders were left in its dust. What worked for books at Amazon, quite quickly moved and extended to just about everything else! Further new businesses and business models were added, including third-party selling, Cloud services and many other offerings. Interestingly, what did not change with Amazon book sales was the actual book (until Kindle was developed)! Same 'book' product, different ways of getting it, additional services that go with it, and clearly the market has spoken: just ask Borders ex-shareholders. Amazon makes extensive use of advanced ICT, especially AI and (its own) Cloud.

2. Uber created a network effect of personal transport offerings, and while Uber and its competitors have grown dramatically, the service is not that different to long existing taxi services, and the use of a vehicle to transport people as a service is certainly over 120 years old. Uber's business model relies on advanced ICT and could not exist without it. Pure ridesharing goes even further: where Uber uses paid drivers, pure ridesharing uses ICT to connect regular drivers of vehicles with those needing a ride in real time, offering obvious cost advantages.

3. Airbnb uses ICT to create a market for casual rental of accommodation, and what is new is the business model of how demand and supply is efficiently connected online, using existing accommodation assets that are indeed not new. It's a pure business model play, now competing with and dwarfing the capacity of the world's largest hotel chains.

4. Apple revolutionised many things, including how consumers accessed music and video content through its online distribution service iTunes and then AppleTV. Others (such as Spotify) have also further innovated here. Music is still music, as are movies, and consumers still want to listen and watch as before.

Blockbuster once employed over 80,000 people renting videos on tapes and is no more.

5.   Dell Direct entered a tough competitive industry and allowed customers, first business then retail consumers, to buy customised PCs and peripherals online, have them assembled-to-order quickly, and delivered with pre-loaded software to their consumers within days. Dell's market entry with this innovative business model gave the industry a significant shake, with entrenched participants such as IBM, Compaq, HP and others restructuring in attempts to respond. What was different was the innovative business model of a customised 'make-to-order then deliver' approach of Dell, and what was not really different was the actual computer and what it could do.

It is interesting that the examples above and many others like them are of new businesses, or in Apple's iTunes case, a new industry for it to come into and dominate. Why didn't Blockbuster, at the height of its powers, invest in renewing its services and business model? Same for Kodak. Is there a 'curse of incumbency', or at least a significant inertia that makes it hard or uneconomical for companies with existing and successful operating models such as Borders, to be highly innovative, or even, once it sees the writing on the wall, to be a fast follower? Are incumbents 'blind' as a result of their real-time success, to potential transformations? This then leads to the question of how many and which of our major operating companies in Australia, which are often significantly profitable and sometimes exist in the cocoon of cosy oligopolies, are ripe to be knocked over by those which have superior business models. This question is especially pertinent at a time of Industry 4.0 inception, where powerful technologies such as AI and Cloud bring opportunities for those who can effectively deploy them. Such threats can come from international companies who have already moved down the path of such advanced technologies, or in the present world where capital is cheap, from start-ups.

The potential threat for Australian incumbent companies that do not invest, or that underinvest in technologies that keep them at the cutting edge of cost, quality, service and delivery performance are at least threefold:

1.   Start-ups will pick off their profitable segments, niches and service lines, leaving them with 'the rest'. Start-ups have the opposite of the 'curse of incumbency', and often are risky propositions themselves, but for those that succeed, it's a case of 'incumbent beware!'. Start-ups don't generally have the inertial drag of legacy systems and old-world culture that can dog the incumbents.

2.   New product categories that threaten incumbent's markets, such as Afterpay and ZIP's foray into purchase financing that takes market away from credit card issuers, and Bitcoin that offers an alternative payment system. ZIP and others are further developing these alternatives from retail purchasing to corporate procurement platforms.

3.   International incumbents that have invested in technologies beyond our local businesses, and therefore may have cost/quality/delivery (CQD) advantages,

underpinning better value propositions can enter Australia, with our relatively high disposable incomes, oligopolies and solid profit margins, and even some lazy balance sheets, and either through acquisition or organically, can challenge existing players. For example, what would happen if Walmart chose to aggressively bring its capabilities to Australian retailing? Costco, Amazon and Aldi have done so in relatively recent times, but as yet it can be argued that these have become niche plays, with less than 20% market share. Walmart has invested heavily in new technology, has a global footprint, and presumably at some point will notice the small but profitable niche 'down under' and bring its cost structure and AI and Cloud-based intelligence to our shores, along with its global supply chain power, that dwarfs that of local companies.

While we observe these three categories of threats as very real, we note that they are far from 'sure things' in any category. For example, foreign banks have entered Australia on previous occasions, mostly without success to date, especially when they attempted organic growth.[2] Other large multinationals have entered the Australian market only to exit after being unable to attain the necessary critical mass. Furthermore, we have seen the exit of the major automotive OEMs (Original Equipment Manufacturers) from Australian shores, when those OEMs determined that other regions in the world offered better options for their capital. Yet clearly for Australian incumbents, the best defence against the three categories of attack described above, is to drive CQD (Cost-Quality-Delivery aspects of value creation) hard, striving for international best practice levels of performance, and embracing any new technologies that can transform them towards achieving improved competitiveness. Further beyond pursuing CQD improvements in their existing operations, comes the big prize of innovation in their business models that technologies such as AI and Cloud can bring. Walmart and Amazon are investing significantly in highly automated AI-enabled retail stores, that drive service offerings, food freshness, stock and supply chain efficiency and productivity. It is certainly a challenge that Australian retailers should not ignore, and many similar examples exist in other industries.

Looking back and looking forward at ICT

Through briefly reviewing some elements of the history of ICT and innovation progression as described above, we can observe with the wisdom of hindsight, how innovations were initially in tangible goods, then services, and more recently in the use of ICT to create and enable new business models. From the early days of unsophisticated information networks, both public and proprietary, innovations have led to E-commerce, E-business, and a range of technology platforms. Cost structures were shattered. For example, the commission fees for buying a parcel of shares in the 'pre-internet' world was 1.5% for retail consumers, i.e. broker fees were $300 for buying or selling $20,000 of shares. When online straight through processing directly connected buyers and sellers to the market more efficiently and speedily. Transparency increased markedly, and share brokers were disintermediated because the transaction fee was reduced from $300 to $10, i.e. a 97% drop! That was certainly an early case of ICT-enabled radical transformation.

Looking forward, the technological capabilities have continued and, in many ways, accelerated. Moore's Law has guided us to understand the large and continuing increases in processing capacity at lower costs. Huge amounts of data are generated in businesses and economies, and with electronic transactions and increasing uses of sensors of all types gathering data (from video cameras to RFID, Internet of Things and other sensors), opportunities arise about how such data can best be used to create business and consumer value. This is where and how the next set of promising technologies, principally Artificial Intelligence and Cloud computing/processing, are coming to fruition this decade. This begs the question of how business models can best make use of such capacity. From raw data, adding some intelligence can produce useful information, leading to more effective decisions, when it is effectively harnessed. For example, one of our case study businesses in this book, Kogan, has developed a machine learning capability that offers highly customised offers to millions of people in Australia every day, without any physical storefront. Whereas a physical storefront is standardised for every person who walks in, Kogan's sophisticated data analytics and AI provides a unique storefront to each potential customer, based on large amounts of data.

Innovation in business models: how and what?

There are many ways to formulate candidate business model innovations. The Doblin approach has proved useful to many executives when considering innovation opportunities and choosing which aspects of their business model they should transform. It categorises business model innovations as where a business leadership team can change/transform potentially any of:

1. *Profit model*, changing market segment and price point, or moving to a subscription model, charging membership fees, creating a network or switchboard, selling by auction, letting customers set or offer prices, offering some services for free, flexibly pricing, financing, licensing, bundling, disaggregating elements/features, and various risk sharing or allocation mechanisms.
2. *Network innovation*, involving merger/acquisition, open innovation, consolidation, alliances, partnering, supply integration, franchising, coopetition, or other forms of connection and collaboration.
3. *Structural transformation*, including uses of incentives, transforming organisational design, IT integration, outsourcing, centralising or decentralising, standardising, or creating centres of excellence, using knowledge management or competency centres.
4. *Process transformations*, including operating process standardisations, localisation, offshoring or onshoring, flexible production, mass customisation, crowdsourcing, on-demand production, lean systems, co-creation of services

with consumers, intellectual property, logistics changes, and use of predictive analytics.

5. *Product transformation*, including superior product specification, ease of use, safety, feature aggregation, simplification, additional functionality/features, environmental sensitivity/performance, recycling/conservation, design styling, niche focus.

6. *Product system*, including adding complementary offerings, bundling, including services, modular product, platform approaches, and integration of services.

7. *Services*, such as guarantee, free trials, loyalty initiatives, leasing, solution provision, self-service, and ongoing or superior services.

8. *Channel*, including direct-to-consumer, flagship outlet, innovation of store design, pop-ups, third-party marketing/sales/distribution, cross-selling, make-to-order auto-replenishment.

9. *Brand repositioning*, such as co-branding, sub-branding, leverage across categories, certification, private label, showcasing.

10. *Customer partnering*, including customer task simplification, duration, disintermediation, supply chain repositioning, mastery provision, personalisation, network creation.

This set of items above is not an exhaustive list (although it may seem exhausting to the reader), but rather a showcase of many of the main ways in which innovative transformation can be attempted. This begs the question as to how such potential transformations, from relatively minor (but still transformative), as against incremental, to 'heavy transformations' can be enabled by technology choices such as AI and Cloud. Here is perhaps the central point of this book, that the potential for transforming any aspect, as listed above, of a business should be considered first and then connected to the power that can come from technologies. Some transformations will only be possible with the use of technologies. Some do not need advanced technologies at all, and indeed are such that the cost of implementing technologies would exceed the benefits. Therefore, we suggest that the use of technologies such as AI and Cloud should be considered in terms of their value-creating potential for any contemplated transformation.

Further, some innovative transformations will not only be more effective when they are 'tech-enabled' but will also be infeasible or ineffective without the technologies. That infeasibility might be technical or economic, or both. The most important high-level point is that without technology as a potential enabler, the types and sets of transformation options will be more limited than with those technology enablers in place. Further, for some of the specific transformations that executives might be considering, the degree of required tech-enablement can vary from small or even zero, to overwhelmingly large and indeed necessary. For example, repositioning existing offerings to a different market segment, and changing price point and volume may not necessarily need advanced technology, unless it brings cost advantages for example, but on the other hand, going from a mass-produced standard product or service to a mass-customised, highly personalised service may well require Cloud capability, and AI enablement (think Kogan and Netflix). Machine learning might be effective in making personalised recommendations to customers as an enabler of moving to a differentiation position in a financial services sector, or in offering 'fitted' customer suggestions as to specific holiday packages in the tourism sector. Such is less likely in the commodity end of each of those markets. This is where we can observe that 'technology push' enablement capability, needs to be well fitted to the 'value proposition pull' of the proposed transformation in market requirements planning.

What can new technologies do, disrupt, add value to, and what are their limitations?

Industry 4.0 is a term often used to describe the fourth industrial revolution of which AI and Cloud are key elements. In this book we focus on business models that can be transformed when enabled by these new technologies, meaning we focus on incumbent companies rather than start-ups. Building a new business from scratch or close to scratch is, by definition, not truly a transformation. Incumbent companies often have brand equity, customer base and goodwill, significant assets and physical resources, and a workforce. These elements can be either great assets, or else when significant transformation is called for, liabilities dragging against progress. Perhaps this is why so many examples exist where 'creative destruction' is brought to industries by new companies that disrupt the old equilibrium.

For executives working in existing firms being wary of start-ups (e.g. major banks being wary of fintechs), it is of great importance to understand the business implications and opportunities of new technologies, as an input to strategy making and transformation. C-suite executives and those who inform and support their decisions should be able to understand enough about what their technologies and engineers are able to provide, so they can formulate strategies that make the most out of market opportunity and matching technical enablement. If new technology is seen as a completely opaque black box by senior executives, how can they really know its innovative capabilities? We hasten to say that senior decision makers need not know the details, but should be literate, as against illiterate, in having an accurate high-level view of what technologies such as AI and Cloud can, and cannot, do, where they are powerful and in which directions they are developing.

How new technology has created new challenges and opportunities for business model innovation

Technology has continually driven change in customer value propositions, market structures, and consequently, organisations. As each decade has gone by, innovations in computing power, networking, core business systems and digital interfaces, have transformed the way that we all do business. Over the past ten years, this has resulted in the elevation of various technology roles to the C-suite, e.g. Chief Technology Officer, Chief Data Officer, Chief Analytics Officer. This elevation reflects a recognition that the effective use of data, information and related technology is critical to the future success of an organisation.

Despite these recent elevations, the way in which 'the business' interfaces with 'the technology team' is still evolving, and often problematic. The gap between business and technology functions is a recurring theme in many organisations. This book seeks to create some common language and a set of principles for the business to identify and lead the critical innovations for which technology support is required. We aim to provide clarity for how business leaders can drive benefits from technology. While there are many efficiency gains to be had through a range of technology innovations, e.g. automating an existing process, genuine innovation of a business model must come from changes in the way the business operates.

To that end, we believe that business leaders must have a working knowledge of the critical technology building blocks, so that they can practically understand the ways in which technology will disrupt the markets in which they operate. Over the past 20 years, the job of investing in information technology (IT), has primarily been the responsibility of the IT leadership group, whether that technology was needed for delivering 'table stakes' capabilities, or for a genuine competitive advantage. In order to generate material and sustained competitive advantage, we believe business leaders will need to proactively bring forward potential IT-powered innovations, ideally in a co-development process with their IT counterparts. Put in simpler terms, there needs to be a recognition that not only will business strategy inform technology choices (as has always been the case), but also that emerging technology capabilities should create new strategic options and pathways for a business to transform. We have listed a high-level summary of these technology evolutions in Figure 1.1. Looking forward, we suggest that all business leaders should assume that rapid further changes and transformation potential will continue, and perhaps accelerate!

One of the inhibitors of technology innovation and technology investment has been the relatively low success rate and challenging business cases for typical technology-led change over the past 20 years. Countless organisations have

1970s	1980s	1990s	2000s	2010s+
Core systems come into existence	Technology becomes widely accessible	Databased & connectivity gain momentum	The internet era begins	Cloud, AI & the growth of new devices
• Mainframes • Distributed terminals • Core computing	• Office computing • Mini-computers • Word processing • Spreadsheets • Home computing	• Network computing • Email • Relational databases • Client-server applications	• The internet revolution • Increasing consumer engagement • Intranet development • Widespread broadband	• Cloud computing • Big data platforms • Deep learning & AI • Mobiles, tablets & wearables • Social media

FIGURE 1.1 A high-level summary of 50+ years of ICT developments

announced large scale technology transformations, only to find that after several years and $100 million plus budgets, they receive little benefit and face painful feedback from analyst commentators and shareholders. Such history creates a 'I'll believe it when I see it' attitude amongst key stakeholders, which creates headwinds for these initiatives. An alignment between business and technology on what specifically needs to be done differently to innovate the business model is critical to the success of these investments. To deliver this outcome, more business leaders need to provide a business-led view on how technology can help them drive change, together with confidence that they are likely to deliver future vision they have painted for their investors. This requires knowledge of what is possible, together with a practical understanding of why the transformation is likely to be delivered on time, and within budget.

What's different with AI and Cloud technology?

Before the growth of AI and Cloud technology, each organisation would need to install and manage its own software, on its own, self-maintained hardware. Technology vendors designed their own solution stacks, which provided a base level of capability, which was often customised. Those customisations created a competitive advantage and were often perceived to be an asset to the business. AI described a set of algorithms that could be developed and run using specialised software, run on expensive hardware, programmed by even more specialised statisticians and research specialists.

Over the past 15 years, the process of developing and deploying a wide variety of AI models has become simplified through improved software interfaces, automated algorithm development, and a dramatic increase in the number of people who are trained in the relevant model development skills. In parallel, a set of emerging algorithms (which we will explore in detail in a later chapter) have enabled machines to classify, predict or simulate outcomes in a way that clearly surpasses human capability. This nexus of machine capability and human capability is often recognised as core to success. Key questions are of what tasks and activities can machines do better, and which can humans still do better, with this being a moving interface, since machines are getting smarter and more capable every year! Further, how can a business best be rebuilt to most effectively take account of rapid improvements in automated processing and machine-learned decision making, alongside human capabilities? This is no longer the stuff of science fiction: businesses such as Bank of America have rebuilt themselves based on astutely and correctly deploying answers to these challenges (see Chapter 4).

In parallel, the development of Cloud-based technology (i.e. technology 'born in the Cloud' and accessible via the internet), has forced technology vendors to innovate and collaborate. Monolithic platforms have been replaced by composable architectures, which allow businesses to connect a variety of building blocks together, to create a much more tailored solution. In particular, the creation of Platform-as-a-Service (PaaS) solutions, which provide hardware and a configurable environment with a wide array of end-to-end capabilities on a scalable platform, have dramatically reduced the required skill levels and investment cost, for building and deploying advanced AI solutions. These solutions provide pre-built libraries of statistical models, interfaces, and much more user-friendly tooling that dramatically commoditise 'infrastructural technologies'.

These developments have led to the frequent use of the term 'technical debt', to describe the process of IT customisations and bespoke coding, going from an asset and competitive advantage to a liability and burden for the business. Companies that adopt open, Cloud-based technology, tend to have less technical debt, in addition to the increased agility that comes from accessing best practice services and technologies. This set of opportunities should not just be considered for larger businesses, e.g. from ASX100: one of the exciting AI/Cloud-enabled transformations described in this book is of a family company, Canningvale, that moved from wholesaler (mostly of bed linen) to Cloud-based retailer, capturing a much larger slice of the value-add in its value chain. ICT, specifically Cloud, was core to its transformation, and value-added AI going forward would allow it to add even further value in a Netflix-like or Kogan-like way to its customers, via intelligent product suggestions, price optimisation, and better demand prediction and management.

These changes have created new avenues for differentiation, and new solutions to previous problems:

- *Can't connect with the end-consumer?* Cloud platforms, in combination with AI technology, dramatically reduce the cost of direct-to-consumer digital interfaces. These technologies have enabled Formula 1 (racing) to sell its media direct to consumers.[3]
- *Don't have data about the external market?* A broad range of third parties now provide a wide range of data, at highly granular levels of detail, sometimes with real-time integration. This is what enables businesses to confidently launch in new markets they hadn't previously operated in.
- *Don't have data about your own operations?* Service providers now provide data from their operations as a value-add, while machine learning techniques are commonly being used to infer process information based on 'data exhaust' from transactional systems.
- *A computer can't do that?* Off the shelf Deep Learning algorithms are now more effective at diagnosing tumours than a doctor and are probably better at reading their handwriting.

These examples are a small subset of the ways in which organisations are working through a range of previously intractable problems, which would otherwise have stopped or significantly increased the cost of some of these business model innovation opportunities. They are also examples of why traditional incumbency advantages are fading away in so many industries. The dynamism and turbulence of new business applications of new technologies such as AI and Cloud mean that business strategies have a shorter shelf life and if left unattended, will increasingly 'date' within a year or two. The 'good old days' when business strategies and plans were devised to last over five-year or longer time horizons now seem laughable in many instances. This new, tech-enabled dynamism and turbulence brings opportunity, and of course, threat. Having strong market share and brand used to be a highly protective asset: no longer is that the case.

Why AI and Cloud? Why not other disruptive technology?

A critical decision when updating any strategy, is defining the boundary of what should or shouldn't be considered for change purposes. The authors of this book are firmly of the view that the combination of AI and Cloud technologies have created a unique opportunity for market disruption and business model innovation. We have also chosen to draw the boundary at this point, without including other disruptive technologies.

When compared against a range of other technologies, AI and Cloud technologies (together with the advances in networking and Application Program Interfaces [APIs[4]] to simplify interconnection between technologies and data) each have far greater applicability across a broader range of sectors, are more ready for commercialisation, and most importantly, have a greater ability to differentiate the way in which an organisation serves its customers, i.e. they provide innovations that can drive a material level of competitive advantage.

Over the last 10 years, the growth of PaaS in particular, have provided a wide range of capabilities that accelerate the development and application of AI solutions. These innovations are one of the primary reasons why machine learning solutions have become much more commonplace, as the barriers to development have reduced (see Figure 1.2). They have also provided a far wider range of advanced algorithms, which often come 'pre-trained', and avoid the need to provide very large and often costly training datasets.

For all these reasons, we believe that AI and Cloud technology provide both an opportunity and a threat to incumbent organisations, which executives and boards need to tackle head-on. In a later chapter, we will provide greater detail on the ways in which these technologies allow organisations to serve new markets, in ways that they were previously unable to do.

AI: some development directions and limitations

In December 2020, panels of experts gathered in Montreal[5] to debate the future of AI where some fascinating points were made as the sharpest AI experts peered into the future:

1. Deep learning is far from the end point of AI; indeed AI has a great deal of further development potential in front of us. Deep learning was reported as a great point of progress, but still requires a lot of data, lacks generalisability across applications, and is not a reasoning-based approach.

Disruptive technology		Multi-sector impact	Commercial availability	Ability to differentiate at scale
Autonomous vehicles		◐	◐	◕
Blockchain		◐	◕	◐
Quantum computing		◕	◐	◐
AR/VR		◑	◕	◑
3D printing		◐	●	◐
Drones		◑	●	◐
IOT & 5G		◑	◕	◐
Cloud	SaaS	●	●	◕
	PaaS	●	●	●
	IaaS	◑	●	◑
AI / ML		●	◕	●

Individually, each of AI & Cloud can have a significant impact, however in combination, there is a multiplicative benefit of these technologies

FIGURE 1.2 Potential disruptive technologies for consideration

2. Hybrid approaches that combine algorithms with rules-oriented software were seen as a next development field within AI, improving its interpretability, trustworthiness and clarity in application. Combining logical reasoning with deep learning seems promising.

3. Much of AI is currently substantially limited to acting on human-curated data sets, with new developments being where algorithms and perception actuators can facilitate their intelligent interaction directly with the world at large.

4. AI was recognised by experts as missing what are essentially human capabilities of common sense, still unable to fully exert and use knowledge, to which we would add that innovation and indeed business model transformation is still a human activity, requiring lateral thinking, much more than deep learning.

5. Yet AI steams forward in its capabilities, and as it becomes more cost-effectively available, including with thanks to Cloud, its use in combination with human capabilities continues to evolve. AI can unquestionably be superior to using pure human capabilities in highly structured tasks, with growing ability to move towards richer and less fully structured applications coming, fast.

How widely are these technologies being applied?

Many surveys are undertaken of practices and intentions in deploying new technologies. *Forbes* magazine reported on Algorithmia's 2021 survey[6] of over 400 business leaders of major businesses, with headline findings that:

1. 83% of enterprises increased their budget for AI in 2020, over 2019, including 20% that increased these budgets by over 50%.
2. 10% of businesses currently use ten or more AI applications.
3. Chatbots, fraud analysis and process optimisation were common application areas. These volumes are similar to reports from other studies, for example Salesforce' 2020 study found that 69% of enterprises report that AI is transforming their business.
4. The demand for data scientists is growing at high double-digit rates with 29% of major enterprises already having over 100 such people working on development initiatives.
5. Half of major organisations are using AI to deal with fraud, expected by most to increase.

In business value creation terms, AI went almost nowhere for 50 years since its first serious conception in 1955, and in the past decade, and particularly since 2015, it has really jumped forward, partly because of the Cloud capability now in place that complements it and increases its return on investment! There was indeed only a small prospect of AI creating significant business value when computing in general and telecommunications capabilities were immature. Everything from data processing capabilities through to real-time distributed systems have now advanced to where AI is at last able to deliver business value, as evidenced by the investments referred to in the survey findings above.

Where our findings differed from the conventional wisdom

As we began this research, the authors came in with a set of viewpoints, developed across a broad mix of experiences in industry, consulting and academia. As we have furthered our understanding, a range of findings appear to contradict the conventional wisdom on a variety of topics.

Topic 1 – The pathway for AI and Cloud adoption

The conventional wisdom would suggest that the best approach, is to develop a series of proof points, which allow the organisation to build confidence in the potential (and manageable risk) of these technologies.

There is nothing wrong with pursuing initiatives with near-term benefits. However, undertaking a series of proof-point and limited deployments seems to be answering the wrong question – that of '*how might these technologies benefit our organisation?*'. It can lead to incrementalism: that can become a debilitating limitation. Additionally, a carefully sequenced development approach which primarily learns only from the organisation's experiences, is likely to result in a net decrease in capability, in comparison to competing organisations that gain insight from a broader range of organisations and application instances.

We think the better question to ask is: '*How will my organisation be successful in the medium term, what changes do I need to undertake, and how will AI and Cloud technologies support these changes?*'. By anchoring the ambition in the transformation of the business model (i.e. the way the organisation creates value for its stakeholders), the underlying technology is more relevant to the organisation's stakeholders, is a more integrated part of the solution, and the transformation is more likely to be successful.

Topic 2 – These technologies are complex and require significant organisational scale

A common pushback to the adoption of AI and Cloud technologies, is that they are highly complex, and as such, only large organisations have enough 'slack'[7] to enable their consideration and effective adoption.

The case studies included in our research, include small organisations as well as large organisations, across both the private and public sectors. We believe the question posed above (specifically, '*how will my organisation be successful in the medium term*') is relevant to all organisations. Indeed, each of our profiled organisations implicitly addressed this question.

The technologies associated with supporting the answer come in a range of different price/performance points. We also believe that technical advances are actively reducing the cost of these technologies, making what was recently state of the art, available to all. Moore's Law essentially continues, and most aspects of ICT costs are declining fast. Platform and shelf-based solutions are increasingly available to all.

Topic 3 – The constraints of technical debt

Many established organisations perceive the developments and innovations in their newly established competitors, as only being possible through the absence of legacy technology. This issue of technical debt has been a major inhibitor of innovation in the past, and we agree that technical debt is a challenge to be worked through.

However, we see technical debt as a tactical issue to be resolved as new candidate business models are being evaluated. Not only have many organisations been able to resolve these issues, but the use of Cloud-based technology in particular can act as a mechanism to simplify the legacy technology stack and allow for elements of the legacy stack to be progressively decommissioned, while providing users with elements of a modern technology platform.

Topic 4 – The skills required in the boardroom

Over the past ten years there has been a desire for boards to have 'Digital NEDs (non-executive directors)'[8] to appropriately guide AI- and Cloud-enabled business model transformation. Unfortunately, not many boards have such skills within their board teams.

Our perspective is that while having a sufficient number of Digital NEDs is certainly beneficial, three non-technical board member attributes have a greater impact on organisations considering how best to revitalise their organisation: exploration mindset, discomfort with the current basis of competitive strategy and seeking a future focussed strategy.

By focusing on these three non-technical skillsets, we believe that a board is well equipped to perform its duties in approving and providing the appropriate support for the organisation's strategy, to transform in a way that is enabled by these new technologies.

Topic 5 – The balance of actions versus ideas

Some commentators believe the most challenging (and most important) part of the transformation process is the development of the idea and supporting strategy. Others say that implementation (and adaption) is the critical element of success. Yet other commentators say that the traditional approaches to strategy development and implementation are no longer appropriate as we enter this 'new paradigm'.

Our view from this research is that organisations need a balance of each of these capabilities. While there are nuances in the methodologies behind strategy development and program implementation, some which need adjustment in light of these technologies, most of the fundamentals still hold true.

Our recommendation is for organisations to have a bias towards *what to do* and *how to proceed*, rather than waiting for a perfect strategy or an optimal implementation approach. In regard to the growing focus on experimentation, we believe that this is an important capability with growing relevance, however *experimentation is not a strategy*, and while it does have a place in shifting the organisation, *experimentation is not going to transform the incumbent organisation*.

Summary

In this introductory chapter, we have considered the Industry 4.0 revolution that is upon us, and in particular, have begun to unpack the issues and opportunities that AI and Cloud can bring to organisations that wish to use them to enable transformation. New business models can be formulated by such radical capabilities. Such formulation is best built based on solid antecedent capability conditions (see Chapter 2). As in the diagnostic in Appendix 1, executives should consider the extent to which these antecedent conditions will support or hinder their potential AI- and Cloud-enabled business model transformations (abbreviated to BMT throughout this book). There is tremendous opportunity for businesses to gain advantage through BMT, and conversely, threat for those who fail to act.

Notes

1 *CIO* magazine, 27 Jan 2017. 'Banking on bots: The move towards digital labor in financial services', www.cio.com/article/234110/banking-on-bots-the-move-towards-digital-labor-in-financial-services.html

2 Foreign banks last major incursion into Australian consumer banking was pre-internet, and certainly before AI and Cloud could be deployed. Barriers to entry and cost structures are very different in the 2020s to what they were in the purely bricks and mortar days of the 1980s.

3 *The Strategy Story* (9 March 2022). 'Marketing strategy that revived the fate of Formula One'. https://thestrategystory.com/2021/07/19/formula-one-marketing-strategy/

4 Many organisations are also generating significant benefit from robotic process automation (RPA), a specific form of technology that allows machines to act like a human operator integrating various manual tasks.

5 MONTREAL.AI. (23 December 2020). 'AI debate 2. Moving AI forward: An interdisciplinary approach'. Montreal, Canada. https://montrealartificialintelligence.com/aidebate2/

6 https://info.algorithmia.com/email-state-of-ml-2021

7 Jansen, J. J. P., Van Den Bosch, F. A. J., & Volberda, H. W. (2006). 'Exploratory innovation, exploitative innovation, and performance: Effects of organizational antecedents and environmental moderators'. *Management Science*, 52(11), 1661–1674. https://doi.org/10.1287/mnsc.1060.0576

8 Korn-Ferry, 'The digital board: Appointing non-executive directors for the internet economy', 2013, http://static.kornferry.com/media/sidebar_downloads/The_Digital-Board_Final.pdf, accessed 28 May 2019.

2
ANTECEDENT CAPABILITIES OF AI- OR CLOUD-ENABLED BUSINESS TRANSFORMATION

While a significant body of research exists related to AI and Cloud technologies, alongside an equally thorough examination of Business Model Innovation (BMI), there is currently limited literature that focuses on the drivers that lead organisations to choose and successfully implement AI- or Cloud-enabled Business Transformation (abbreviated to BMT in this book). We refer to these drivers as the necessary ingredients or antecedent capabilities to BMT.

It is important to make a distinction between antecedent capabilities and success factors in the context of transformation. For this review, antecedent capabilities are the building blocks that organisations need to possess prior to making a decision to undergo transformation, while success factors are seen as the required elements to achieve a successful implementation of BMI. Our focus for this chapter is on antecedent capabilities and how they enable the decision-making process for BMT. Figure 2.1 shows these antecedent capabilities. We have derived these elements from both literature review and from examining case studies, and our own experiences in a variety of technology-based and other transformations.

Our purpose in describing these antecedent capability elements is to stimulate thinking about them in the sense that executives can assess them and take them into account, and in some cases change, improve and develop them, prior to planning BMT work, especially involving AI or Cloud. We note that most of these antecedent factors are internal to the organisation and may be readily able to be changed to some extent, and others may be structural or outside the control of the business' executives. In Appendix 1, we provide a self-assessment table that executives can use to consider their strengths and weaknesses on these antecedent capability factors.

DOI: 10.4324/9781003255529-2

FIGURE 2.1 Conceptual model of antecedent capabilities for BMT

Capability 1: Leadership proactivity

The ability of leaders to make strategic decisions well, exercise effective judgement in doing so, then carry out oversight and control of such BMI transformations is at the heart of AI or Cloud-based or indeed, any other form of transformation.

Most literature related to BMI and AI/Cloud leads to the conclusion that leadership is a critical enabler on its own as well as a key influencing factor for all the other antecedent capabilities. The decision to pivot business models significantly, particularly if enabled by dynamic new technology, requires strong leadership that can shape a culture of change acceptance and willingness to learn and innovate, with leaders educating themselves about those technologies and how these could be used to enhance business models.[1] Leadership is also seen as crucial in making decisions leading up to business model transformation, as Augier and Teece[2] recognise: 'in the dynamic capabilities framework, management plays distinctive roles in selecting and/or developing routines, making investment choices, and in orchestrating non-tradable assets to achieve efficiencies and appropriate returns from innovations'.

Just as we observe the importance of proactive leaders in building and transforming successful organisations, such as with Steve Jobs, Bill Gates, Jeff Bezos, Eiji Toyoda, Henry Ford, Jack Welch, Alfred Sloan, Henry Ford, Elon Musk and a host of others, the other side of the coin, equally valid, is that where this proactive element of leadership is of low quality or is absent, significant transformation is unlikely to be energised, resourced, governed and implemented. All the other influenceable elements of BMT hinge on proactive leadership as the glue that brings them together, aligns them and spurs them on. We are not saying that 'proactive leadership is everything', but we do suggest that it is a necessary condition, although not on its own sufficient to ensure success.

Capability 2: Innovation culture

Some organisations are welcoming of all sorts of change, and some shun it. The overwhelming sense of how Google, 3M, CSL and Apple achieve their innovations is because the accepted norms of behaviour are that change is expected, and generally embraced, when it is implemented well. Business model transformation is 'Big C' change and will have a much higher likelihood of succeeding if people welcome change, are prepared for role changes, new structures, new technologies, and see the glass as half full rather than half empty. Sometimes characterised as a growth mindset, as against a fixed mindset, such an internal cultural dynamism will help a great deal with implementation and hence give executives increased confidence to attempt BMT. If, however, the organisation has a history of being tradition bound and resisting change, then maybe this antecedent capability needs attention first!

Capability 3: Balancing exploration versus exploitation

The balance that organisations try to maintain between exploring new opportunities and exploiting old certainties influences an organisation's ability to innovate and is considered an antecedent capability to BMT.[3] Some organisations spend a great deal of money and effort on exploration, such as Google, Apple, Samsung and CSL. Others, such as Malaysia's oil/gas company PETRONAS, spend relatively less on innovation and exploring for new products, services and business model approaches, focussing more on productivity and the cost efficiency of their existing assets while keeping the OEE (overall equipment effectiveness) pumping those assets, literally as fast and hard as possible. AI- and Cloud-based business model transformations require significant work on their development, and indeed much exploration, hence businesses that have little strategic interest or resource intent in 'new opportunity' exploration would be expected to undertake less transformation using such means.

Capability 4: Risk tolerance

Organisations that undertake BMT must take into account risks associated with major transformation. As such, a necessary antecedent capability is also a sensible (non-zero) level of risk appetite. The saying 'nothing ventured, nothing gained' applies in the sense that in the search for superior returns through a business transformation, success is not guaranteed, and we certainly do not have certainty when we explore and develop successful new BMIs. Overly conservative approaches are likely to mitigate against exploring new approaches such as BMT, perhaps in favour of more incremental initiatives. Great leaders will be able to put such BMT initiatives into context, assess risks as part of the overall 'big picture' of the portfolio of exploration and improvement activities, and use both sound analysis and effective judgement in taking some sensible risks. Furthermore, great leaders apply Cicero's adage 'he plants trees, which will be of use to another age' – they consciously consider the organisational risk/reward relationship beyond the period of their individual involvement of the organisation while avoiding the legacy monument trap. Sophisticated tools such as risk analysis and decision trees can be useful here to support judgement processes. It is not trivial to 'fly the plane and rebuild the plane at the same time', requiring excellent strategic change and risk management capability.

Capability 5: Strategic process strength

By strategic process strength, we mean that great businesses have formal processes for formulating and reviewing strategies, executive decisiveness in choosing initiatives, and sound analytic capabilities supporting their choices. Poorly performing firms can be seen to dither over decisions, fall prey to 'analysis paralysis', and hence often miss the boat on opportunities, even where they become apparent. Businesses that effectively scan the environment, including that of emerging technological developments, create strategic ideas, test and evaluate these, then crisply choose to pursue the best of them, do so consciously as part of their overall business strategy. They are systematic and thorough as a key part of this strategic process strength. For transformation, being careful yet decisive is to advantage, since being first or at least early into the new market space can be of great value. Uber, Facebook and Apple are global examples, and Kogan and SEEK are local Australian examples of fast, decisive early movers.

Capability 6: Foundational data and information systems readiness

Another fundamental antecedent capability to BMT is having the appropriate level of foundational data and information systems. By 'appropriate', we mean 'not perfect, but good enough for the use case of that data'. The firm's information architecture needs to be ready and up to a standard where the AI or Cloud transformation can be grafted on, without being overly plagued by dreaded legacy system anchors. A range of 'dealbreaker' technology limitations could be considered, for example:

- Digitised data – Critical current state data must exist in a digitised format. For example, filing cabinets filled with paper based annual leave and training records, need to be digitised in order to enable the transition to a modern,

Cloud-based HR system. The use of Cloud technologies in environments with incomplete data only serve to exacerbate the organisation's current state limitations.

- Well understood data – Research conducted by Deloitte[4] found that AI leaders understand that superior data management is a necessary precursor to successfully implementing AI. As powerful as modern AI algorithms are, they don't have any 'common sense'. For example, if data about a customer's preference for home delivery is only known *after* they choose to buy a product, an AI Price Optimiser using that data, would incorrectly assume that all home delivery customers are willing to buy the product, at any price! Organisations don't require 'perfect data', but a robust and practical understanding of what is and isn't reliably populated is critical when using advanced algorithms.
- Connectivity – Many Cloud-based platforms will invariably need to interface with existing platforms, which may not be adequately set up for Cloud connectivity. For example, a Cloud-based Customer Relationship Management (CRM) system, sending customer orders into a fax-based service delivery platform is a problem. Many legacy systems haven't been designed for these modern requirements, and will therefore require some foundational connectivity improvements, to take advantage of Cloud technology.
- Security – Another capability to focus on is security, especially for digital transformations. As companies' access to data sets on customers, employees and suppliers grows, there is an increased requirement for a fundamentally safe layer of data security. Many layers of dysfunction will occur when a firm's security is found wanting, from customer trust issues to business partners and suppliers wanting out.
- Flexibility – Tallon et al.[5] found that flexibility across IT infrastructure is a crucial antecedent capability to an organisation's ability to transform quickly, and enables staff to quickly build, test and deploy new or changed applications. This flexibility is in contrast to traditional, rigid technology capabilities, which were more appropriate when the cost of IT development and experimentation was considerably higher. It is more an 'agility capability' at the present time.

Capability 7: Market and customer sensing

Another antecedent capability to BMT is an organisation's ability to stay tuned in to, and hopefully ahead of the needs of their current and potential future customers, and their requirements, both known and emerging. There is an important balance to strike here between current and future customers. Working with leading edge customers, and potential new customers, seeking their inputs, asking them about problems they foresee and would like to solve, are all part of the creative process that brings the 'voice of the customer' into the potential BMT. It then needs to meet the capability set brought by AI or Cloud: then a 'sweet spot' can be developed by astute executives, where capabilities, hopefully unique or difficult for others to replicate, meet customers' existing or new requirements, hopefully efficiently and effectively.

Further, the additional opportunity brought by BMT is to tap into a new market segment!

Capability 8: Opportunity/threat drivers

BMT involves significant resources, taking some risk, disturbing the status quo, and likely means taking some people out of their comfort zone, whether this be the board and executives, or operating staff, or all of the above. Hence there must be significant motivation for the organisation to do something significant as against just pursue 'business as usual' along with some incremental improvements. Motivation usually comes from opportunities, threats, or a combination. Relating to the 'sensing' part of strategic process maturity, this antecedent capability involves recognising opportunities and threats early enough so as to make it worthwhile acting strategically on them; if this sounds easy and obvious, then what explains Kodak, Blockbuster, Borders, and a host of others that didn't see, or if they did see, didn't act on the freight train that was coming at them?

Whether it is primarily opportunity or threat, or, more usually, a combination, the sensing can swiftly be followed by the framing of the transformation initiative, in which once again, strategising about how far the transformation should go into AI and Cloud use must be decided upon. Some executives want to go towards the 'bleeding edge', some the leading edge, and others are even more conservative, which boils down to judgements about risk and return.

In this realm, it is important to not fall into any of a number of traps that can befall the inexperienced team. First, consider the sunk cost trap. Basically, this means being wary of chasing initiatives such as transformations that haven't been going well and throwing good money after bad. Disciplined executive teams regularly evaluate and are prepared to 'kill off' strategic initiatives that deserve it. They know that one cannot change the past, and they take full and realistic responsibility for the future path, putting emotion aside and concentrating on future value creation.

Second, it can be fallacious to assume a 'status quo' as the base case. So net present value estimates that work from a zero base over anything beyond a very short term, can present a picture of comfort and stability that isn't justified. A key question about any BMT evaluation is 'what will happen if we don't do this?', and the answer is highly unlikely to be 'nothing much', except in the very short term.

Capability 9: Industry dynamism

Industry dynamism as an external antecedent to an organisation preparing to undertake BMT. While all the other antecedent capabilities are primarily inwards focused, it is important to understand how the industry and market in which organisations operate also drive decision making towards BMT. We consider industry dynamism in relation to competitive intensity and its innovation opportunity set.

When firms exert significant pressure on their competitors, it is reasonable to assume that motivation for BMT will be higher than when such forces are more 'relaxed'. Porter's Five Forces[6] provide broad elements of competitive intensity drivers, including the primary pressure from existing competitors, and also that exerted from customers, suppliers, new entrants, substitute products and others. On an operational level, switching costs by customers and the ability to differentiate in the market are other elements driving competitive intensity, and hence industry dynamism. Industry concentration ratios and growth rates may also impact the degree of rivalry between incumbent firms. When competitive intensity is high, we would expect proactive leaders to search for ways to innovate and transform as a manner of combating pressure on margins. Business model transformation is expected to be motivated by high levels of competitive intensity or the potential for it. For example, the global automotive sector has strong competitive intensity, with consumers having very many choices, and suppliers striving to find any sort of an edge that is possible, thus spurring innovation investments. Although it is not a transformed incumbent but rather a new player, Tesla is an example of how capital markets price radical innovations in mature industries. In automotive, GM, Ford, Toyota, Mercedes and others are striving to transform from fossil fuel propulsion systems to pure electric products, essentially chasing the 'E-pure play' Tesla. Chinese electric vehicle makers are moving fast, at scale, with high dynamism. Compare this with railroad operators or regional airlines, where in any rail business and region, there may be only one or few operators, and local competitive intensity is relatively low.

The integrated nature of antecedent capabilities

The antecedent capabilities shown in Figure 2.1 and described above, do not act independently. We have already stated, and we re-emphasise here, proactive leadership is the glue that acts on and through the other elements. There are many other connections, for example risk attitude and preparedness to engage in exploration projects go strongly hand in hand, as does the internal culture-setting of change readiness/willingness.

Industry dynamism and the levels of threat/opportunity that exist may be interrelated. Highly dynamic industries may well portend higher levels of threat, and for the proactive, higher levels of opportunity.

Strategic process strength itself draws upon a number of the other antecedent capabilities, and likely goes strongly and positively with sound approaches in many of them, even of having a suitable existing state of IS and data architecture. The reason is that firms with sound strategic decision processes are more likely to have considered and invested previously in their IS and are also more likely to have had the means to do so.

The elements of Figure 2.1 can best be considered as components of the necessary and integrated foundation for incumbent firms wishing to succeed with BMT, and executives should consider which of these are their corporate strengths, and their weaknesses, remembering that with these components, at least to some extent, 'a chain is as good as its weakest link' (see Appendix 1).

Notes

1 Lee, J., Suh, T., Roy, D., & Baucus, M. (2019). Emerging technology and business model innovation: The case of artificial intelligence. *Journal of Open Innovation: Technology, Market, and Complexity*, 5(3), 44. https://doi.org/10.3390/joitmc5030044
2 Augier, M., & Teece, D. J. (2009). Dynamic capabilities and the role of managers in business strategy and economic performance. *Organization Science*, 20(2), 410–421. https://doi.org/10.1287/orsc.1090.0424
3 Augier, M., & Teece, D. J. (2009). Dynamic capabilities and the role of managers in business strategy and economic performance. *Organization Science*, 20(2), 410–421. https://doi.org/10.1287/orsc.1090.0424
4 Deloitte. (2020). *Thriving in the era of persuasive AI.* www2.deloitte.com/content/dam/Deloitte/cn/Documents/about-deloitte/deloitte-cn-dtt-thriving-in-the-era-of-persuasive-ai-en-200819.pdf
5 Tallon, P. P., Queiroz, M., Coltman, T., & Sharma, R. (2019). Information technology and the search for organizational agility: A systematic review with future research possibilities. *The Journal of Strategic Information Systems*, 28(2), 218–237. https://doi.org/10.1016/j.jsis.2018.12.002
6 Porter, M. E. (1991). Towards a dynamic theory of strategy. *Strategic Management Journal*, 12(S2), 95–117. https://doi.org/10.1002/smj.4250121008

3

LOCAL CASE STUDIES

Introduction to the case studies

We selected organisations, large and small, public and private sector, in order to illustrate what has been and hence what can be accomplished in existing organisations that wish to transform their strategy, operations, marketing, or even their entire business model through AI, Cloud, or perhaps both. Some of these organisations have been in existence for many decades, some for only a few years, but in all instances, the use of AI and/or Cloud was motivated by a desire to improve outcomes for stakeholders (often customers or employees), or to improve the competitiveness and effectiveness of their offerings and processes thus improving outcomes for shareholders.

We selected case studies across a range of industries and collected information from interviews with executives and examination of documents. The case studies each present some unique issues for readers to consider, in terms of the particular costs, benefits and risks of their transformations. Yet in all instances, these initiatives represented net forward progress for those organisations. This progress should not be evaluated against the 'status quo' of business as usual, because of the general progress being made in virtually all industries, but rather we reemphasise here that 'standing still is going backwards in relative terms' (see Chapter 1).

Further, there is a potentially large opportunity cost of not venturing into new technologies, when they are available, in absolute terms. For example, if SEEK or Kogan had chosen to not venture into using AI to add value to their data, analytics and decision-making processes and services, then the value contributions brought by these technologies would have simply been uncaptured or lost. In addition, their competitive positioning would have been weakened. Similarly with Cloud, if Yarriambiack Shire or Canningvale had not moved onto the Cloud, value would have been lost in the opportunity forgone, which would have led to reduced value to many of their respective stakeholders. In some instances, not making progress and

DOI: 10.4324/9781003255529-3

not using such technologies for advancement leaves the door open for competitors to take advantage of such laggard behaviour. We refer here to the moving 'efficient frontier' that exists in essentially all sectors of the economy. AI and Cloud uptake are providing adopters the opportunity to improve their organisational effectiveness, including cost efficiency and service/quality, and the only reasonable assumption is that this will continue, and possibly accelerate. AI is making decisions and resource use more effective, and Cloud allows for it to be deployed more effectively, while also improving the reach of its deployers, at lower cost. Surveys of company executives continue to strongly show such benefits that are material, often improving organisational effectiveness by 20% or more,[1] and indeed reported by Ericsson[2] as 'cost savings ROI of 10x to 20x'.

The case studies of exemplar companies in Australia described below demonstrate such advantages.

These case studies are presented in an order that illustrates the importance of the antecedents. However, we recognise that readers may wish to jump directly to the case study(ies) of most interest or relevance to their situation. As a means to facilitate this, we provide a very brief synopsis of each case in Table 3.1 below:

TABLE 3.1 The case studies of exemplar companies in Australia

Case study	Description	Key Points of the Case
Deloitte	Large, established partnership focussed on business services seeking to develop a new business offering that was not accessible through traditional service model	• Market opportunity identified by empowered business unit leaders • Cost efficiencies through AI and Cloud technologies enabled Deloitte to open up a substantial market segment that it was not able to profitably serve under legacy approaches • Significant use of RPA and APIs • Not just technology … success required 'what is possible' style thinking coupled with a fundamental, granular review of workflow • Involvement of a large range of skills (including information security) as well as changes in staff expectations for initiative success
Moula	Emerging Australian fintech seeking to serve an underserviced sector of the market through the use of advanced algorithms	• Founder-led executive team providing proactive leadership • Identified specific competitive advantage (credit risk assessment) enabled through AI and dataflows • Development of new business/IT/data operating model key to success • Culture of 'open experimentation' with tolerance for 'fail but learn' • Non-legacy culture allows incumbent to realise what is possible rather than hold onto 'what we have'

TABLE 3.1 Cont.

Case study	Description	Key Points of the Case
SEEK	Established ASX50 operator of online employment classifieds and education and training proactively positioning for possible future competition	• Former disruptor (of print classifieds) observing disruption in other markets triggers executive attention and investment ahead of the curve • Started with a 'proof of concept' approach, but benefits of that approach plateaued … thus sparking SEEK to embrace core platform refresh initiatives under a common team, thus breaking down organisational and skill silos • 'Thin slice' pilot approach generated confidence in the emerging solutions • Recognised that eliminating risk is not feasible, so initiative progressed with a sense of tolerance about clarified risk
Kogan	ASX300 online shopping platform investing in foundational IS platforms to enable the next wave of growth	• Entrepreneurial approach to innovation with ideas sourced from all layers of the organisational hierarchy – seeking asymmetric bets • Although digital-native, executive management does not see technology as a source of advantage per se – rather, technology is a set of capabilities to enable innovation • Legacy technology stack had become inhibitor to business growth • New foundational IS and data layer provides the means for decentralised decision making
Bank of Queensland	Established mid-tier Australian bank using technology to create a competitive advantage from what others might consider a competitive disadvantage	• New 'growth and challenger' mindset executive team onboarded • Saw an opportunity to get out of the competitive 'no-man's land' through a different cost structure and operating tempo enabled through technology • Senior executive commitment to change ('enterprise commitment') felt through the organisation and key to overcoming reluctance • Simplified, modern Cloud tech stack reduces data silos, improves process effectiveness for customers and enables BOQ to quickly capitalise on inorganic growth opportunities

(continued)

TABLE 3.1 Cont.

Case study	Description	Key Points of the Case
PEXA	A newly listed firm established by key industry players as an effective means to resolve an industry-wide issue	• New organisation established to fulfil 2010 COAG commitment to improve the property conveyancing process • Complex environment – seeking a national platform that supports legacy state-based practices • Success due to considering this not as a technology platform, but rather as an industry-wide evolution supported by technology. Majority of capital spend associated with process design and industry engagement rather than technology build • Required design leadership to overcome challenge of reimagining an existing diffuse set of processes • Targeted specific transaction types to get up the adoption curve associated with such a network business • Resulting process compressed in time (and cost) and elevated in quality – not 'digitisation' but rather 'collaborative space'
IAG	An ASX50 general insurer seeking to fundamentally redesign a critical pain as the first step of a broader journey	• Longstanding goal to enhance customer experience and satisfy customer needs, while managing the cost of claims and supporting overheads • One specific area (total loss claims processing) seen as ripe for renewal • AI used to determine probable event outcome, thus enabling streamlined and efficient digitised engagement with customer and other parties • Such an approach requires proactive management of risks as well as engagement with external stakeholders and regulators to manage perceptions of bias in AI • Success in this area marks the beginning of IAG's AI adoption journey
Canningvale	A privately held family firm using Cloud technology to respond to changes in their position in the soft home furnishing/ Manchester (household linens/ cottons) value chain	• Increased retailer pressure forced Canningvale to reconsider how it engaged with customers, moving the value chain closer to the end-use customer where much of the profit margins lay • This strategy was heavily enabled by the new technologies in the Cloud • Smaller size (in people) of organisation enabled transformation success through more responsive decision loops

TABLE 3.1 Cont.

Case study	Description	Key Points of the Case
		• Preliminary business analysis ('mapping it all out') enabled Canningvale to understand current processes as a means to identify what might be required from future tech stack, an example of which is a machine learning inventory software forecasting management tool • New platform supports culture of visibility, and the organisation continues to grow at acceptable EBIT margin
Caesarstone	An international firm executing three parallel regional digitisation initiatives (one of which is Australia – thus allowing some compare/contrast with other regions) to proactively reduce the risk of commoditisation	• Legacy 'distance from customer' business model associated with being a manufacturer exposed the group to disintermediation (and possible declining margins) • Leadership agreed to move towards a model that provided greater customer intimacy as well as additional value provided to end-customers and channel partners • Solution was to develop an ecosystem across the value chain that would serve as a platform for collaboration • Digitised collaboration platform also enabled Caesarstone to understand emerging issues (for example lower than expected conversion rates) • Initiative seen as a business model change rather than a technology initiative • Highlights desirability to have required skills available 'in house'
Scope	A non-for-profit entity positioned to take advantage of market opportunities enabled through scalable Cloud technology platforms	• Management decision to invest in overhauling antiquated technology stack • Cloud technologies adopted as better/faster/cheaper than traditional on-prem alternatives • New platform enables capabilities not previously available as well as an enhanced consistency in client experience • The revitalised business processing platform has enabled Scope to pursue a range of opportunities (in a rapidly changing environment) that it simply could not pursue with the legacy approach

(continued)

TABLE 3.1 Cont.

Case study	Description	Key Points of the Case
Service NSW	A government executive agency that sits within the Department of Customer Service, providing each access to government services in New South Wales	• Using agility as the catalyst for change, Service NSW reimaged the service delivery process • Due to the lack of government organisations embarking on large scale transformations of this nature, Service NSW turned to digital natives for best practise • The uplift in their internal capabilities meant that they could design, build and implement systems at a rapid pace, which was vital as the COVID-19 pandemic hit
Yarriambiack	Small regional local government shire with limited funding adopting Cloud technologies to enable improved and more responsive citizen services	• Renewal of tech stack spurred by new leadership and a review of the Local Government Inspectorate in November 2019 • Investment limitations encourages Yarriambiack to explore disruptive approaches such as SaaS • New platform addresses the process concerns flagged by the Local Government Inspectorate as well as improves the ability for shire staff to meet the needs of the local community
Urban Art Projects (UAP)	A small organisation leveraging disruptive technology to create unique artistic works	• UAP makes used of a range of disruptive technologies, including 3D printing, robotics, augmented and virtual reality • The use of Cloud platforms, has enabled UAP to dramatically reduce its cost of innovation and take a much more experimental approach to tackling new projects

Each case study provides:

- an overview of the organisation,
- a summary of the opportunity the organisation was pursing,
- a description of the initiative undertaken,
- a view as to the situation today,
- a perspective of how the case study demonstrates one or more of the antecedents,
- and some closing thoughts of the key insights of this case study.

Case study 1: Deloitte self-managed superfund

We start our discussion with a case study of Deloitte Australia.

An overview of Deloitte Australia and the self-managed superfunds (SMSFs) audit market

Deloitte Australia is the Australian firm within the global Deloitte organisation. Deloitte Australia has over 900 partners and 11,000 staff, and provides services across the audit, tax, risk, financial advisory and consulting domains.

Financial audit, historically known as 'attest', was the original offering of the firm founded by William Welch Deloitte. In 1849, Deloitte was named Accountant to the Great Western Railway, one of the earliest joint-stock companies in Britain. Thus, Deloitte became the first independent accountant to a public company.

In the proceeding 172 years, Deloitte has evolved into a member of the international 'Big 4' professional services firms. Audit and assurance services continue to make up a large proportion of revenues, contributing approximately 20% of the Australian firm's FY21 revenues of $2.3B.

As a partner-based professional services model, the firm grows through the entrepreneurial actions of its partners and staff. Partners and staff continuously identify and source new opportunities, capabilities and innovation ventures for existing or prospective clients. Deloitte's identified opportunity for Self-Managed Superfunds (SMSFs) highlights the importance of reimagining traditional offerings using the power of Cloud and AI.

Self-Managed Superannuation Funds (SMSFs) are a key component of the Australian financial landscape. Over 600,000 individual SMSFs manage A$750B of assets, representing nearly one third of Australia's $2.76T retirement savings system[1].

In essence, a SMSF is an investment vehicle established for the sole purpose of providing financial benefits to members (limited to four) in retirement and their beneficiaries on death. A SMSF will have its own Tax File Number (TFN), Australian Business Number (ABN) and transactional bank account, which allows them to receive contributions and rollovers, make investments and pay out lump sums and pensions. A SMSF is a trust, and therefore requires trustees to establish and execute investment strategies for the fund. All SMSF investments are made in the name of the fund under the control of the trustees.

A SMSF auditor is an independent qualified individual responsible for considering and assessing a fund's financial statements and the SMSF's compliance with superannuation law. The auditor must report any non-compliance issues to the fund's trustees and the Australian Tax Office, the regulator for the sector.

The professional fees for a SMSF audit vary substantially and are usually dependent upon the complexity of the fund. The Australian Taxation Office[2] reported that the SMSF audit fees ranged from $200 to over $2,000, with a typical fee in the order of $500 – $1,000. Taking the mid-point of this range, one could estimate the total SMSF audit fee pool in Australia to be in the order of $450M p.a. This audit fee pool was typically serviced by smaller scale accountants through a retail client service model.

The opportunity

Originally, when the concept was being developed, Deloitte used a Cluster-Based Growth management approach[3]. In this approach, the large firm was broken down into smaller communities of fellow practitioners, defined as 'clusters'. These clusters contained two to ten partners generating $5 to $50M in revenue that were seeking to lead in a particular sector or sub-sector. Within its broader audit practice, Deloitte had an active superannuation cluster with substantive client presence, including large superannuation funds. Audit fees for such engagements ranged from $100,000 to $1M+ p.a., and the client service model was oriented towards servicing such significant clients.

In addition to its superannuation audit services, Deloitte provided broad-based accounting support to large family and private firms, another priority cluster prioritised for client service. Deloitte occasionally provided SMSF-related audit and accounting services as part of broader client relationships and engagements but had not actively targeted the sector with offerings.

Deloitte arguably had less than 1% of the overall $450M fragmented SMSF audit market. Using existing relationships and cluster priorities, the firm questioned: could Deloitte capture market share for the adjacent SMSF audit services?

The initiative

Frances Borg, a partner with Deloitte, previously led the Financial Services Audit team. By 2014, Frances had already dedicated multiple years to auditing large super-annuation funds. She was aware of the scale of the SMSF market and the relative fragmentation. In her words:

> We saw an opportunity to come up with an offering that made the most of the data available. We saw that other SMSF participants (like administrators) were starting to use the Cloud, and the account service providers and our clients were using the Cloud. There was data being made available through various data sources. We saw an opportunity to funnel this data from third parties that could be used in an audit.

In addition to this, an opportunity was identified; to set up a system that allowed for communications – 'the exchange of information and the workflow' – to be done in the Cloud which would provide a 'seamless interaction from an audit and client perspective'.

This vision eventually became the SMSF Audit platform[4]. There are three main technical elements of this platform:

- A secure web portal for audit and client participants – one of the first platforms on which Deloitte mandated Multi-Factor Authentication.

- A set of Application Programming Interfaces [APIs] to grab and pull data from a range of participants – banks, administrators/accountants, share registries, etc.
- A set of robots (Robotic Process Automation) to address those areas where APIs could not be deployed to obtain data or documents.

However, this was not a case of a 'build it and they will come'. The initiative would alter how an audit was conduct, from end-to-end. 'It was really thinking about who was best placed to do each aspect of the audit at a very granular level and designing towards what we wanted the end-to-end auditor and client experience to look like'.

Such a desire to re-visit and re-design an existing offering is not uncommon. Indeed, the concept of Business Process Reengineering became formalised in the 1990s to reconsider how things should be done, given advances in technologies and value chain capabilities and changes in business partner expectations. However, such initiatives can be difficult to justify when there is no need for significant cost reduction or service improvement – which was the case here.

Fortunately, Frances and Deloitte had found an opportunity to think through how to address a market adjacency through a specific market opportunity. 'We had a relationship with one of our major superannuation administrators', she explains. 'They were large scale, with also very manual processes. They were willing to engage with Deloitte if we were able to solve some of that problem for automation. That was the first trigger'.

The second was the identification of a bigger market opportunity; the audit process had not yet been digitised which offered a large offering Deloitte could service. The third trigger was in regards to exploring what was possible when it came to 'digitising an end-to-end audit process, wrapping workflow around an audit, communicating with clients in the Cloud, because that would inform the broader Audit Transformation initiative that we were concurrently conducting on a larger scale'.

This kind of 'what is possible' thinking was not just about redefining and automating process and workflow. All aspects of the service model were open for discussion: clients, channels, service, team, partnership, and markets. Importantly, clients had been involved in the initial rethinking of the model, which has since been continuously refined.

This rethinking also redefined roles and expectations of individual professionals within audit client service teams. Spending significant time with the methodology and risk teams, many options were explored. There were choices to be made around whether to standardise or automate every aspect of the audit, where to use the back office, and where to use more skilled practitioners to be able to focus on areas of judgement and risk. 'There was a lot of training required, outlining the end-to-end process and tweaking oversight to get the right outcome from a quality perspective'.

Additionally, a targeted strategy of change management for professionals had been undertaken. It was a big ask.

We had to change expectations of the average auditor about their day-to-day task. We were trying to get them out of the habit of doing the lower-level work themselves, instead giving them comfort that the work had been done. They didn't have to review everything end-to-end before they picked up the audit – the team had followed a standardised process so the work should be at the level of quality that they needed. It took time for professionals to get that faith.

While Deloitte was aware of what its competitors were doing throughout this process, it did not change its program. In fact, competitive risk was not a strong consideration. 'We were really just running, doing our own thing'. There was a dual purpose. 'Yes, we were building an SMSF audit platform to make the most of the SMSF opportunity, but it was also about exploring – exploring what could be done from a standardisation, automation and digitisation perspective for audit'.

Cloud technologies and their rapid evolution were vital. Without this change, the type of volume that can be currently undertaken could not have occurred. There was this need to 'push the boundaries in terms of how much we could use data and digitisation in our end-to-end audit process whilst at the same time maintaining – if not enhancing – quality'. Frances is adamant that this could not have been possible without Cloud technologies. 'We were always pushing as hard as we could to make sure if there was a new technology to be implemented on the platform to make it more secure, we would do that'.

The situation today

Several years on, Borg acknowledges the impact of this development and its pathway to success. It's a process that has taken time. While clients love the portal, in order to reap the full benefit of the standardisation process, everyone needs to use the portal and provide the data in the same way. It's a process that encompasses not only the team but also the clients, with onboarding having been called out as an important element. 'There's no doubt that the process has become more profitable. It has taken time'.

A retrospective view of the timing is also illuminating. Four elements had to exist for success:

- There had to be sense of wonder within a set of leaders at Deloitte about the potential of some of these technologies to help address a market opportunity.
- There had to be a client with scale that had sufficient confidence in the state of the technologies to be willing to go on the journey with Deloitte – this allowed the development team to work to a set of specific constraints rather than build an idealised solution.
- Other counterparties (such as banks and share registries) had to have the ability to digitally link (typically through APIs) with the Deloitte platform, or at least have been willing to build those digital bridges.

- The technologies had to be sufficiently robust enough so that Deloitte could deliver upon its commitments for quality and risk, including security of client information.

In the end, the technology met the promise and enabled business model innovation.

> I think the timing was right. Sooner? We may not have known. What we built, seven years ago, it was leading edge at the time. It still is great right now and it compares really well to what is being built [for corporate audit] now.

Antecedent alignment

The Deloitte SMSF case study demonstrates a number of the factors for success discussed in Chapter 2. Three strongly demonstrated factors are discussed below.

Proactive leadership

Leadership does not have to be top-down. Partner-led businesses should empower leaders to identify and pursue opportunities. This is a good example of a (then) mid-level partner at Deloitte recognising an opportunity and engaging the broader organisation to make the vision a reality. Whilst the involvement of many senior individuals was vital for its success, the business model transformation would not have occurred without the drive of one individual who was empowered to act, regardless of their position within the hierarchy.

Exploration and exploitation

Exploration was a key element within the team. It was this intellectual curiosity that sparked the initial exploration of what might be possible. Tethered to the need to deliver results within a specific period, the launch of the initiative could only occur when there was sufficient confidence that it could be exploited, which in this case came from the alliance with a keystone client. As such, this exploration was enabled by corporate resources and 'permission'. Once proof of concept had been identified, the focus was on 'how do we rapidly scale to fully exploit?'.

Market and customer sensing

This initiative came about because a group of partners saw a market opportunity that could enable incremental revenue as well as deepen relationships throughout the SMSF ecosystem. There was also a concurrent opportunity to use SMSF audit to pilot what could be possible for the future of corporate audit.

Closing thoughts

The SMSF initiative at Deloitte is a good example of business model innovation within an established (and highly regulated) business context. We now turn to a relatively recent entrant of an established industry segment to explore how emerging organisations can also redevelop their business model.

Case study 2: Moula

We now move from an example of business model transformation in a well-established industry to a case of using AI (in a way different to its competitors) as a key differentiator in a crowded fintech market.

An overview of Moula

Moula was founded in 2013 to 'help hard-working business owners in Australia access the business finance they need to grow Moula' (n.d.)[3]. Drawing on their experience in the financial services sector, the three founders, Aris Allegos, Andrew Watt and Piers Moller, felt that the existing processes for small to medium enterprises to obtain a business loan were cumbersome, paperwork-oriented, security-oriented and slow. As a result, a very sizeable part of the Australian economy was not able to access credit. The founders had a vision that the loan origination process could be digitally enabled such that it could be simpler and quicker. In turn, this would address the credit availability gap and allow business owners to spend their time on what mattered – building their business.

Moula's original offering was a form of unsecured business lending. Provided that a business had some history (an ABN or ACN, GST Registration, six months of trading history, $5,000+ in monthly revenue), business owners could apply to borrow between $5,000 and $250,000 on a 12- to 24-month loan term. The application process itself could be completed in as little as seven minutes, and a credit decision would typically be reached within 24 hours. As part of its commitment to fair lending, Moula had transparent pricing, with no fees such as administration, direct debit or early repayment fees.

Moula wrote its first loan in 2015 and grew its business deliberately, given the founders focus on credit quality. The Moula founders determined early that they would lend on the basis of the health of the business rather than on asset security. To do this, Moula's credit decisioning team had to have an understanding of the near-real-time financials of a business.

Initially, such an understanding of an applicant's financial health was derived through interfaces with a company's supporting bank. In 2015, Moula established a relationship with Xero in which business customers utilising Xero's Cloud-based accounting platform could choose to share financial data with Moula for the purpose of assessing credit worthiness. In 2017, Liberty Financial partnered with Moula, providing additional equity for product and team build as well as a funding facility. This enabled Moula to accelerate its growth. By 2019, Moula was processing over 20,000 business loan applications and grew its loan book by 124 percent.

In 2019 Moula introduced its second product, MoulaPay. MoulaPay is a merchant credit facility in which MoulaPay merchants can allow their customers to pay for their business purchases using their MoulaPay facility and manage their repayments within a 12-month cycle. Like Moula Business Loans, MoulaPay experienced rapid acceptance and growth in the Australian market.

The opportunity

Like any other loan makers, managing credit risk is a critical task. Moula's traditional processes used experienced human underwriters to review an application's information (such as through a Xero Cloud-based information) and make a credit assessment. Over time, the credit underwriting team developed significant intellectual property around how to assess credit risk in this environment. Could this human-oriented intellectual property be transitioned into an artificial intelligence environment to achieve better decisions faster?

The initiative

The Moula founders recognised that data could be very insightful, but it took time to build sufficient data assets that could then be leveraged by machine learning engines. Whilst many fintechs had been exploring the use of AI to ease the data collection process, in early 2018, the Moula founders felt that they were ready to explore what else might be possible.

Paul Pesavento joined Moula in April 2018 after a significant number of years building origination platforms for major banks. Paul established the data function of Moula with an initial focus on understanding how and where real-time data might influence a modern credit decisioning workflow. In time, the team was able to build a machine-learning based credit decisioning system.

> We were fortunate to be able to start from scratch and we've developed a capability we call Hector in which the data that exists sits within what I would call our data ecosystem so that the decisioning team can transform and engineer the features that we use, which then drives the machine learning models that responds to those features and facilitates an automated decision.

Moula offered him an opportunity to build a next generation origination platform unconstrained from typical limitations. As Paul notes:

> The traditional approach to credit decisioning automation in the consumer space was to go to a lending vendor such as Experian NBSM or SAS, who would provide you a pre-built system that you would configure and apply your own rules.

This approach would render lenders dependent on the internal technology function to provide data in the shape that was required. As such, lenders would be reliant on technology to change the data to fit to their strategy as it evolved.

Paul stresses that success in building a machine learning credit decisioning platform was not a simple matter of hiring a data team. The learnings established by the business over the years were the cornerstones of success. The features in Hector were developed over the prior years of experience in business.

> One of the founders took the lead for credit – he had the background on how these small businesses work, how accounting data works, where the risks lay. Over time, the IP on what the risk characteristics developed as they worked through a manual solution. So, when I turned up I could convert that into an automated solution. The ability to learn isn't just machine learning. It's also business learning, which is probably 80% of the solution. Machine learning is easy when you have everything set up.

Moula did not immediately cut-over all its credit decisions to Hector. Instead, Moula trialled Hector's effectiveness through adopting a 'zero delegated authority' approach to compare how Hector's decision compared with human experience. As the team gained more confidence in Hector, the delegated authority was progressively raised to such a point whereby Hector is now a key part of the overall process. Moula sees Hector as a critical differentiator, as Moula considers their credit decisioning process to be significantly more effective and less intrusive on their customers than competitor approaches.

Paul considers Moula's de facto operating model to be a key building block for the success of the Hector development:

> By virtue 'well, how do we get this done', you develop an operating model that works really well. It's a bit like the apple falling on Newton's head when you realise that in other organisations, you grow up doing something you have been taught to do … the way the business does things. You don't really think about how to do it differently. It's important to have the expertise and leaders working with you, and have the trust and empowerment to just try and experiment and not feel that you have to have everything perfect on day 1.

Paul asserts that while these models were great, the operating model they chose was something he is most proud of. The operating model encompasses how he and the data team work with the chief underwriter and their team; how they operate and work on a day-to-day basis. They sit together, work through issues, receiving and acting upon feedback in an agile way.

Moula's operating model has a strong emphasis on co-location and empowerment of professional teams to address issues in a highly empowered environment. Not only does this operating model enable rapid resolution of current issues, it also provides an informal mechanism to encourage experimentation. Paul explains:

> I don't think it's a conscious thing that we allocate time or space or persons or whatever to deliberate exploring. I think it's the opportunities that present themselves that force you to explore and solve that thing that you hadn't been thinking about yesterday.

The experimentation this model enables isn't driven by top-down innovation mandates, but rather through a dynamic approach to addressing challenges. In fact, Paul concludes that such an approach – of 'getting thrown challenges'– initiates innovation, such that they were being forced to iterate 'in a direction that you may not have been considering'. This approach leveraged their strengths, adding to what they are capable of doing.

Whilst much of this discussion has focussed on the use of machine learning (a form of AI), Cloud technology was also a key ingredient to Moula's success. As part of the plan to enable rapid scaling of business loans, Moula migrated from an on-prem environment to the Microsoft Azure ecosystem in approximately 2018. In addition to this, the move towards Azure enabled the Hector development team to utilise the broader Azure ML capabilities as they developed Hector.

The situation today

Like many organisations, Moula was impacted by the exogenous shock of the COVID-19 pandemic. While some organisations had a significant need for additional funding to realise the opportunities in front of them, others needed to quickly adjust their operating tempo and their finance repayments. Through this, Moula's Cloud-based operating platform (powered by Hector) continues to grow and provide critical finance to Australian organisations.

The capabilities of Hector continue to be refined as the business identifies and pursues new opportunities. The Moula team is also considering opportunities across the SME credit lifecycle as well as supporting the growth of its second offering (MoulaPay).

> We're now segmenting and optimising more. For us, it is still early days. We're scratching the surface of a lot of things. As our business grows and scales and as we grow our products, you see how you can tailor things. We need that scale to happen, but this will enable that as we move. It's just 'what is the right solution at the right time'. Having the business context and the ability to develop the platform as one team as opposed to handoffs is really important.

Antecedent alignment

The Moula case study demonstrates a number of the factors for success discussed in Chapter 2. Three strongly demonstrated factors are discussed below.

Proactive leadership

It will come as no surprise to our readers that – as a founder-led company – proactive leadership has been identified as a key factor in Moula's success to date. There are three specific nuances to highlight.

First, the founders had a clear sense of an opportunity in the market and were able to complement their individual skills with the skills and resources of others (employees and partners) to bring their vision to life.

Second, the founders realised they did not have all of the answers. As such, they sought to inspire others to do their best work. They instilled a corporate culture of trust and empowerment, enabling the individuals within the organisation to solve the problems they saw as they pursued the market opportunity. The founders – in particular, the CEO – continued to communicate the vision and allowed the broader Moula team to strive to keep the vision and the idea alive.

Finally, the founders had an 'instinctive' sense that data would be an important corporate asset in the medium term, and they invested early, without the certainty of return. They designed their origination and servicing platforms to capture data, trusting that the captured data would eventually be used to create a competitive advantage. In the words of Paul Pesavento:

> When the founders first established the processes they understood that they didn't know everything. So, because they were storing digitised data, they could go back and extract insight to questions you didn't know back then, that you may now choose to try to solve different questions with that data.

Overcoming process inertia

Moula is not the only market participant in this area. In addition to the incumbents (the big 4 banks, Macquarie and the mid-tier banks, the credit union movement, and others), there are a range of other fintech companies seeking to win a share of this market segment. However, these organisations tend to draw from a common pool of talent, which is steeped in the traditional ways of doing things. There is a strong attitude that 'unless we are moving forward and trying to make things happen, they are not going to happen'. Paul asserts that it's this mindset and culture that distinguishes them from other banks.

> They'll have ideas. The same ideas will come by because it always does. But, there is some fundamental organisational permafrost that will just stop an initiative. They will throw things on what they might think important because that's what always has been important, but it really isn't that important. It's less important than the opportunity they are not capitalising on.

Risk tolerance

Through much of this case study we have considered risk from a credit risk perspective. Moula's ability to manage credit risk has matured as its machine learning platform matured. As an emerging company, the Moula management team was very conscious of the need to manage credit risk and minimise losses, even within during a historically benign credit environment. Over time, while the theory of how risk is managed has not necessarily changed, the automation has built a lot more confidence in their approach in regard to understanding how risk is and how it's measured. 'You could say that it is the application of our agreed risk appetite that has improved'.

In addition to managing credit risk, Moula takes a collective approach to resource allocation risk. 'Resource allocation risk is something that we collectively manage by virtue that there is a risk that you are not doing the right thing'.

Closing thoughts

Although Moula could be considered a typical fintech disruptor, this case study highlights the challenges incumbents face regarding overcoming process inertia. We believe this is a key antecedent for all incumbents to consider as they contemplate how they might revitalise their business model.

Case study 3: SEEK

We now turn to SEEK. Across industries there is a genuine need to answer the question of what do major incumbents need to do, and what processes must they have in place to successfully incorporate Cloud and AI. Examining SEEK, and its journey from early disruptor to one of the leaders in the market, can help articulate what one successful approach looks like in a real-world sense, and bring to life elements of the toolkit that incumbents need to develop to thrive in this world of Cloud and AI. They are an example of an established disruptor disrupting themselves through Cloud and AI.

An overview of SEEK

In 1997, SEEK was founded by Matt Rockman, Andrew Bassat and Paul Bassat in Melbourne, Australia. It began as a disruptive online marketplace leveraging the internet and technology to build a low cost and highly effective online employment platform.

SEEK was publicly listed on the Australian Stock Exchange in 2005 and continues to be an Australian owned and operated business employing more than 1,000 people in Australia. The SEEK Group's international portfolio of employment and education businesses gives exposure to approximately 2.9 billion people. The portfolio primarily comprises of online employment marketplaces which are geographically situated in Australia, New Zealand, Hong Kong, Malaysia, Singapore, Thailand, Indonesia, Philippines, Vietnam, Brazil and Mexico.

Since its inception, SEEK has become Australia's number one jobs, employment, career and recruitment site in the ANZ online marketplace, holding market leadership on key metrics such as monthly visits, brand awareness and placement share.

Post the sell-down of its share of Zhaopin, SEEK expects to generate more than $1B of revenue in financial year 2021/2022. SEEK holds the largest market share in Australia (34.3%) and has double the unprompted brand awareness relative to its closest competitor, and SEEK also holds the largest market share in South East Asia (23%).[4]

The opportunity

Whilst some might see SEEK as a relatively recent disruptor, the reality differs.

SEEK's original vision was to be outstanding at both sales and marketing as well as delivering outstanding, customer-oriented service to candidates and hirers. Broadly, SEEK's history can be viewed in stages, with phase one primarily focussed on winning in what was, as Simon Lusted, SEEK's Managing Director – Strategy, Product and AI – says, 'a relatively simple market along the dimensions of sales and marketing'. During this phase, sales and marketing through traditional print was the most effective way to solve the information problem at the heart of their business – ensuring that employers and employees are aware of – and have access to – the best candidates or jobs.

Over time, this customer-orientation enabled SEEK to achieve its leading position in the market. This sales and marketing focus translated to a relatively immature product and technology capability, a defining feature of this phase. 'When I joined SEEK someone senior said to me, we are not a technology business, we are a sales and marketing business, and we both actually agreed that that might be a problem'.

The trigger for SEEK's journey into its second phase was in 2012 after it underwent a strategic review to determine whether a proactive approach needed to be taken, given the shifts in the basis of competition identified across the US and European markets. While they weren't under pressure in Australia and other core markets, there were some dramatic shifts in the US and European competition. 'We could see businesses with the same pedigree and history as us were being run over the top by far more technologically advanced disruptors'.

Specifically, these disruptors were outcompeting traditional players by using technology to collect job ads from employers, attract candidates, and connect the two roles previously defined by sales and marketing efforts. 'Increasingly technology such as search aggregation, social and mobile were creating ways to break the constraint, and innovative players were using that against the more traditional players'.

In order to future-proof its business, SEEK has committed to major, ongoing investment into AI and technology to develop world class products that ultimately help solve information problems between candidates and hirers. SEEK proudly shares that their innovation, empowerment and collaboration-led company culture has facilitated the successful operation of its technology-based solutions. Their philosophy is to be 'world leaders in applying the state of the art'.

The initiative

With the basis of competition clearly shifting, SEEK identified that its position as a sales and marketing focussed business was untenable, and so it decided to invest ahead of the curve and build up its product and technology capability to augment its strengths in sales and marketing. From here it was a matter of identifying how product and technology show up in customer needs and use cases, and identifying what technologies can or are being used to satisfy those needs. The solution identified was to focus on machine learning and AI:

> We are at our core a business that is about solving an information problem for candidates and hirers, and we were seeing that there was very high leveraging of certain types of data technology, whether you want to call them machine learning or AI on the information problems that we care about.

As such, SEEK's second phase was defined by its decision to build out the necessary product and technology capabilities to enable the adoption of AI and machine learning, with the main market constraint shifting to become its 'ability to access, understand and leverage data and apply AI'. In this phase, customer needs and uses cases determine which AI software and products were created and(or) outsourced for SEEK to implement. From 2012 onwards, SEEK's investor reports outlined the decision for significant capital expenditure and investments to be made that would primarily focus on developing and improving AI products and technologies.

The situation today

SEEK's adoption of AI began with them taking a centre of excellence (COE) approach – this allowed expert teams to embed AI into specific select workflows and take new products to market in a 'non-controversial way from an organisational perspective'. Essentially, the COE approach allowed SEEK to build products that recommended jobs to candidates as a proof of concept that they could do a better job than they could without AI.

This approach was highly successful to begin with, however benefits began capping out after 12 months. This is because the proof-of-concept products that were showing great promise were not able to be applied to the core product of the business – the core results page.

> We really struggled to actually address problems in our core, so things like 60% and 70% of the value that we create is generated from the core results search page. We couldn't get a COE team in, partly because we had a vendor there that was delivering traditional IR based search.

Another contributing factor to the benefits of the COE model capping out was the dissonance that began to emerge between the vision and expectation of product leaders and AI subject matter experts in terms of what could and should be achieved. There was 'this knowledge gap' between product leader and a subject matter expert AI analyst.

> The product leader might want AI to do something, but they don't know what is possible. The subject matter expert AI analyst wants to do something, but they do not understand the customer problem. So you just have these two wheels spinning and an interface between them that is just pure gridlock.

SEEK's leadership noticed these issues and decided to steer away from the COE approach and towards an integrated centralised AI product team, with AI viewed more as a product. These centralised product teams included engineers, product managers, analysts and data scientists who contract with experience teams to jointly solve problems.

SEEK also faced a strategic choice when determining the leader of this integrated centralised team. SEEK felt they had a choice of appointing either a 'tech' leader (who is oriented towards understanding and delivering the possibilities of the technology) or an 'enterprise' leader (a leader that balances strategy, people, process, stakeholders, and organisation). SEEK selected Grant Wright, an enterprise leader, as the leader of the group. As Simon relates:

> Many companies go with the data person. It's a mistake in my view unless they are genuine enterprise leader. Grant has a key part of the journey – he is a non-data leader who managed the team and stakeholders for last four years or so.

Stakeholder management in this context goes beyond the typical 'stakeholder management' described in management textbooks. In this emerging area, data science, software engineering, and 'product' professionals didn't have an agreed set of norms about how the groups would work together. Furthermore, in the SEEK situation, the tools, processes and decision rights were all in flux. SEEK felt that they needed an enterprise leader such as Grant to lead them through that discovery process.

> There's no established pattern to copy. There is no 'Spotify model' – just idealised blog posts. We had engineers with 20 years of deterministic process clashing with new data science types, who are inherently probabilistic and use less established tools and processes. Add on to that tension a product team that is focussed on experiences and not information products. That's what Grant has helped us navigate.

This centralised approach coupled with enterprise leadership was able to break down the team silos that previously existed and allowed for innovation and solutions to be industrialised and applied in a standard way across all problems, including those in the core. This approach also ensured that engineers were not disconnected from use cases and were solving actual business problems. On top of this, the concept of having contracts in place was essential to SEEK's success as it aligned teams on what had been agreed for a service in terms of delivery and built a collective sense of responsibility for outcomes and trust between and within teams. 'To enable ownership of the information problem end-to-end you need data scientists, engineers and product managers all thinking about the same problem in the same team because that is where the innovation happens'.

On top of this, the perspective that AI should be seen as a product (e.g. the core search product), resulted in SEEK's 2-step approach, with the first step being to build a product that solves a customer problem, and the second step being to combine this product with a broader experience. This process required the experience and AI teams to work together, however the team with the data scientists and engineers was held accountable for solving the information problem – again ensuring that there is clear accountability.

It is important to note that the first step of this process relied on SEEK's 'Thin Slice' approach to thinking about building and delivering AI enabled products. This was essentially a modified Minimum Viable Product (MVP) model, an approach used by other organisations to demonstrate the 'do-ability' of a change in process in highly complex organisations, similar to what Commonwealth Bank did in the 2000s during their core banking modernisation.

In practice, the creation of a 'Thin Slice' required all key components such as a contract to be in place, a process to monitor Service Level Agreements (SLAs) to be identified and a feedback loop of data to improve the product to be sourced – without these things a proof of concept could not be called a 'Thin Slice'. And so, the creation of a 'Thin Slice', was able to demonstrate both the value of a new product, as well as its practicality and feasibility. This in turn enabled the speed at which products can be developed to increase and ensured that leaders and the team more broadly was confident that the product would work. SEEK's aim was to then increase the speed of 'Thin Slice' delivery cycles, to further accelerate this process.

In short, SEEK's adoption of AI has brought about profound and long-lasting successes across the entire business, and it is thought to be one of the reasons that they have not lost market share. Three key examples of this success are:

1. Premium ads which could not have been introduced without SEEK's improved AI capability, and its ability to enable value-based pricing.
2. Increased search efficiency, through the rollout of Smarter Search which delivered a 20% uplift in search efficiency across eight markets, meaning that 'the search function is so much better that candidates apply for roles 20% more often than they used to'. This led to significant share growth in Australia, 'and now forms the basis for at least 4–5 years of really significant innovation runway'.

3. AI is now woven through SEEK's product experience from smart contextual suggestions and nudging in flows, to core search and personalisation, recommendations, monetisation and pricing, candidate selection (highlighting key skills qualities), to underlying taxonomies and normalisation. SEEK's leadership team feels that this could not have been achieved under the previous COE approach).

Antecedent alignment

There is a genuine need to inspire and provide a toolkit of what needs to be in place to successfully incorporate AI into an incumbent. The SEEK case study demonstrates a number of factors that are essential for the success, with 4 strongly demonstrated factors discussed below:

Proactive leadership

Despite SEEK being an 'organisation that does not like change more than any other', leadership was able to proactively look to future-proof their organisation against disruptors before any pressure was felt. This approach has prevented SEEK from losing market share, and indeed allowed them to win in the market.

On top of being proactive in terms of getting in front of problems, the SEEK case study also stresses the importance of having leadership that proactively seeks to understand the relevant technology in order to understand the strengths and limitations.

> You need a leader that understands enough about what might be possible (for example, the different types of neural networks, their potential and their limitations). This leader needs to know this to some level because they need to be able to constructively engage with those people who do know this stuff. That is the 'hens teeth' challenge.

Strategic process strength

SEEK, as an organisation, was very strong in terms of its strategic process, especially at the leadership level. The organisation was strategy led, and has a high level of strategic clarity, due in part to the willingness of leadership to engage in robust debates. The continuity of this strategy was also important, with leaders being supportive and committed to the AI outcomes, and willing to back themselves over multiple financial cycles. Because of the leadership support and commitment, the team was clear as to why they were doing what they were doing and the benefit it would derive. 'We held ourselves pretty accountable to do it'.

That said, room for this strategic process to improve was identified, specifically in terms of ensuring that strategic thinking penetrates deeper into the organisation outside of leadership.

Exploration and exploitation

The explore-exploit aspect was quite strong. At the beginning of the AI journey, SEEK had an explore focus, as there was no accumulated knowledge or expertise. Small teams of 5–10 people owned a space, innovated, and delivered and optimised services. A critical element during this explore phase was the patience of leadership, who would fund and support AI products even when things were not going well.

However, SEEK has discovered that, due to its scale, small autonomous teams cannot continue to explore whilst they also undergo exploitation work. This has meant that some teams explore function has been starved, whilst exploitation work has been carried out. In the short term, this has been quite positive because teams have been motivated by constantly seeing the benefits of releasing products. However, the problem is that the forward-looking roadmap is less specified and defined, as less explore work is being undertaken. Essentially, the current organisational structure had limited the degree to which teams could explore and exploit, and so the organisational structure evolved to unlock this potential. SEEK expects that this organisational structure is not the end-state and will continue to evolve to support the needs of the business as they evolve.

Risk tolerance

SEEK's outlook on risk was that it exists in every action and decision, so completely eliminating risk is not feasible. When taking risks, it is essential that leadership, and SEEK as an organisation more broadly, has clarity around what the specifics of the risks are being taken are. It's not that there isn't risk, 'because everything is [a] risk'. But rather, there was more specific clarity over the risk.

Closing thoughts

The experience described in this case study, highlights the need for perseverance and long-term investment in order to deliver long-term value. At various points, SEEK had all the technical and technology capabilities required, but there was still a need to drive the appropriate alignment and collaboration across teams, to deliver the right customer outcomes.

Case study 4: Kogan

We now turn to Kogan. In many ways, Kogan is following SEEK's path, only to be delivered faster and with a culture of opportunistic entrepreneurialism.

An overview of Kogan

Kogan was born from a home garage in 2006, starting with the contract manufacturing of two models of television units in China. Since then, it has placed an aggressive focus on growing through asymmetric opportunities with significant upside and limited downside. Today it is an Australian Securities Exchange (ASX)-listed business with 230 employees in Melbourne, 20 in Shenzhen, and over 140 outsourced staff members in the Philippines, plus more than 200 staff members in New Zealand who operate the Mighty Ape business that Kogan acquired. Kogan has grown to become a portfolio of retail and services businesses with nearly $1B in annual revenue across Australia and New Zealand. To do this, Kogan has significantly transformed its business model and supporting technology platforms and systems over the years.

Kogan's business model is organised into a set of verticals, each of which provides consumers with either a range of services (such as Kogan Mobile) or physical, white-labelled products. Kogan has over ten million products for sale, the majority of which sell through their marketplace by third parties. Kogan manufactures less than one percent of all products listed on their marketplace channel, and the products sold by Kogan are predominately private label or inventory taken from third party brands. Notwithstanding that less than one percent of all products are sold by Kogan, these products reflect more than half of total product sales on Kogan's platform.

The opportunity

Kogan takes an entrepreneurial approach to innovation, with broader management receptive to new ideas and insights from across the organisation. Some of these innovations are tactical and specific focussed, such as initiatives designed to improve efficiency within a specific department. These ideas are often sourced 'bottom up' from within the organisation and prioritised for development using a 'value card', where the likely financial or non-financial benefits associated with execution are defined. If Kogan finds initiatives that have the potential to, for example, generate $50,000 of additional net profit, or save the equivalent of one FTE over a year, it will be prioritised based on value to the organisation. This approach generates an ongoing and prioritised backlog of improvements, which leverage the benefits of automation and process improvement.

The process of gathering these inputs is free of hierarchy, however larger investment decisions tend to be made by a set of senior leaders, who are constantly scanning for opportunities in the market. Ideas or strategies for starting a new business vertical, making an acquisition or launching major products such as Kogan mobile are typically discussed at the highest level of the organisation. Launching a marketplace, for example, required a detailed market and competitor analysis, followed by an internal assessment of competitive advantage levers. This was supported by an execution assessment, where delivery capabilities, cost, lead times and required internal expertise are considered.

In some cases, Kogan's approach is opportunistic, such as when the company bought Dick Smith and Matt Blatt, distressed businesses with valuable brands. These acquisitions were separate to Kogan's existing strategies, however they identified that there was an asymmetric opportunity to salvage struggling businesses, broaden their market reach, and scale profitably without disrupting operations.

Given Kogan's heritage as an internet business, and a mantra that Kogan are 'statisticians masquerading as retailers', each of these changes in the business model have a few things in common, specifically an element of newness, with business decisions replicated on an ongoing basis over their last ten years of operations. Kogan do not rely on emulating another business model or methodology. Because this approach relies on novel business innovations, they have taken an experimentation-based approach to business development. In the words of David Shafer, chief financial officer, chief operating officer and executive director 'by thinking about the way things should be done, trying an approach, learning along the way and letting the data prevail'. Shafer says:

> In our organisation, we have a culture where the data prevails, and it doesn't matter whether an idea is presented by me or Ruslan (Kogan) or anyone else, ultimately there's a test and learn scenario, and the test fails, and we pivot. The truth prevails in the organisation and I think having a metrics data-oriented culture is helpful in a truth prevails context, because the data is everywhere, and if you can tap into it, then you can demonstrate a point for or against.

Despite their brand for being a tech-based business, at points in their development (in particular, before they had their Initial Public Offering (IPO)), their prior, legacy technology stack had become a bottleneck for growth, which necessitated significant investment.

The initiative

When Kogan was a ~$200M revenue business, the company still relied on downloading sales and spreadsheets from the website, periodically amending elements, manually emailing sales orders and using outdated accounting systems. These back-end limitations caused a range of bottlenecks and inefficiencies: unnoticeable from a customer's perspective, but no longer appropriate for a publicly listed company seeking automation. These processes resulting in warehousing and dispatch inefficiencies, customer service errors and poor order visibility. The desire to be a publicly listed company and access additional capital to grow, necessitated a change. As Shafer states, 'necessity is the mother of invention, and we were operating on spreadsheets'.

To manifest this change, Kogan implanted SAP Business One, a Cloud-based ERP (Enterprise Resource Planning), to improve data integrity and enable central storage. A layer was then created around SAP, with their own software constantly polling SAP for information and presenting it to internal stakeholders in a more useable format, such as user-friendly dashboards and reports.

The situation today

Having this underlying technology provide a layer of reliability was critical. Between 2016 and 2021, Kogan grew from about $200M in gross sales to approximately a billion dollars. Having a significant degree of automation and high data integrity reports was essential to power the business to grow. The foundational IS platform was subsequently connected to a raft of best-in-breed tools, tailored to the needs of each department's unique needs. The people who lead specific teams and projects have the autonomy to select the tools used in their department, in-line with Kogan's decentralised leadership culture.

This approach differs from many others as part of a distributed ownership concept, as Shafer says, with:

> the people best equipped to make software decisions the people who are actually operating and tracking business metrics and KPIs in that team. We find that this approach means that they are getting the latest and best tools ... using an open concept driven by KPIs.

Kogan's combination of a data-led culture, together with best in breed tools, has led to significant personalisation based on what customers are clicking, browsing, and purchasing. Today, this level of personalisation is powered by machine learning, and thorough data analysis beyond which an individual person could ever do.

Antecedent alignment

Market and customer sensing

The primary motivator for Kogan's use of AI and Cloud technology, is purely to capture market opportunities. Since its founding, Kogan has focussed on identifying opportunities for 'asymmetric returns'.

> The essential principle is that we want to make a large number of educated bets in spaces where we think we can provide value in a significant industry where there's a lot of consumer demand and where we can have a huge amount of upside for a very limited downside.

The combination of that approach, together with personalisation from a single data source, guides their understanding of the customer's current and future preferences. Kogan has one cohort of customers within one data lake, which includes all of the data from each of our different divisions, providing a valuable source for data analytics. These insights create future opportunities for Kogan to build new verticals with data providing a digital footprint of customer behaviour across their digital channels: browsing, purchasing or clicking, and using that information to create a better experience for consumers.

Risk tolerance

A critical enabler of this strategy is Kogan's degree of comfort with quantified, risk-based decision making. The company is trying to adopt a risk mitigation approach to growth, by pursuing many opportunities, failing fast and pivoting before identifying additional asymmetric opportunities. Over the history of the business, this has led to a range of successful new ventures, 'including the launch of Kogan mobile six years ago, in partnership with Vodafone, now capturing more than 2% of the telecom market in Australia and hugely profitable'.

A critical aspect of this, is their focus on measurable, hierarchy-agnostic, data-led decision making driven by the desire to achieve the right outcomes for the business in the most practical way, enabled by technology.

Closing thoughts

Kogan, and their data-driven, decentralised culture, are a great example of 'opportunistic innovation'. While they have a digital-centric brand, they were very selective about when to upgrade their systems, and view technology as a means to an end, not an end (or differentiator) itself. The combination of this culture and strategic approach, have enabled them to drive significant top and bottom-line growth in the highly competitive and challenging retail sector.

Case study 5: Bank of Queensland

An overview of the Bank of Queensland

The Bank of Queensland (BOQ) began in 1874 as a building society. Until recent years, it was best known as a mid-tier regional bank, predominantly servicing Queensland and New South Wales customers. The business was very people-dependent, serving retail and small business customers.

In addition to an accelerated branch opening program between 2001 and 2004, the bank also grew through a series of wide and varied acquisitions including the acquisition of UFJ's equipment finance business (2003), Home Building Society (2007), Pioneer Permanent Building Society (2007), CIT Vendor Finance (2010), Virgin Money (Australia) Pty Ltd (2013), and Investec Bank (Australia) Limited (2014) among others. These acquisitions were kept relatively unintegrated due to the high cost of developing a single set of consistent systems across each (at the time those businesses were acquired). As a consequence, BOQ lacked the scale advantages of their big 4 competitors and were also hobbled with technology systems described by their previous chairman Roger David as a 'bowl of spaghetti'.

Like any bank, their business model was relatively straightforward, and was being increasingly commoditised. As they were so people-dependent, they were also challenged by the increasing use of brokers (for retail customers) and customers' expectations of an improved digital experience.

The increasing desire for digital-first interfaces had a dual-impact for BOQ. For one, it created a disadvantaged customer experience relative to competitive alternatives. It also increased the number and range of competitors that BOQ had to compete against. In this landscape, digital competitors like Macquarie's Banking and Financial Services arm, were growing at multiples of the 'system' growth rate.[5]

Simultaneously, and in light of the Financial Services Royal Commission, regulators were increasing standards for risk management and executive accountability. The fallout from the Royal Commission was immense. Serving as a catalyst for numerous conduct, remediation and transformation programs across almost every Australian bank, particularly the big 4 banks,[6] it significantly increased their cost-to-income ratios for the banks, while driving a general culture of risk aversion across the sector.

Like most banks, BOQ had also embarked on a core banking platform redevelopment, called Denovo. In its case, BOQ was re-platforming the Virgin Money Australia (VMA) branded bank, such that it would serve as the channel to bring on a younger, digital-first customer cohort.

All this is to say, these challenges put BOQ in a position where it was underperforming against its competitors. In a statement to the ASX, outgoing chairman Roger Davis said, 'We have seen enormous regulatory, technological and economic change. I believe now is the appropriate time to transition to a new chairman'. This change was the first in a series of deliberate changes to reposition the strategy of the bank. This change in strategic direction has led to its transformation and repositioning in the market as a genuine competitor to the Big 4, with a far stronger strategic position than its mid-tier competitors. These changes began with Patrick Allaway, the new chairman, bringing on George Frazis as the new Group CEO, who subsequently brought on Ewen Stafford, as the group chief financial officer and chief operating officer.

The changes in the executive provided the group with some diverse perspectives on where the market was heading, particularly given the diverse background of the new executives. Frazis had an extensive background in banking, with experience heading a variety of organisations and brands in different parts of the market. Likewise, Stafford had deep experience in banking, but was also a senior executive in other organisations, including Telstra and Australia Post. This combination of experience was a critical part of a group-wide strategy refresh, which would reset the position of the bank, within a very mature sector of the economy.

The opportunity

BOQ's transformation journey began with proactive leadership. Each of its new executives brought a growth and challenger mindset. This culminated in the development of an aggressive new strategy which addressed their fundamental market positioning challenges. In the words of Ewen Stafford, 'If I roll back 2 years or even 18 months, I don't believe that view was the prevailing view. In fact, I think people very much saw us in no man's land. That's very different from today'. In his 'glass half full' view of their strategy, BOQ could 'have scale and the customer numbers and balance sheet in a way that a fintech couldn't. We're also small enough to really take advantage of the technology, the environment and the macro trends around the customer choice'.

Achieving this would require:

> at the core of the strategy ... a whole different cost structure. A cost structure that's much more akin to the start-ups than it is to the major banks, but with a really differentiated set of customer propositions across the multi brand strategy.

The initiative

Key to this was leveraging the existing Denovo programme, such that it would transition the larger part of the bank to a single core banking platform. This platform would be part of a fundamental change as to how the bank would reinvent itself and its cost structure:

> We were fortunate that we inherited the Denovo programme ... At that point it was being built as a standalone technology stack for that particular brand, and we've since taken that strategy and made it a certain hall of retail banking, and potentially in time, it will also include the business bank as well.

The commitment from the Board and Executive Committee cascaded through the organisation:

> There were certainly different reactions within the organisation. Some saw it as a threat, some saw it as an opportunity. That enterprise commitment was the way forward. It fundamentally changed the way in which people then interacted with the transformation programme. It was no longer a silo; it was the path forward for the organisation.

While this change meant the BOQ Board and executive were taking on additional delivery risk, that risk was a fundamental requirement to its transformation:

> A key learning I would say, if you want to get your digital programmes to be taken seriously, is that you need to actually take the risk that they are meaningful for large parts of the organisation, even if they're going to be disrupted by them.

Cloud technology was also a key part of the successful acquisition of ME Bank. This was an instrumental element of BOQ's multi-brand, growth strategy. ME Bank and BOQ had a clear path to a common core banking platform 'That was a very critical part of the consideration set. It certainly was heavily reflected in the valuation models'.

Successfully executing on this acquisition has dramatically shifted BOQ's position in the market. It now stands near-5th in terms of size, drawing clear daylight with its traditional competitors, all the while diversifying its customer base.

> Geographically, we were heavily skewed to Queensland and NSW. This now provides a very strong presence in Victoria and in the mobile market, so it gives us a much better balance across the across the eastern seaboard as well. So that [was] an important part of that business model build out.

The situation today

BOQ continues to operate through five main channels: Owner-Managed Branches (OMBs) who run similarly to franchisees, Corporate-run branches, mobile bankers, brokers, and call centres. Many customer-facing processes were heavily or completely dependent on people-led processes. While this resulted in strong relationships and deep understanding of customer needs, the lack of digitisation and technology created inconsistency in the customer experience. Additionally, bankers and support staff were burdened by a significant workload. Despite having an abundance of data, BOQ was unable to leverage benefit from those assets.

The lack of system integration and channel complexity at BOQ was at the extreme. Within the Retail business, there were two core systems, and even greater complexity within the Business Bank. This complexity resulted in slow processes with significant amounts of manual intervention. In contrast, now it takes only four minutes to sign up to a VMA bank account. The process and customer experience on the website is tracked through the journey; this helps BOQ inform its transformation program as to where investment should be made in its ongoing system and process improvements. The adoption of Cloud technologies has enabled the bank to scale its customer data and develop standardised processes that systematically improves the customer experience and maintains a high quality of service.

One unique aspect of BOQ's technology adoption is the focus on embedding a, 'purpose-led, customer culture' in a technology driven way. Rather than simply replacing the current state ways of working with technology, there was a deliberate focus on leveraging the strengths of each channel and focussing their digitisation efforts only on the areas which were most suited to automation and machine led decision making.

Antecedent alignment

Industry dynamism

BOQ's position as a mid-tier bank sitting in between the big 4 and the smaller fintech/start-ups presented unique opportunities and risks. BOQ chose to be proactive and leverage its scale and access balance sheet (relative to fintechs), and its relative efficiency and nimbleness (relative to the big 4), to acquire ME Bank and consolidate its back-end to reduce its cost structure.

Risk tolerance

The new leadership team has been actively 'moving out' the risk appetite, convincing the board to improve their comfortability to take on risk. The key driver of this was the senior management team who fully aligned and supported the refreshed strategy and the need to take on necessary and well managed risks successfully deliver transformation.

Opportunity/threat drivers

Macro circumstances, the post-Royal Commission environment, and a perceived structural disadvantage for the mid-tier banks, formed a critical threat. By leveraging a common, cloud-based platform, BOQ were able to fundamentally shift that view. In Stafford's view:

> Even 18 months ago, there were a lot of questions about structural disadvantages. I think there were absolutely those. That view is starting to disappear, and in fact, given some of the legacy challenges the big banks have, not that we don't have our own, by the way, but they're nothing compared to them relatively.

In addition to this, the cloud-based platform constituted a key part of their focus on a multi-brand strategy which simplifies and consolidates their supporting systems:

> change in strategy last year to go from wanting to build a sort of a standalone, rather than we're going to take our existing retail bank and potential acquisitions, and put this on the digital stack in a multi-brand format, to take advantage of that cost-to-income, that economic scale and simplification benefit, and then being the engine for effectively that digitalized growth … which non-digital companies just can't match.

As a result, this simplification created a significant opportunity for BOQ Group to have a competitive advantage in the acquisition of ME Bank, due to the common T24 core banking platform.

Closing thoughts

A few years ago, BOQ was facing significant challenges in the market due to their technology limitations and significant technology debt. This backdrop did not suggest that BOQ would be able to transform its business model using new technology. The combination of proactive leadership, together with a business-wide shift in strategy, mindset, and risk appetite, have had a dramatic impact within a short time span. This further highlights the importance of business leadership and culture, when taking advantage of these new AI and Cloud technologies.

Case study 6: PEXA

The previous case studies have explored organisations seeking to develop and/or refine their competitive proposition. PEXA is an unusual case, in which an industry collectively formed a new entrant as a means to overcome intractable process inertia issues … powered by the Cloud.

An overview of PEXA

Many of our case studies have explored how incumbents have renewed their business model through AI and Cloud. Our next case study is slightly different – a situation where the incumbents realised that a new paradigm would benefit all parties and therefore, founded an independent organisation to develop, deploy and operate that new paradigm, enabling those incumbents to commence their own business model renewal. PEXA (Property Exchange Australia) was formed in 2010 to fulfil the Council of Australian Governments' (COAG) initiative to deliver a single, national e-Conveyancing solution to the Australian property industry. PEXA – originally known as National e-Conveyancing Development Limited – recently listed on the Australian Stock Exchange with a market capitalisation in the order of A$3B.

The opportunity

Prior to 2010, transferring a real property in Australia involved a number of parties working through a conveyancing process. Once a buyer and seller had committed to a contract (an extensive process in and of itself), a range of specialists were retained to enact the agreement. Both parties would typically employ solicitors or conveyancing agents to handle the paperwork, and frequently both the buyer and seller would have a lender involved. At an agreed time, the buyers' and sellers' agents as well as agents of the respective lender would meet in a settlement room to exchange signed documents, bank cheques, paper title documentation. Prior to exchange, the parties would check the relevant documentation to ensure all was in order. Following this, the parties would exit the settlement room to deposit the cheques and lodge documentation with the relevant land registries office.

However, approximately 30% of settlements had to be delayed or rescheduled. There could be documentation issues such as differences in names and amounts. There could also be issues with the titles, or situations where someone had lodged a caveat on a title. Given this was an in-person activity, settlements could also fail to complete for the simple reason that one of the many participants did not attend on time.

Even with this physical exchange of documentation, various challenges could occur. It takes time for funds to clear and for land registries to process changes – it was possible for a caveat to be placed on a title after physical settlement had occurred but before the title transfer had been actioned.

The land registries had seen this hazard, and at least two registries (New South Wales and Victoria) had initiated digital conveyancing initiatives to cure these issues.

Australia has an interesting combination of state-based land registries and national banks. These national banks have to deal with eight different land registries with their own processes and expectations. The banks were concerned that they would have to link into a variety of state-based systems, essentially replicating in the digital world the silo processes that existed in the paper world.

The issue of how best to move to a nation-wide digital conveyancing platform was brought to the attention of the Business Regulation and Competition section of the 2010 Council of Australian Governments.[7] The result was the PEXA predecessor, which was established by a consortium of four state land registries (New South Wales (NSW), Queensland, Victoria and Western Australia). Each vended in the intellectual capital associated with their past efforts. The big 4 banks invested shortly thereafter, and the development began.

Could an entity independent of any of the key participants successfully deliver a lasting solution?

The initiative

As Todd Reichmann, PEXA's Chief Strategy Officer, explains, 'the whole experience needed to be rethought and brought into the digital age'. Like New South Wales and Victoria, several land registries in the world had been exploring exactly how to achieve this digital enablement:

> If you look around the world, what you typically see are land registries digitising elements of the process. For example, you might be able to submit a form digitally, or you can sign a form digitally with a digital signature.

However, no geography had managed to solve this problem in a holistic sense. Nowhere in the world had been able to 'provide a digital environment where all of the essential participants [could] collaborate, [could] verify and validate information'. In other words, no one had been able to develop a platform that combined lodgement of title documents and financial settlement, one that could be 'the nexus of everything you need to do to take a buyer from having signed the contract to getting the keys'.

Success wasn't a simple matter of deploying technology – a sense of industry transformation was required.

Our founding CEO, Marcus Price – who oversaw the first ten years of PEXA – thought the reason past initiatives failed was because these projects were seen as a technology project to effectively enable paper processes. His view was that this was really an industry evolution and we needed to create a solution that will create value for all stakeholders. It was really his drive and sense that this was a whole industry transformation rather than a technology enablement project that allowed PEXA to get to where it is.

Significant investment was made, yet only a minority of this was on technology. As Reichmann explains:

Of the investment required to get to profitability about a third of that was on the platform itself and the other two-thirds was on industry engagement and all the other spending needed to get to that point, which was seeking to convert the industry.

In addition to this, PEXA brought in additional funders to help it realise its ambitions. Initially, PEXA raised money from participating banks, then eventually receiving more funding from commercial shareholders like Macquarie Bank and the Little Group.

It was in some regard a public-private partnership. The states were effectively given equity for their existing IP and early contribution. However, it was very much a private sector attempt to build this as past public-led efforts had not succeeded.

As one could imagine, the conversion of an entire industry wasn't without its challenges, particularly given the network economics of a platform organisation such as PEXA. 'In the early days, first of all we had to get people signed up to the platform. We had to get them their certificate. We had to get them registered and we had to verify their identity'. This process in itself involved a number of steps. The training of people came next, in order to have them start to use the platform. What was particularly pertinent was getting both sides to use the platform. 'You might run a digitally savvy conveyancing business, but if the vendor of the property your client bought is using a conveyancing agent that does everything by fax, then you couldn't use PEXA'. In order to overcome this 'chicken or the egg' situation, PEXA initially sought out instances that only required a single member as opposed to two or more.

Lodging a caveat is a good example – you can lodge a caveat and there is no counterparty to that. The banks might also have single party transactions – perhaps someone pays off their mortgage, or someone gets a line of credit on an unencumbered house. Whilst the volumes of such transactions isn't significant in the grand scheme of things, at least it got people using the platform.

This initial foothold was then expanded by pursuing transactions with a focussed user group.

> The second big one was refinance. Effectively that's a bank-to-bank transaction. Again, both banks need to be on the platform, but the banks saw the efficiency in that. We were able to progressively get all the banks to migrate to PEXA for these transactions.

Even with this approach, a change to the opt-in model was required to get the platform through the top of the adoption S-curve.

> Even if you had 50% of conveyancers on both side of the transaction, willing on any given day to use the platform, that meant that only 25% of transactions could be performed on PEXA if that was randomly distributed. We had parts of the industry frustrated at the pace of development – lawyers are not renowned to be quick adopters of technology.

This slow-moving transition didn't purely cause frustration for users. Those who had transitioned had to effectively support dual processes with incrementally elevated costs.

> Increasingly, the industry lobbied the government. In response, states like Victoria and New South Wales announced timelines by which certain categories of transactions had to be conducted electronically. The later geographies saw what was happening in Victoria and New South Wales and started to migrate naturally.

Once the adoption wall had been overcome, people's sense of 'what is normal' helped subsequent adoption.

> It's interesting to see how people's attitudes have changed. For a long time, the banks were still doing only 10% of their work on PEXA and 90% on paper. So culturally everything was set up around processing paper, with banks having big mortgage ops teams.

However, as volume grew at a rapid pace, the paper approach gave way to the digital approach. PEXA became the industry normal. Noticing how much more seamless and easier this new digital way was, the traditional paper-based method felt 'painful'.

Cloud technology was an important building block given the transaction growth expectations.

> Cloud was very relevant. Scalability was #1. We realised as the platform grew from being still relatively low levels of transactions to a level where

the platform was going to be mission critical for the Australian economy that we needed far more resiliency. We've been on the AWS Cloud for the past four or five years. That allows us to scale, as we are now doing 15 times as much volume as we were doing even three years ago. In the recent times with COVID, property transaction volumes are probably up in the order of 20% as well. We've been able to absorb all that demand with 99.99% uptime. We could not have handled a fraction of that volume growth without AWS or a similar service.

Participating in the AWS ecosystem also brought technology advantages. There was significant cross-pollination of skill sets and development tools between AWS and PEXA's development team. Beyond this, Cloud technology also lowered a potential barrier to use for potential participants, given its easy useability.

PEXA also utilises AI.

There are two ways that we are using AI. One is security. We are using AI in our monitoring of security. The second thing is that we are enabling other participants use of AI through the use of APIs. If you are doing mortgage discharges or something similar, then much of that can be automated through RPA or other machine techniques. We expect that there will be more AI/ machine learning at different junctions in the process.

The situation today

PEXA has succeeded in its goal to become the de facto settlement platform.

We now have as members 150 financial institutions, which is pretty much every ADI [Authorised Deposit-taking Institution] in Australia and every non-ADI lender directly or indirectly. We've got more than 9,000 legal and conveyancing firms using the platform, which we reckon is close to all of the legal and conveyancing firms that conduct property transactions.

The new platform extends far beyond a simple digitalisation of the old way of doing things. Rather, it provides an entirely new service adept in connecting people. 'We are not just a digital platform. In a nutshell PEXA is a collaboration space. It's a B2B platform with a whole bunch of verified users'. It makes a once-problem laden, time-consuming paper-based process into a seamless digital one. 'The process has been both compressed in time and elevated in quality'.

It is an achievement that is unique. 'No one else has brought that all together in one package that can be done with a high degree of security, reliability and validation of data'.

In addition to delivering efficiency and quality in the core process, the digitisation of the process has enabled access to additional value through data. A host of new class products have been built. The data lost in paper shuffling is now retained through technology.

> We can now be able to tell authorities key market trends ... we will also be able to provide prospective views on market activity based on what's due to settle. We will be able to provide banks and other stakeholders assurance that they are registered on title to all the properties that they lend against. We can let mortgage insurers know when a mortgage is being paid out. All sorts of insights that can now come as by-products of a systematically structured Cloud-based approach in the middle of it.

This has also enabled the participants to evolve their own business models.

> The success of PEXA has also led to the states being able to privatise their land registries. If they hadn't had the digital enablement that PEXA brought, they would still be processing roughly 500,000 property transfers and 300,000 refinances manually.

Antecedent alignment

Whilst the PEXA case study confirms several of the factors discussed in Chapter 2, there are two factors that we would like to highlight.

Proactive leadership

Earlier in the case study, Reichmann discussed the importance of the CEO's vision of PEXA being an industry transformation rather than simply a shared technology initiative. Pricing services in such an environment could also be quite challenging, and once again, the leadership was proactive in identifying and addressing such a critical challenge.

As Reichmann reflects:

> How would you price the service? It's not something that had previously existed. The genius of the early management team was to effectively estimate what's the value being delivered in terms of freeing up people's time, minimising the costs of re-work, etc. We came to a particular figure. That total value was then allocated amongst the various participants and those became the prices of those services. It created an incentive to take up the service because it is matched to the value. There are fees associated with using PEXA, but it is well aligned to the value created for that participant.

Overcoming process inertia

One interesting nuance of the PEXA situation is the challenge of being able to reimagine an existing diffuse set of processes. By creating an industry that previously didn't exist, PEXA had a lot of design leadership. They provided for a myriad of special cases that were required to be catered for. One in particular that Reichmann recalls was in regard to the nuances of how the legal framework interacted with the financial framework.

> It's such a complex area – property law and land registry transactions. There's a particularly small set of subject matter experts. We had to build what we call the national e-conveyancing data standard. It didn't exist, but we needed to build a super set of messaging that would go back and forth between PEXA and all of the eight land registries. There's an equivalent messaging standard with the state revenue offices that didn't exist previously – it had not been codified. You need a lot of heavy infrastructural thinking. Our SMEs had to both understand the process which means you are stepped in it. But you had to be inventive enough to step outside the process. It is very difficult to get the best of both worlds.

Whilst PEXA may be an extreme example, it highlights the challenge of identifying those specialists with the greatest depth of knowledge in existing platforms, particularly when they may have the most to lose through the digital transformation.

Closing thoughts

PEXA is an interesting example of an industry encouraging business model refresh through the establishment of a new capability that, in turn, enables industry participants to refresh their business models. Whilst not all readers will have such an option available for their organisations, we think some might be able to utilise a similar approach. In addition, the impact of COVID-19 as a driver of transition to a digitised platform, highlights the impact of non-technical factors, to either delay or drive uptake of a new and unarguably more effective technical solution.

Case study 7: Insurance Australia Group Limited (IAG)

IAG is an example of an established organisation, in a highly regulated industry, taking an innovative approach to leveraging AI and Cloud technology to improve a particularly challenging part of the customer journey.

An overview of Insurance Australia Group Limited (IAG)

IAG is the largest general insurer in Australia and New Zealand. It provides a variety of products across its brands, as well as distributing insurance for third party partners. In order to acquire and maintain this status, IAG has had to undergo substantial change and transformation over its 160-year history. In recent years, this change has taken the form of new and innovative technologies, including Cloud and AI.

IAG's origins can be traced back directly to the 1920s, where it provided insurance to its members across New South Wales and the Australian Capital Territory, through its National Roads and Motorists' Association (NRMA) brand. IAG, as it operates it today, was established in the year 2000, when NRMA was demutualised in order to launch the insurance business (NRMA Insurance Group Limited) on the ASX. After rebranding to IAG in the early 2000s, IAG grew through several acquisitions in the pursuit of being Australia's largest general insurer. This has proven highly successful, with IAG's businesses (NRMA Insurance, CGU, SGIO, SGIC, Swann Insurance and WFI) presently underwriting more than $12.5B in premiums per annum.

The opportunity

A key priority for IAG is to continuously enhance customer experience and satisfy customer needs, while remaining aligned to commercially viable outcomes. To do this, IAG conducted a portfolio assessment to understand the greatest challenges faced by customers based on claim volume. IAG analysed the claims by assessing the impact of those claims on customers' lives, and existing pain points in customer engagement.

Through this process, management of total loss claims under automotive was identified as a high priority area well suited to experience innovation using AI. Total loss claims from motor vehicle insurance products represent a particularly difficult time for the customer, as they have often gone through a highly stressful and potentially traumatic experience. Statistically, total loss claims account for approximately 10–15% of the total annual claim volume.

Historically, the manual process to serve a total loss claim involved multiple stakeholder groups. The process relied on customers lodging a claim over the phone or online. This assessment was dependent on human inspection and analysis, which could result in inconsistent processes and outcomes. If the assessment determined that the claim was a total loss, it was manually triaged and sent to the total loss team who calculated the value of the offer sent to customers. The non-standardised nature of this process meant that the time between claim lodgement and settlement averaged around three weeks but could vary between a few days to more than a month. This lack of consistency and largely customer-driven process resulted in dissatisfaction.

IAG felt that improved management of these claims could improve customer experience outcomes, reduce IAG's internal costs, and improve employee efficiency over the long term. The existing legacy claims management process was complex, highly manual, and transactional, which limited the potential impact of more simplistic process streamlining approaches to address these challenges.

The initiative

Considering these pain points, IAG looked to redesign the claims process by incorporating AI. Doing this effectively and responsibly was part of an internal and external drive for IAG to influence the broader business community's approach to adopting AI technologies in an ethical and productive way. This included supporting the development of the Australian AI Ethics Principles and applying those principles to the areas where AI is transforming its business model.

In the context of this business subfunction, IAG piloted a program in late 2020, which used AI to predict whether a motor vehicle is a total loss after an accident and to fast-track the process in those cases. The pilot used a combination of the techniques described in Chapter 5, to leverage AI techniques to predict the likely outcome of an event based on several triggers, from the data provided about the incident.

The situation today

Once a motor vehicle claim is lodged, a notification is automatically sent to the customer, advising them of the possible total loss outcome (provided the total loss model scores sufficiently high), setting up the appropriate customer engagement journey from the start of the process. The automated process also provides customers with a clear list of documents and information they need to provide for their claim to be processed.

Because the process is more digitised, if the vehicle is ultimately assessed as a total loss, customers are also offered the option to settle their claim digitally, with supporting information sent automatically to the customer. Automated system rules are used to send triggers to customer claim consultants during key moments where human interaction is likely required. These changes were able to streamline the claims process and reduce the number of customer-initiated interactions from six to one, reducing the need to contact a call centre.

This customer experience has the potential to reduce claims times by up to 1.5 weeks, and substantially improve customer experience by automating a traditionally manual process (IAG, 2020).[8] In total, this resulted in NPS (Net Promotor Score) increases of 10% for trial participants. The notification process for potential total losses prior to formal claims assessment could be applied with a 90%+ accuracy rate.

The success of this development served as IAG's statement of intent to adopt new and emerging technologies and marked the beginning of the group's AI adoption journey. While the total loss solution has been rolled out and is being continually improved, IAG's broader AI ambitions are expected to work through the same human–centred design process and transform the next most impactful functional area. As IAG continues to invest in this area, and the supporting risk management, we expect there to be an even more rapid business impact.

Antecedent alignment

Other large incumbents can take valuable learnings from this case when exploring AI for efficiency and improved customer experience, while ensuring the responsible application of AI technology in their business.

Proactive leadership

IAG's executives made their strategic intentions clear by putting in place an organisation-wide focus and identifying how the business needed to transform its current state through technology enablement. This collective focus was to develop the capability to provide customers with a consistent end-to-end experience – spanning across claims operations, technology, and customer. IAG's leadership understands that customer needs should be the driving force for choices across the entire company. This compelled IAG to openly seek ways to improve customer experience by adopting an end-user focus, as opposed to executing internal ideas. Without collective commitment across the organisation, it is unlikely that the solution would have been developed, as input from cross-functional teams, proactive investment in improved risk management, and innovating thinking were critical.

Risk tolerance

Another important factor to consider is the risk appetite of a company and its willingness to explore new opportunities. IAG's experimental mindset, together with their proactive investment in risk mitigations like the Responsible AI Index (Fifth Quadrant, 2021)[9] and their broader contribution to the effective and responsible use of AI (Chris Dolman, 2021),[10] was essential to the creation of this solution. A minimum viable product was produced by primarily focussing on messaging updates, followed by interactions and claims settlement. Whilst developing this solution, IAG iteratively tested and updated the algorithm sensitivity and thresholds to ensure the final build satisfied customer needs. Automatically updated dashboards, reflecting relevant performance outcomes and metrics, were built to enable demonstration of and monitoring of the resultant efficiency and improvements.

Foundational data and information systems

Finally, the foundational data and information system readiness of a company is an important factor to consider in terms of the ability to introduce technological change. For IAG, the core systems were in a state that meant AI could be adopted with minimal change. This is because, whilst there are still several legacy systems to work around, over the past few years IAG has updated its core systems – simplifying them from 30 down to 5. A core part of this experience was the work that IAG has done around the simplification of their systems, and without this work, this solution could not have been implemented without major changes being made.

Closing thoughts

IAG's application of AI is in some ways quite novel and unexpected. Given the highly regulated and sensitive nature of insurance claim assessments, there was a material risk that needed to be managed through this process. IAG chose to navigate these risks, because of the significant negative impact of the existing process on their customers. Rather than shy away from this, they made significant investments into the fundamental capabilities required to responsibly manage these risks.

Confronting these impactful moments for a customer in a thoughtful and creative way, is what's given IAG the ability to differentiate against its competitors in a highly competitive market.

Case study 8: Canningvale

The organisations underpinning the previous case studies have been either businesses with scale (and therefore a potential for what academics call 'slack') or organisations with investment mandates from their shareholders. We find Canningvale very interesting, as it is a great example of how an organisation without such slack responded to the existential threat of disintermediation through creating a new business model.

An overview of Canningvale

Canningvale, a family company, began as a manufacturer of soft home textiles. Products like Terry towels were produced in Western Australia. Due to globalisation and the increasingly competitive prices of offshore products, manufacturing in Australia became increasingly tough. As such, Canningvale transformed into an importer, exporter and wholesaler of soft home textiles, servicing brick-and-mortar retailers of Australia.

When Jordan Prainito joined his family company Canningvale, in 2013, the company was a contract manufacturer and wholesaler of soft home textiles. These products, like bedlinen and towels, were sold by traditional retailers, including discount and department shops, as well as specialist shops like bedding chains. At that time, in 2013, Canningvale was a small business enterprise with a total of 18 employees. Jordan recalls:

> I started to get my hands dirty and examine all different parts of the business. I actually worked in all different parts of the business, and I was really surprised at how much manual data entry was involved, whether it was from auto processing to inventory management, forecasting financials, et cetera. If we were going to achieve a great experience for our consumers, we had to have real

time information, not just for them, but for ourselves, in order to have a really speedy and accurate fulfillment process, to have excellent customer service, avoid overselling inventory and be in stock with our best-selling items at the right times of the year.

At that time, Canningvale had not been a technologically intensive company. Similarly, they were facing growing pressure from retailers. Small suppliers, akin to Canningvale, had little power in their relationships with major retail chains. Retailers would dictate the terms, focussing heavily on price, and often overlook quality and value. As terms were becoming 'tougher and tougher', there was a looming prediction that 'this could only go one way'.

This challenging landscape, coupled with the business' predominantly manual processes and systems, were a catalyst for radical change. This change also came with a significant learning requirement:

> I set out to educate myself on what other businesses do, what was out there in forms of products, digital products, software, and I came across the notion of ERP. They're not really a new thing, they're getting a lot more mainstream for small to medium businesses today. But essentially, I started looking into what they used to exist for and what they were used for and what was coming out at the time, these new and exciting products that led me into a self-education journey and research journey, where I discovered this concept of Cloud-based systems and their inherent flexibility, the real-time information that these platforms could provide.

A new strategy began to emerge – one that saw Canningvale move down the value chain closer to the end-use customer where much of the profit margins lay. This strategy was heavily enabled by the new technologies in the Cloud.

The opportunity

There was a strong motivation to transform. As explained by Jordan, 'it was the strategic direction that drove that journey and then our ambition to be one of the best at this, being an online retailer'. At that stage, direct to consumer sales through Canningvale.com sales were approximately 10–15% of revenue, with the remainder coming through retailers such as David Jones, Target, Spotlight, and the like. While there were also up-and-coming marketplaces, such as Catch or Kogan, the primary channel was through wholesale relationships with traditional brick-and-mortar retailers.

The initiative

The business strategy was mobilised through the overhaul of technological systems. Canningvale engaged in a NetSuite ERP build, and invested in working on a new platform, akin to Shopify, BigCommerce Enterprise. These systems were automated and efficient:

> The way I sold that to the business – as in to the board – was that essentially the investment over time would save us so much time, energy, effort and overhead and improve our overall business visibility and processes. So, it really was a no-brainer, and I think a lot of small to medium businesses out there today assume that these sorts of systems cost too much, but really they're half a salary in today's market and they can save you upwards of three, four, five people. So, with NetSuite specifically, we started about four years ago, focussed on establishing a great operational foundation and then we took online marketing seriously six months after the NetSuite implementation'.

Additionally, Jordan attributes the smaller size of the business at that time as being an enabler for their transformational success.

> In our size company, one of the most important things when a business is transforming itself is the ability to make decisions quickly and to have one person making those decisions. I didn't know this at the time, but I look back on it and that was a luxury of being a smaller business, we were agile, we were able to make these decisions. Essentially, the board was happy to give us a mandate focussing on the end outcome and say, 'Go on, get this done'.

Planning and execution were also key. Engaging in a business review process, 'mapping it all out' gave Canningvale visibility of how their current operations. This map became a workbook of sorts, allowing them to approach software companies and consultants. By showing them where they were then, software companies and consultants pitched their services and capabilities, to show them where they could be.

Ultimately, Canningvale worked with JCurve (a Systems Integrator) and implemented the system of NetSuite (a mid-market focussed ERP) to improve their technological capabilities and incorporate technologically induced efficiencies into their operations.

> One tool we use which is really good, is called NETSTOCK, a fantastic machine learning inventory software forecasting management tool… this tool essentially would take what is happening in your business at the current time, as well as overlaying historical information and you can order with a click of a button.
>
> Essentially it's an automatic inventory data collection algorithm that processes all the information, both current and historical, and also what you're forecasting, to potentially give you your ideal order recommendations with one click. This can do it all the way up to ordering the correct raw materials

at the right time, the right quantities, to fulfill that forecast of demand on those finished goods and items.

Similarly, automating their fulfilment was another 'key piece' of the business model's success. With all their stock stored in their warehouse and third-party logistics provided in Melbourne, once an order was placed from their online store, it would be shipped out either the same or following day.

While the back-end of the business was being overhauled, so too was the front-end. Moving from a wholesale business model to a direct-to-consumer business model identified a need for a B2C marketing uplift.

> Regarding online, we had a small, dedicated core customer base. But after you moved away from those people and you looked towards new active customers, or customer growth, it really came down to marketing and execution. So, for us being an ecommerce player, this was all about focussing on the end customer, managing our paid channels well, striking up partnerships with other online retailers in different verticals and swapping vouchers to cross pollinate our databases.

The financial outcomes of the technology investments, new business model and strategic positioning were impactful. 'Our profitability and cashflow significantly improved. We've been growing at 60% to 70% year on year pre-COVID-19, and when COVID-19 hit it was just crazy'.

Even when COVID-19 presented challenges to the supply chain, delaying timelines and stock availability, systems like NetSuite were incredibly beneficial.

> [With NetSuite], we could adjust the variables to what was happening at the time and then it would reforecast our needs and we could action that very quickly. It didn't take an army of analysts to do that for us, we had a system that did it for us and really made our life better. It made us a lot quicker to respond and react when these things were happening. So, it was a tough time from a supply point of view, but otherwise, the top line was strong, and also our capability meant that the bottom line was strong.

The situation today

While Canningvale has evolved immensely, the growth continues. The immediate future sees a focus on five key strategies in the business. The first being range expansion, using data from Reddit, Google Trends, SEM rush, Subreddits, and Google AdWords to ascertain demand and 'market validate' new categories.

> Essentially, we'll market validate the product, we will try and find a key differentiator about that product or that category, find our hook. And the way you can do that is you'll find your hook hidden in the underbelly of

competitor reviews for that new product category. Look at the common complaints that customers have about other competitors in a certain category you're going to go into. It could be my product arrives damaged and crushed in its packaging or something. If you see that a lot, then you know that's something you have to fix within that category if you're going to go into it, and make sure you can do that well, and then talk about doing that on your marketing ad copy.

Following this, they run Facebook ads – three separate ads, in fact, all with the same audience but with slightly different taglines and hooks. Whichever has the highest click-through rate to identify the most compelling hook. Utilising this data, they will work their product category launch or new product line around solving those issues. Only six months after this, they will be in the market.

The second strategy is around their overall value proposition. This will see improvements to the user experience, from improvements to the online store to the development of greater brand authority. As Jordan explains, 'it [is] about how we can improve our conversion rate and keep our website traffic on the trajectory that it's been on for the last couple of years'.

Scalability and the cost of doing business is another focus.

> We wanted to deliver a 20% EBITDA relative to sales. So, what we did, and this was about 12 months ago, we established a recurring internal process that looks at repetitive tasks and the costs associated with them, and not just the dollar cost but an actual time cost as well. The opportunity cost of someone doing, say data entry for a broad kind of idea, and what we did was, 'Anything that takes more than 15 minutes to complete, is repetitive, will be independently reviewed and assessed to see if it can be automated, or if it's an integration, improved.

The fourth strategy is centred around developing a stronger hold on small B2B and commercial trade accounts.

> What we're looking into is essentially providing the wholesale pricing we used to provide to say a Target or a David Jones to small Aussie businesses, anything from Airbnbs, to bed and breakfasts, to gift registry businesses, wedding registry businesses, and this has been quite exciting. There's a massive demand for this and given we're a vertically integrated business, we can afford to give them best in class pricing and still make a little bit of money ourselves, but also support them. And obviously the average order values for those accounts are five, six, seven eight grand every order, so it's quite a exciting strategy of ours that again diversifies a mix of revenue and our risk.

The fifth and final immediate focus will see the empowerment of people within their business. Being a people-centric business allows them to grow an empowering environment that allows the business to remain agile as people are encouraged to put forward ideas and make quick decisions.

> What this strategy is about is creating a delegation of authority matrix, a risk matrix, and then being able to work on that each quarter and revisit it and make sure that people feel empowered to do their jobs to the best of their ability.

Antecedent alignment

Proactive leadership

There is no doubt Jordan's leadership was instrumental in the company's transformation success. As a leader, he attributes his success to an ability to forward plan and critically think about the future.

> I think it's important for someone in a leadership position in a business, you're dealing with a lot of people, a board, business activities, all at once, and then you're also responsible for steering the company in that right direction, I think having the ability to forecast what could happen. Or, maybe it's imagination where you can imagine what could happen in the next few months or even a few years from now and then prepare the business for those possible outcomes is probably one of the more important things that I've learnt, that that's part of the job.

Akin to thinking outside the box in a visionary way, visibility to the people in the team is equally as important.

> It enables that individual to feel heard and it shows them that they're important because it's your time you're giving to them. And whether it's 15 minutes or half an hour, that's been something I think that's really enabled us to get buy in from everyone in the business. And to this day, I'll still do on-on-ones with every single person in the business once a month.

Risk tolerance

Ascertaining the risk of implementing this new technology was important. As Jordan explains:

> We saw it as a win-win in the sense of whether or not we succeeded at executing the e-commerce side of the business … we still had room for improvement in terms of managing the way we went about managing our wholesale orders, purchase orders, and other things like that.

Ultimately, Canningvale decided that adopting Cloud technology would only enable the business. Or as Jordan exclaims, 'there was no reason why we shouldn't shift to a Cloud-based ERP system'.

Closing thoughts

Canningvale executed a fundamental shift in its entire business, including customer channels, supply chain, marketing and support services. While some of the solutions adopted by Canningvale won't suit all businesses, the case study highlights the way in which smaller organisations can access industry-leading capabilities at a fraction of the previously required investment.

Case study 9: Caesarstone

Like Canningvale, Caesarstone saw change coming. They decided to move in advance of this change with a set of business model transformations across its three regions (North America, Europe and Australia). In addition to the insights about the transformation process, the Caesarstone case study provides a valuable insight into 'how things are done' in Australia relative to other parts of the world.

An overview of Caesarstone

Caesarstone is a manufacturer of engineered stone that is used in high-end kitchens and bathrooms. The company started in 1987 in a kibbutz in Israel, at which time the use of engineered stone (as opposed to mined stone from a quarry) was a major innovation. That innovation enabled the company to grow from its base in Israel to new markets overseas, with a strong focus on Australia, Canada, the UK, and the US as growth engines for future expansion. As a manufacturer, Caesarstone relies on a vast number of installers, designers, stone masons and distributers to connect their product with the end consumer. Prior to their transformation, the network of distribution centres, installers and interior designers was largely organic, made up of a vast number of small businesses and contractors.

The opportunity

While Caesarstone was a consumer-facing brand, they were still critically reliant on third parties for their success. They were a manufacturer, with little direct connection to their consumer. This 'distance from the customer' created concern around the potential for future irrelevancy created from competition in the market. This was particularly pertinent given the way in which competitors entering the market drove margin compression across the value chain.

As Izhar Gilad, VP, Global Digital Ventures, explains:

> If we [were to] stay in this position, where we will it lead us?... We under-
> stood that we want to change that. As a manufacturer, to survive, or to grow,
> or to expand in the next five, ten years, we need to change something in our
> position, and the value that we are giving to our partners and to our end
> customers. The way that we tackle that is, in some extent, through digital
> transformation or digital innovation.

At a more specific level, the assessment process began with 'mapping the current
value chain and where we play, and identifying the pain points that we have, in
order to grow'. The primary pain points were around price management, and
brand erosion. In order to remain competitive and maintain their strong brand,
Caesarstone decided to create new competitive advantages, through digital innovation – tools, platforms and capabilities; to help its partners do better business with
them, and better business with their customers.

The initiative

Rather than follow the traditionally linear and disconnected process present
throughout the industry, Caesarstone's solution was to develop a 'digital ecosystem'
across the value chain that would serve as a platform for collaboration.

The process of developing this platform first began with a detailed review of
the existing pain points for everyone involved in the end-to-end process. This was
detailed and practical. Most critically, they needed to avoid offsiding the existing
players in the value chain so that they could create a win-win situation. 'We [were]
solving to the K&B [Kitchen and Bathroom Retailers] – the headache of, let's call
it, of running around for the specific service provider ... [as] there's a lot of headache in this specific point'.

For many of these retailers, the process of managing a sales pipeline and the
varying specifications of each customer, with its own countertop design, was a
practical challenge that could be addressed through a digital platform with 'an end-
to-end solution from their management perspective, meaning from the quotation
process, the CPQ [configure, price, quoting solution]'.

In other words, these enhancements went beyond what was traditionally
offered. There was the ability to have a 'visual element' that allowed the K&B to
'play around and visualise how the kitchen benchtop will look like with different
colours, different cabinets, different accessories'. This could also be transitioned into
'an official quotation, with the SKUs (Stock Keeping Units) and prices, and so on'.
It also gave them 'the option to manage and control their pricing, margins, and their
overall relationship with the fabricators'.

The ability to manage pipelines and product visualisation isn't fundamentally
unique, however many of these retailers are small, trade-focussed businesses who

lack the time and ability to invest in digital tooling. To create a compelling value proposition for these organisations, Caesarstone developed a one-stop-shop on a Salesforce-based platform, which provided all these capabilities in a way that was simple and intuitive for the retailers. As it was developed based on Salesforce, the platform was 'open for integration' allowing the retailers to connect it to their existing digital solutions; for holistic, seamless experience.

> From a consumer-facing point of view, the digital front-end opened up a new range of opportunities to ease the process of managing that element of a home build or renovation. It also enabled Caesarstone to address feedback across the entire value chain if any issues arose: '[the customer] is always aware of what is going on – as your quotation is being processed, your measurement date is being scheduled. And you know everything is being coordinated with the end consumer. At the end of the installation or upon closure, we also collect the feedback from the end consumer. By that we're reducing the uncertainty and lack of knowledge of the consumers, keeping the in the loop all times'. Questions such as, 'how was your experience with the overall process?', are asked, providing a direct response as to the end-to-end process, from the fabrication to the K&B, and Caesarstone as the manufacturer.

This allows the K&B to not only better manage its own operation, but also that of its fabricator, ensuring customers are satisfied. 'For us, it's very important to start and collect feedback from the end consumer'. These enhancements are seen by the consumer as significant value-adds that go beyond the core product of engineered stone, providing them with peace of mind. This platform allowed them to have 'a win-win-win situation' for all three parties, as 'each one is getting its own share of the pie'. This focus on all the parties winning has made for a smoother transition to this new, platform-based approach.

The situation today

Cloud technology was critical to Caesarstone's transformation. It was an accelerator, a source of low-cost innovation that connected many disparate sources of information onto one platform. 'Many of these systems were on premise, and many of the systems did not exist'. In particular, the ability to connect transactional data across systems in a Cloud environment created the ability to drive a more seamless customer experience that enabled Caesarstone 'to understand the end consumer intentions, directions, thoughts, at the beginning of the journey'. Even if a customer goes onto the website and searches for a certain product, regardless as to whether they leave their details, 'we use cookies or similar mechanism' to 'touch' the end consumer at the beginning of the journey. Similarly, if a consumer:

> goes to our showroom, and puts [their] details over there, in Sydney, or in Melbourne, the colours, trends or products that consumer likes are able to

be attributed back to their details. This means that when they then go to the K&B, all that information as to their preferences and browsing behaviour is already there, assuming of course they gave the consent.

These insights have very practical implications. Namely, they can largely improve the customer experience 'We can say, "Okay. You've been to our website, we know what's your taste"', or 'if you also visit our showroom ... we know which colours you picked over there'.

Antecedent alignment

Proactive leadership

Caesarstone's focus on creating a platform-based business model was led from top down, and bottom up as well:

> Our CEO, who understood that the way that we are managing our current business and our go-to-market right now, if we keep on doing that. Einstein was cleverer than all of us and said, 'You cannot do the same and expect different results'. So, at the end of the day, we need to change something. In addition, our field team saw this opportunity of missing link or the gap in the value chain, which we, Caesarstone, can come in and bring value.

To highlight just how important this change was on the organisation as a whole, this new model and the focus to get 'closer to our end consumer' was one of the three strategic pillars in the organisation.

The delivery of this transformation as part of a critical, CEO-led program enabled Caesarstone to put in place the right risk tolerance, inject new capabilities and skill set and look at this change as a fundamental transformation, rather than an IT project.

By framing the need to transform the business model in this way, the business had a significant platform, enabling it to accept the practical risks of making such large-scale change.

Because Caesarstone's historical differentiators were based around their product capabilities, there was a clear need 'to bring onto the team people with different skills that we used to have, with different backgrounds. Including myself, I'm coming from a technical background, from the high-tech industry in Israel, from a digital background'. The injection of new talent went beyond pure skills requirements.

> There's no other way; if you want to scale up, if you want to move forward and make it a competitive advantage, then we [needed to] have the right skill set in-house. And this is not something that [existed] today in our organisation.

The commitment to the transformation was also fundamental to their success.

> You need to understand that it's sort of an 'all in', you're going in. You started this journey, you're probably going to end it in a bit of a different way that you started it. You need to invest time, money, [and] people into it. And it's not a small investment. It's not a sprint, it's a marathon. And you need to keep on investing.

Risk tolerance

Risk tolerance was critical to the success of the transformation, because of the inevitability of problems arising in the transition. Patience is integral as they are addressed: 'you will have issues and you will need to evolve in it, and the fix cycles and the adjustments are very quick. We are releasing new features every month now. So, it's something that is very fast'.

The perception of these risks differed heavily depending on the incumbency and dominance of Caesarstone in the market:

> Because we are a market dominant [in some of these markets], and we have the benefit on one hand and the disadvantage on the other hand too. That people are looking at you, and you cannot fail on some extent.

Closing thoughts

While Caesarstone has a positive reputation and brand, the traditional business model it used to occupy was both a universally accepted norm and a driver of ongoing commoditisation. This example should highlight the new ways in which Cloud technology is being used to drive new relationships with customers and change the roles of various organisations in the ecosystems in which they participate.

Case study 10: Scope

Scope is another example of the old adage of 'necessity being the mother of invention'. In Scope's case, a necessary IT platform upgrade provided an option benefit due to the use of Cloud technologies.

An overview of Scope

Scope was founded in 1948 by a group of families wanting to provide enhanced support to their children with cerebral palsy. Today, Scope is one of Australia's largest not-for-profit disability service providers, supporting thousands of people with complex intellectual, physical, and multiple disabilities. Scope's mission is to 'enable each person we support to live as an equal and empowered citizen'. Initially based out of Victoria, Scope has grown and is now expanding its presence into the New South Wales market.

In 2013 Scope was registered as a National Disability Insurance Scheme (NDIS) approved provider as it continued to grow and provide enhanced support services. Today, Scope provides key services including supported independent living, therapy, early childhood intervention, short term accommodation, and day and lifestyle options. Furthermore, Scope is active in the research field with over 30 years of active research, aimed at improving the lives of people with a disability and their families and carers.

In 2019, Scope tendered for the Victorian government outsourcing contract. This saw their staff increase from 1,500 to approximately 3,500 staff, and in turn, bring on another 2,000 customers. Their services are now delivered from 350 sites across Victoria.

The opportunity

Prior to the transformation, the IT infrastructure was basic. As David Branch, the then-chief information officer of Scope, explains, 'I went to do a presentation on how to use pivot tables in Excel and half the people in the room didn't have a new enough version of Excel in order to be able to support pivot tables'.

As evidenced by that 'eye-opening' example, the antiquated infrastructure and systems posed significant inefficiencies and risks throughout the organisation. The customer management and finance systems were hosted out of the office in Box Hill, with documents locally stored, no backups and weak security processes. Furthermore, sites were run in a decentralised way, which included manual rostering of front-line workers, manual customer interfaces which resulted in inconsistencies across sites.

The initiative

Scope's first step in their transformation was to transition the servers into data centres and create a centralised filing system. Scope decided to go to market for a managed services provider to transition them to a private Cloud, making them one of the first not-for-profit organisations to opt for this approach.

As Branch explains:

> We underwent a massive operation of going out to every single site, backing up the local drive of every PC and copying contents up to the central service, which formed the basis of our centralised, secure and backed-up filing system.

Working with a small Melbourne company in that first instance, it wasn't immediate success 'They didn't really have the bandwidth to support an organisation of our size'.

Going back to out to the market, Scope opted to go to market with an RFP (Request for Proposals) a few years later, signing with Harbour IT, to overhaul the antiquated systems and make Scope a pioneer in this space.

The situation today

Today, Scope has dual data centres with immediate fail-over to the secondary if required. This provides industry-leading access, uptime and system reliability. They are currently in the process of putting backup links into every site which will cut over to 4G if National Broadband Network (NBN) fails. There is also consistent data backup, with 'all our data being backed up every night'. There are multiple layers of security managed by external providers, which reduced the need and cost for Scope to have those resources inhouse. Utilising external providers also ensures the 'depth of expertise', for niche skills which Scope wouldn't be able to econom- ically employ directly.

As part of the NDIS compliance requirements, Scope was required to move to a new service delivery system, Lumary, which was built on a Salesforce CRM plat- form. The new system allowed them to record and gather more detailed informa- tion on the services provided to customers, the location, and the staffing. The new system provides a level of configurability which enables Scope to understand effi- ciencies through workflows and automation. This is a fundamental transformation from their previously decentralised and disparate approach to process management.

The transformation and shift to a Cloud platform have provided customers with a more consistent service delivery experience, from first enquiry through to service delivery –with more ongoing improvements and enhancements expected to be made, complemented by Lumary and Salesforce's quarterly software update process. Since embarking on the Salesforce journey, Scope have been able to bring together various touchpoints for donors, customers, employees, and stakeholders all on to the one platform, increasing their ability to connect and communicate with Scope.

Employees have also enjoyed efficiencies and new functionality, staff are now able to access their roster through a new app, log timesheets, request leave and pick up new shifts. Furthermore, resource allocation has been optimised from a decentralised process requiring 70 staff members, into a centralised rostering and resourcing capability. 'When we have shifts available as well, it enables us to have a much more direct contact with the frontline worker and label them to respond much more quickly to us'. Furthermore, resource allocation has been optimised from a decentralised process requiring 70 staff members, into a centralised rostering and resourcing capability.

Antecedent alignment

Leadership proactivity

By being the first movers in the Not for Profit (NFP) space onto private Cloud technology, Scope's leadership displayed exemplary proactivity. The Board was accepting of the need to invest in technology at an early stage. In fact, in Branch's view, the technology 'wasn't available any earlier' or that Scope was indeed a very early adopter in its sector. At that time 80% of sites didn't meet some key SLA requirements for performance. The executive team's support of the new IT requirements enabled the transformation to occur.

Industry dynamism

The industry itself at the time was in a period of significant consolidation. The industry was highly competitive and challenging to differentiate in, with strict compliance requirements which meant scale and size was increasingly important to its long-term future. Cloud technology enabled Scope to be compliant while managing unit costs as their organisation scaled. Four years ago, Scope Victoria changed to Scope Australia, operating in a federal scheme. This capability is a critical enabler for that expansion.

Risk tolerance

While upgrading systems and employing new technologies may be considered risky for most organisations, Cloud technology for Scope was a significant risk mitigation against existing technology and operations platforms. The centralisation and codification of processes and workflows significantly reduced risk, resulting in fewer errors and greater efficiencies. While Scope is still working through additional mitigations, such as document management solutions, with their SaaS Cloud platforms such as Salesforce and Office 365, they still 'trust and verify', backing up their own versions of critical data in the event that they require direct access to that critical information.

Culture/internal dynamism

Scope had a culture of 'relentless change' that went far beyond applying solely to technology. The culture fostered within the organisation was a 'continuous improvement culture'. Similarly, its forward-looking market and customer focus ensured the company was open to change and transformation.

Closing thoughts

Scope demonstrates that business model refresh through Cloud technology is a feasible strategy for those in the not-for-profit sector.

Scope also provided two additional insights that resonated with our research. First, for a more seamless transformation, partnering with similarly sized partners who are driven by similar values is key. As was displayed with Scope, choosing the right partner was crucial to their success. The smaller IT partner did not have enough capability; the larger IT organisations (like Telstra) presented challenges working together through the transformation due to the differences in size. Second, the 'Scope approach' provides a guiding framework to drive culture and process change for staff, with a focus on the customer at the heart of it all.

Scope continues its transformation journey to ensure that IT system architecture remains fit for purpose and future-proofed by ensuring rationalisation of systems as technology advances as well as transitioning to a highly integrated and automated environment to ensure quality of information and outcomes for staff and customers.

Case study 11: Service NSW

Service NSW provides an example of how access to a range of complex government services can be transformed, to improve efficiency and customer outcomes for an entire population.

An overview of Service NSW

Service NSW is a New South Wales (NSW) government executive agency that joined the Department of Customer Service on 1 July 2019. It was founded with the vision of being the world's most customer centric government by delivering a world-class, one-stop-shop in-person, online or over the telephone services for its' customers, businesses, and partner agencies across NSW.

Service NSW acts as a single point of contact into several government agencies, include Transport for NSW, Fair Trading NSW, and Births, Deaths and Marriages. Each interfacing agency has its own operating model, structure, and way of working.

Positive customer experience outcomes are of the highest priority to Service NSW, driving its purpose of enhancing the quality of life for the population of NSW by making it easy for them to access the government support and services they need.

Since its inception, Service NSW has become a network leader through the provision of the MyService NSW Account and is leading service delivery and reform through their Service NSW omnichannel and Service NSW for Business. It operates 110 Service NSW centres across the state, with 153 points of presence which extend to include 32 council agencies, 10 digital self-serve kiosks, and 4 mobile services centres, covering 99% of NSW local government areas. Between July 2020 and June 2021, Service NSW assisted over 180 million customers, added 1.69 million new MyServiceNSW accounts, with approximately 4.75 million active users on MyServiceNSW accounts, plus 5.5 million interactions through the ServiceNSW app. With such strong customer uptake and engagement, Service NSW's passionate team are consistently developing existing and new online and offline capabilities to meet customers' evolving needs.

The opportunity

Prior to travelling on this journey, Service NSW was not dissimilar from other government organisations, whereby projects were still being run under old methodologies, and their internal capabilities were out of date, 'We had very little internal capability when it came to digital services'. These limitations had put a ceiling on Service NSW's ability to grow and add value to the community.

The initiative

Service NSW's customer-focussed journey has gone through multiple phases. Initially they began running online and 24/7 phone services in July 2013. Over time, access channels began to include one-stop-shop physical centres, roaming mobile service centres, websites and a dedicated app. Progressive enhancements were made to the platforms, but Service NSW recognised that their ambitions were limited by constraints in their service design and digital development capabilities, as shared by CEO Damon Rees: 'Agility was the driver that motivated us to fully embrace the Cloud and the potential it offered, not because it was in vogue but because if we didn't it would be a ceiling on our capability'.

For all the progress that Service NSW had made in creating a customer-oriented organisation, it still employed a traditional approach to designing experiences and digital services, with significant reliance on partners to bring them to life. Service NSW at the time, 'had very little internal digital development capability when it came to digital services' and were dependant on procuring this skill set from a collection of external service providers which greatly limited their agility.

For Service NSW to continue its pursuit of delivering world class support to communities and businesses across the state, this needed to change. They needed to reimagine the service delivery process in a highly digitally enabled future and did this by embedding Cloud development and engineering capabilities in its workforce. The objective was to amplify the frontline team's existing ability to sense, understand and engage customer needs with supporting platforms, tools and resources that could design, build, test, deploy and iterate digital services just as quickly.

Developing these digital customer experiences became just as critical a capability to the organisation as customer service itself. Building digital skill sets from scratch was key to Service NSW's success, but so too was leading the way in government adoption of Cloud infrastructure that Service NSW could draw on immediately as they built new services. Service NSW achieved this by creating an adaptive and empowered culture of agile and cross-functional teams. This was planned across three horizons: (1) incubation, (2) scale and (3) continuous improvement. Starting with a single product team, Service NSW has now scaled up to 50 product teams since commencing on this journey.

The magnitude of this transformation became clear upon realisation of just how few local or global government entities had established agile development capability internally at this scale or had adopted Cloud environments for government services. Service NSW turned to digital native organisations like Spotify and Netflix, to understand the practices, design philosophies and operations models they had used, and sought to adopt them to aide in their transformation efforts.

Embracing internal engineering skill sets and Cloud development environments has drastically transformed the pace of new service delivery, interoperability of various services and functions and the very nature of the customer service delivered by Service NSW. Cloud and Cloud-enabled coding was at the core of the Service NSW strategy.

The situation today

The uplift in Service NSW's internal capabilities has made the organisation more agile and capable in dealing with changing needs.

As an example, when the COVID-19 pandemic took hold and borders between states started to close, the government needed a solution for managing the flow of people between states and safely closing borders.

They came to Service NSW with an ambitious request to put in place an entirely new border permit service as quickly as possible. 'From the first requests for this capability to that capability being conceived, designed, built and implemented that was 36 hours'. The initial request to deployment took 36 hours, and over the following 90 days the experience and workflows were tuned daily to optimise outcomes and accommodate the regular changes and adaptations of the government mandates. This would have been impossible to achieve with traditional operating approaches and reliance on externals. It needed the digital Cloud capabilities and infrastructure to allow this to happen.

Antecedent alignment

Risk tolerance

Early adoption was always going to come with some risks, and this was well understood by the leadership team at Service NSW. The pace and scale of change required would always come with early inefficiencies or gaps, however these would be resolved as the capabilities matured. Several divisions wanted to maintain strict control over processes and governance; these forums and mechanisms had to be broken apart to not interrupt the velocity that the cross-functional teams were operating at. Breaking down these silos initially, created a sense of angst, confusion, and duplicative effort; however, this was deemed a small price to pay as the change was pushed through.

Strategic process strength

Service NSW had to re-architect the way they thought about how digital services and Cloud would be used as a critical enabler for change. The first horizon in this change was centred around incubating this new capability. 'Let's get one team that shows us what the future looks like, and let's use that to then incubate and grow and build the capabilities'. Horizon two addressed the issue of scale and how these teams can be scaled to meet the increasing demand. Finally, Horizon three was based around industrialisation and optimisation of the capabilities, how do you get not just the individual components working at pace but how does the entire system come together and operate at the same velocity, allowing Service NSW to deliver an enhanced customer centric experience, with reduced re-work and duplication.

Market and customer sensing

Service NSW created open lines of communications and strong working relationships with ministers and other government agencies, which positioned Service NSW as the best option to develop solutions and meet customer demands in a dynamic society. This meant that the collective sensing of government needs and requirements was funnelled into Service NSW, due to the strong track record and success achieved through them with the centralised customer service model. Service NSW established themselves as an ever-growing and learning organisation, capitalising on the vast number of customer interactions they managed, and they flowed this back into experience and service redesign. This iteration cycle was enabled by their agile development teams and Cloud infrastructure.

Closing thoughts

The capability development and organisation transformation journey that Service NSW went through highlights the broad range of nontechnical skills that need to be developed in order to fundamentally transform the way in which value is delivered.

Case study 12: Yarriambiack

In contrast to a large government department, we now shift to the Yarriambiack Shire Council, which demonstrates that small organisations can also benefit from business model transformation through Cloud and/or AI technologies.

An overview of Yarriambiack

The Shire of Yarriambiack is a local government area located in northwest Victoria. The shire was formed in 1995 and covers an area of 7,158 square kilometres. At the

2016 census, it had a population of 7,082 (Yarriambiack Shire Council, n.d).[11] The shire is divided into the three wards, Dunmunkle, Hopetoun and Warracknabeal. Each Ward has two councillors, except for Warracknabeal which has three.

Yarriambiack Shire relies heavily on grain production and agriculture, which accounts for almost half of the workforce. The dry-land farming area produces one-quarter of Victoria's total wheat and barley production and is also known for its production of lambs and wool (Yarriambiack Shire Council).[12] The Shire of Yarriambiack is governed and administered by the Yarriambiack Shire Council.

The opportunity

The opportunity to optimise Yarriambiack Shire Council's technology needs was spurred on by new leadership and a review of the Local Government Inspectorate in November 2019. The review highlighted 'the lack of internal controls, exposing the council to the risk of fraud and/or corruption'. It had previously had a 'Primitive' IT system, utilising Microsoft Office 2007, using manual 'paper-based purchase orders and timesheets' with an outdated server environment.

The council opted to take a non-traditional approach when developing a plan to optimise its technology needs. They decided to reach out to their existing technology partner to understand the costs involved in upgrading. They were quoted approximately $120,000 for the upgrade, yet this excluded automated features payroll, electronic purchase orders and project costings. Using $120,000 as their funding ceiling, Yarriambiack Shire Council explored other options and providers, finally deciding to move away from a traditional ERP system and opting for a collection of Cloud-based software platforms that would give them the same capabilities.

The initiative

CouncilWise, a local government property and rating management platform, was the first platform implemented to assist Yarriambiack Shire Council. For their accounting and financial management requirements, they turned to Xero, a Cloud-based accounting software platform. Even with this, however, the Council would still not have an electronic payroll and timesheet system that met their internal and external audit outstanding action requirements.

They decided to implement Happy HR to help manage their holistic human resource needs, which was, at that time, manual and paper based. Yarriambiack Shire Council also took advantage of the Xero add-on capabilities, opting to use KeyPay, which linked to the Happy HR platform. This allowed the Yarriambiack Shire Council to roll out the automated timesheet capability and get staff onboarded over three months.

Yarriambiack Shire Council encountered some complications due to the type of Xero they were running. They were using Xero projects, which did not have the integration capabilities they desired. To counter this, Yarriambiack Shire Council once again took advantage of the modular nature of Xero and were able to use

Workflow Max, an add-in that enabled them to create 'jobs' for each of the assets under their council.

As the rollout of systems continued and became functional, the next stage for Yarriambiack Shire Council was to shift to the Office 365 suite. Transferring all their files from servers into SharePoint, allowed them to create new structures and assign retention schedules and overlays. This shift helped Yarriambiack Shire Council manage their compliance issues.

Additionally, the Office 365 environment shift provided Yarriambiack Shire Council with a suite of new products, including PowerBI. Utilising the capabilities in PowerBI, they were able to successfully establish dashboards for managers that gave them access to their costings, budgets, reporting and performance without providing them unrestricted access in Xero. The ability to restrict access in Xero was pivotal to ensure that Yarriambiack Shire Council would be able to maintain its compliance requirements.

The situation today

As COVID-19 started to impact organisations and accelerated the need and requirement for companies to have robust work from home capabilities, Yarriambiack Shire Council was in a unique situation. Having just rolled out Cloud and software as a service-based Cloud technology, this adjustment was relatively seamless.

A significant driver for the success of the transformation undertaken by Yarriambiack Shire Council was ensuring that employees were also taken along the journey and were part of the process. By providing regular updates on the progress, employees were given opportunities to ask questions. It also allowed the council to provide insight into why decisions had been made. As the rollout progressed, significant training was provided to all employees; teams had dedicated IT 'champions', who the rest could turn to if they required assistance. The process undertaken by Yarriambiack Shire Council meant that regular feedback could be provided on any updates or enhancements that were needed to ensure they could be rectified.

The impacts of modular and Cloud-based technologies have been felt across the board. Employees have taken the technological advancements in their stride. The removal of paper-based record keeping has reduced manual rework and hand-offs. Employees are also more proactive due to increased analysis capabilities offered by the various software. Productivity has 'exceeded expectations', with 120 manual audit points being reduced to 49; this is expected to decrease by a further ten at the next audit and risk committee. Yarriambiack Shire Council have been able to accomplish and complete more tasks with less effort. This has not translated into employee redundancies, however. In fact, it has opened the door for new opportunities. Whilst some procurement activities have been delayed, procurement compliance has increased, a key challenge per the inspectorate report.

Relationships with customers and ratepayers has also increased over the last 12 months. Since the practices amongst the council has changed, accountability has increased, and an increase in community group satisfaction has been noted. The new technology has provided a central point for customer requests, making it easier to manage customer requests and processes moving forward. While this is still under development, customers have provided 'positive feedback' on the council's changes and the resultant service level improvement.

In terms of the key lessons learned through the transformation, in the words of their CEO, Jessie Holmes 'You've got to be willing to promote the positives and bring people on the journey'. Yarriambiack Shire Council strongly emphasised this statement reflecting upon why their transformation to Cloud-based software had been so successful. Yarriambiack Shire Council ensured that communication and training to all employees was robust and articulate on the benefits that the transformation would enable. The communication was frequent, allowing employees to follow the transformation journey with the leadership team. 'Decisiveness and agility have been key and also inclusiveness and communication'.

Antecedent alignment

Leadership proactivity

The introduction of a new CEO brought a substantial shift in attitude and a willingness to take risks. The approach quickly moved from a conservative and fearful approach to a proactive 'we've got to do something' approach. The refreshed leadership forced a reflection of past failures and forced the team to look at what changes could be made moving forward, ensuring the learnings from past failures were well considered and avoided in the future.

Risk tolerance

There was an acknowledgement that the transformation being undertaken was significant. There was the very real risk that that it may not work, as other councils and companies have realised with ERP implementations. Yarriambiack Shire Council was willing to accept that risk and push forward with their approach. Along the journey, roadblocks and risks did occur, mainly around Xero projects not providing the complete level of functionality required. The risk was actively managed throughout the process, and learnings were taken away to overcome any future blockers. Adopting software that could provide a modular base with multiple add-ons and features was a concern for other councils; traditionally seen as a riskier approach than a standard ERP system. Yet for Yarriambiack Shire Council, this approach helped alleviate some of the common risks in significant transformations.

Strategic process strength

Once a gap is identified in the business, a system failure or process improvement is required, and an idea or concept is developed into a business case. The business case goes to a special Projects and Infrastructure asset group within Yarriambiack Shire Council for assessment and approval. The group will score the business case against criteria and is further prioritised against other projects for budget and CEO sign-off.

Industry dynamism

Yarriambiack Shire Council was following a repetitive path; they were not willing to make accelerated or substantial changes. New leadership and the inspectorate report provided a burning platform and boosted Yarriambiack Shire Council to take bold steps in transforming their organisation and approach to traditional activities. Yarriambiack Shire Council further took a progressive step in appointing a young female CEO to a more conservative area which 'in itself was a huge risk and it has paid off dividends'.

Foundational data and information systems readiness

Like most older legacy organisations, Yarriambiack Shire Council operated in silos with teams 'very territorial over their data' and who could access it. The first hurdle to overcome as part of the SharePoint implementation was to shift the mindset of having documents locally saved to saving them to a single source of truth server and removing the need for document and access restrictions. The introduction of Xero and associated add-ons accelerated this further as it did away with most spreadsheets and lists.

Closing thoughts

A burning platform, ignited by new leadership and an inspectorate report, was the push Yarriambiack Shire Council needed to undertake a significant technology transformation. Traditionally, councils would opt for all-inclusive ERP providers to fulfil their requirements. However, Yarriambiack Shire Council decided to adopt a modular approach utilising Cloud and software as a service technology to shift from a primitive and manual IT system with limited traceability to a Cloud-based environment.

Office 365, coupled with a Cloud-based accounting software in Xero and modular add-ons, has provided Yarriambiack Shire Council an automated electronic purchase order system, electronic timesheets, electronic HR and project management, a CRM system and an asset management system. Yarriambiack Shire Council is still in the nascent phase of this five-year transformation and continues to embrace the solutions offered by Cloud technology.

Case study 13: Urban Art Projects (UAP)[13]

Unlike all of our other case studies, UAP is known for creating bespoke, highly complex made-to-order products, indeed artwork. Due to the nature of its work, UAP doesn't have the ability to standardise mass processes, however Cloud-based infrastructure was a key element of its use of other disruptive technologies, which dramatically reduced its cost of innovation and experimentation.

An overview of UAP

Urban Art Projects (UAP) Group was founded in 1993 by twins Matthew and Daniel Tobin. The pair had spent their university years working at Artbusters, a traditional foundry operating out of the former Windsor Brass Foundry in Red Hill, Brisbane, Australia. Upon graduation they branched out on their own, establishing a facility at Seventeen Mile Rocks on the outskirts of the city. Both brothers trained as artists and built their team from the same talent pool. This first foundry served individual artists and those interested in commissioning public art, leaving an indelible impression on Brisbane's urban landscape.

Over the last 28 years, the organisation has grown to deliver a staggering array of unique projects, from the Oscar statuettes to multistorey architectural façades. Promoting and encouraging 'uncommon creativity' is a cornerstone of the business, which has fostered a spirit of exploration encompassing making, materials, processes, and people.

Today, UAP is a global company, headquartered in Northgate, Brisbane, with a local foundry and another in Upstate New York, USA. Another workshop operates out of Shanghai, China, offering specialist metal fabrication capabilities. Each facility is supported by a team of designers, curators, computational specialists, roboticists, technicians, and tradespeople. The organisation also has a sales presence across Australia, Asia, the Middle East, and North America.

In collaboration with Queensland University of Technology (QUT) and ARM Hub (Advanced Robotic Manufacturing), UAP recently backed FARM (Fabrication Arm), founded by UAP partner Ben Tait. This start-up business offers architects, designers, and creators a virtual factory, in which to collaborate, create, and craft digital twin models ready for advanced manufacture in any location. Recognised worldwide as a leader in public art and architectural design solutions, UAP is now pushing the boundaries of AI and Cloud transformation, driven by strategic partnerships, one-off challenges, and pioneering design solutions.

ARM Hub[14] was founded in collaboration with UAP, in response to the global race to marry advanced manufacturing and robotic innovation, as well as AI and Cloud transformation. The two organisations sit side-by-side in Northgate, and encourage the open innovation model, rejecting a silo mentality in favour of crossing borders and boundaries to explore external innovation via relationships with universities, creatives, and clients.

The opportunity

In 2015, UAP accepted a highly complex commission from the renowned architect, Frank Gehry. Gehry presented UAP with a significant challenge: a stainless-steel staircase with the appearance of a crumpled paper bag – and every crumple was important. UAP's foundry team approached the process in a traditional way, using panel beating, an ancient technique. The pattern makers prepared exact models on which the metal was beaten. Scans were sent to Gehry to compare against his models. While the team remember the project fondly, it was a tedious one, requiring many iterations. Consequently, this project and its inherent level of complexity, got the team thinking about the role technology might play in enabling them to create highly complex work with far less 'friction'.

The initiative

Following on from the company's experience with Frank Gehry, Matt and Dan sought to identify and integrate AI and Cloud transformation into the business. To this end, they visited universities, specifically robotics departments, in the US, China, and Australia. The team that best understood their needs was the Centre for Robotics at QUT. They suggested that robotic vision was essential in automating parts of UAP's workflow, particularly milling and grinding.

UAP and QUT applied for an Innovation Connections Grant under the Australian government's AusIndustry Entrepreneurs' Programme. This scheme enabled the business to embed researchers on the foundry floor, working alongside computational designers and tradespeople. Step-by-step, they began to take a more structured approach to data acquisition, processing, storage and computer modelling.

At the time, UAP assessed their changing systems and processes via a series of design sprints: small projects aimed at testing and embedding these new technologies. The purpose was to leverage foundational investment into a one-system, one-team network, whereby learning was shared across the business and industrywide.

Following on from the Innovation Connections grant UAP, QUT, and RMIT University were awarded funds by the Innovative Manufacturing Cooperative Research Centre (IMCRC) to establish Design Robotics. Design Robotics, established as an Open Innovation Network, focussed on sharing outcomes and facilitating collaboration across the Australian manufacturing sector. This model was then used to establish ARM Hub. Many of the pilots emerging from all three schemes involved the use of robotics to drive automation and improved precision.

The situation today

In contrast to the highly manual, panel beating based techniques used in the Gehry commission, UAP now uses a highly automated, computerised set of processes to create its products, all running off Cloud-based infrastructure, to handle the significant volumes of data and computations required. Instead of sending large volumes of physical documents back and forth to iterate the development of the final product, people across the design process are able to tap into the Cloud-based data and easily see in-progress works, together with overlays of the next steps in the projects.

Two primary robotic processes are used inhouse at UAP: one, mould making, whereby the robot mills exact forms; and two, finishing, in which the robot uses an angle grinder attachment to improve the flatness of a metal surface. Both processes still require skilled tradespeople to apply finishing, but the grunt work is done by the robot; staff are freed from repetitive, labour-intensive tasks. Consequently, robots increased process efficiency around manual operations, but they did not replace jobs. Existing staff benefitted from a commitment to reskilling, whilst every robot purchased resulted in the recruitment of three automation specialists.

Robots are taught to see objects and then perform precise tasks upon them, whilst information on the physical and mechanical properties of the materials was catalogued and reapplied. The team also use mixed reality (MR), augmented reality (AR), and virtual reality (VR) as they interacted with the developing artwork. This technology allows the tradesperson to view computational models as an overlay on the physical form. This interaction removes the need for paper documentation and enhances precision, because the model is literally in the line of sight.

Complex tasks become easier and more efficient. Workers are less inclined to make mistakes, reducing risk and material waste. Matt is quick to point out that none of this would be possible without his staff:

> We have staff who are natural explorers, and we encourage those staff to investigate problem solving, using technology. If they've got a good idea, we will fund that. Sometimes it's a dud and sometimes it's a great success. I think it's a culture of trust – a different way of thinking about problem solving.

Antecedent alignment

Balancing exploration versus exploitation

Due to the nature of their business model, every creative project comes with specific challenges. As such, there is a constant need to balance a combination of Exploration (i.e. pushing the boundaries of new works and new techniques) and Exploitation (i.e. ensuring that their projects can still be delivered to a quality and budget that suits their clients). UAP's jobs vary from costing $5,000 to $20M, and as such, knowing how to balance these capabilities has created a distinctive competitive advantage for the group.

Risk tolerance

While there is a clear opportunity for value to be created across the intersection of digital technology and advanced manufacturing, there is also a significant amount of risk involved, given the unique nature of the artwork UAP creates.

At present, much of the risk inherent in developing new skills, processes, and platforms to gain the value in these technologies rests with industry, which encourages businesses to ring fence R&D investment through intellectual property (IP) protection.

To mitigate these risks, UAP focussed heavily on partnerships under their open innovation model, grant funding, and well-defined design sprints that would demonstrate incremental outcomes as each of these new technologies were applied. These approaches all helped manage the significant risks UAP took when investing in the application of these cutting-edge technologies.

Closing thoughts

It would be easy to look at the artwork created by UAP and not necessarily see a connection to the new technologies that were critical to their creation. While the physical product is now predominantly shaped by robotics, a broad range of other disruptive technologies are part of the process, not least the Cloud-based platforms which enable these masses of data to be transported, processed and manipulated throughout the development cycles.

While some of the technologies discussed in this case are more suited to building low-volume or bespoke products, the design-based approach and focus on experimentation, can easily be applied into a more traditional business environment.

Learnings from the case studies

Every organisation is unique and starts its AI- /Cloud-enabled business transformation from a different point, with a different opportunity and set of challenges being faced. In each case study, we highlight how that case illustrated the importance of specific antecedents.

While each of the case studies tells its own story with its own issues, there are commonalities across these stories. The clearest common antecedent observed is the need for proactive leadership of the organisation and the initiative, whether it is a large government department/agency (Services NSW), through to a family business (Canningvale), or a highly digital-oriented business (e.g. SEEK and Kogan), or a manufactured goods business (e.g. Caesarstone and UAP). Each of our case study participants mentioned proactive leadership as a key reason for success. Beyond the common antecedent of proactive leadership, one aspect of the cases that we found interesting was the repeated themes of why organisations initiated their transformations. We found three distinct sets of 'triggers' (Figure 3.1) across the cases, each with their own characteristics.

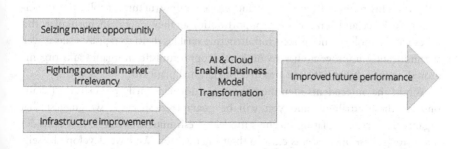

FIGURE 3.1 Triggers for AI- and Cloud-enabled business model transformation

The first trigger type was that of 'Seizing Market Opportunity'. In these situations, we found that there was a very clear recognition across the senior leaders of an organisation that a market opportunity exists. This typically occurs at the board/C-suite level, but we have also seen cases where this recognition occurred further down the organisational hierarchy (such as the case with Deloitte and its Self-Managed Super Fund opportunity, where the opportunity was identified at the Business Unit leader level). This recognition can result in either the creation of a new business, a spin-off of an existing business, or the development of an adjacency to an existing business. In all cases, there was an understanding that a new business model was needed to seize that market opportunity, and AI/Cloud technologies were a critical component to that new business model. However, we caution that several situations that are typically associated with 'seizing opportunity' are not sufficient to meet our definition. For example, we do not consider pursuing similar types of business to those pursued in the past, pursuing adjacencies using the existing business model and infrastructure, piloting technologies to make incremental improvements, or pursuing inorganic growth opportunities to be by themselves good examples of business model refresh.

The second trigger type is 'fighting margin compression/potential market irrelevancy'. In these situations, there is a clear understanding by the board and/or the C-Suite that the existing business model will not continue to deliver the economic outcomes of the past. Accordingly, there is a need to refresh the existing business model to enable ongoing viability of the business. This insight typically results in the development of a new capability that wasn't available in the previous business model, and like the trigger mentioned above, AI/Cloud technologies are a critical component to that refreshed business model. Naturally, using AI and Cloud to revitalise an organisational business model is not the only approach such organisations can adopt – they can explore technologies to make incremental improvements and/or make other changes to the business model (for example target customers, price points, cost base etc). In our view, whilst this is a valuable exercise, it has a limited duration of impact and only delays the future consideration of how to reposition the business model.

The third and final trigger type is 'infrastructural improvement enabling market opportunity seizing'. In these situations, there is a decision by the organisation to invest in refreshing legacy technology, typically through adoption of Cloud technologies. This refreshed technology and process infrastructure enables the organisation to react and seize market opportunities as they occur. In particular, this refreshed technology and process infrastructure enables them to rapidly scale as well as significantly improve ability to undertake opportunistic inorganic and organic growth options given a 'future-proofed' operational platform.

Whilst the antecedents identified above are not necessarily prescriptive ('demonstrate these attributes and you will be guaranteed success') we suggest that organisations contemplating business model refresh initiatives might first consider how strong these antecedents exist in their organisation. We have developed a self-assessment tool as included in Appendix 1.

Furthermore, each of the case studies support our differentiated position from the conventional wisdom.

- *Pathway*: Whilst some of the transformations may have used an incremental delivery model, the 'seizing market opportunity' and 'Fighting margin compression/potential market irrelevancy' transformations were driven from a sense of where the business model needed to be, and then worked back to scope the technical plan to deliver.
- *Scale*: The Australian case studies range from ASX 50 through to small regional shire councils. The commonality of these organisations is not scale, but rather focus on understanding what they need to be to be relevant in the medium to long term.
- *Technical debt constraints*: Several of the case studies are organisations with long-established ways of doing things supported by established processes and technologies. The profiled case studies uniformly recognised tech debt (in processes as well as systems) as something to be pragmatically worked through as a necessary part of transforming their business model, rather than as a showstopper or an exclusionary precondition.
- *Board member attributes*: Not all of our case studies specifically discuss the role of the board in the transformation. However, for those that do mention board members, the attributes that are mentioned are curiosity, focus on the future and tolerance of risk rather than mastery of the digital environment.
- *Balance of ideas and actions*: All of our case studies emphasise a pragmatic balance of strategy and action.

What if we don't support innovation from within?

While this book is focussed on business model innovation for incumbents, we wanted to highlight the importance of supporting innovation, given the short time frames in which a new start-up can begin to challenge large incumbents. To illustrate that argument, we finish this chapter with the case of Verton Technologies.

An overview of Verton Technologies[15]

Verton was founded in November 2014, on a mission to 'change lifting operations by integrating traditional engineering with digital and disruptive technology'. Crane operation has long been recognised as a task prone to inefficiency and risk, specifically worksite downtime, and health and safety concerns. Traditionally, lifting operations involved the orientation and rotation of payloads via taglines – a form of manual load control provided by handlers (doggers or riggers), manoeuvring a rope at ground level, close to the crane.

The idea of a remote load orientation system first came into being in 2008, when Stan Thomson, founder and chief technical officer, was based in Malaysia on an unrelated project. Trained as a mechanical engineer, Stan sketched his prototype for an automated crane, then put it on the shelf to meet the challenges of the global financial crisis. In 2013, following a wave of restructuring in construction management he left his role with an established company and took a risk by starting Verton. During the period between that initial idea and the establishment of the business, the technology caught up, enabling Stan and his cofounder (now a silent partner) to explore the potential of value-added digital tools and Cloud-based systems.

The innovation

Rather than controlling crane operations via taglines, Verton has created a remote control solution that allows a single operator to execute precise control over the orientation of the payload, effectively making taglines obsolete and more importantly removing operators from the drop zone.

Because the transition to remote control necessitated the digitisation of the control process, this also enabled Verton to put 'additional smarts' into the control system. These include inputs from a variety of sensors, together with digital vision and machine learning algorithms which dramatically improve the outcomes and consistently of the crane-lifting process.

This has resulted in close to 99% placement precision, 25% less crane downtime onsite, alongside a 50% reduction in hook time (the time it takes to latch a fixed object, like a pallet of materials or a foundry ladle). Safety and productivity are both significantly improved using this approach.

Where are they now?

Through a close relationship with QUT, Verton was able to fast track newly developed crane products, together with supporting services, to become a global exporter. They have international offices to distribute their next generation remote-controlled load orientation systems in the Middle East, India, Europe, the UK, North America, New Zealand, and across Australasia. Verton has rapidly evolved from a start-up, to an established commercial business with a leading technology over a very short period of time.

Innovate from within, or wait to be disrupted

According[16] to the late Clayton Christensen, who first defined disruptive innovation over 25 years ago: '"Disruption" describes a process whereby a smaller company with fewer resources is able to successfully challenge established incumbent businesses'. The Verton case study description begs the question of why a breakthrough performance improvement in crane operations was conceived and commercialised by a new entrant to the industry, rather than a major incumbent crane designer/manufacturer or operator.

Disruption innovation theory and the Verton case study highlights one of the challenges that all industry incumbents face, being the simultaneous blessing and curse of having market share, cash flow and assets that it wishes to enhance, labelled by Christensen et al. (2020)[17] as a focus on 'sustaining innovations', that are incremental in nature. For example, while major steel companies were trying to make their blast furnaces incrementally more productive, along came steel producing mini-mills, usually started by new industry entrants. While major hotel chains were competing on price, location, features and loyalty programs, along came Airbnb, now bigger than all those incumbents in the accommodation market for travellers.

Disruption can be a threat, whether it is Verton, Uber or Airbnb, and the best defence strategy for incumbents is to convert disruption from a 'potential enemy', usually brought by start-ups such as fintechs in financial services, into a 'friend' and disrupt oneself! This means setting up, as does Proctor and Gamble, an innovation resource aimed at disrupting one's own market. Just as our international case studies, described in the next chapter, of incumbent businesses Rolls Royce, Samsung, Netflix, DBS Bank and Bank of America engaged in various forms of self-disruption, so have some of the successful local case study organisations described above. Canningvale disrupted its existing and long-standing business model when it used Cloud technology to disintermediate its customers who were major retailers and reach out straight to consumers. Scope used Cloud technology to drive its service levels, managerial controls, reach and productivity, beyond previous bounds, giving it the competitive edge to rapidly expand with efficiency.

There are many examples of best practice in using Cloud and/or AI to self-disrupt. In Chapter 4, we describe a traditional and successful company, Rolls Royce that produced and sold jet engines, using both Cloud and AI to disrupt its own business model and sell 'power by the hour', and related additional services. Netflix disrupted itself from distributing DVDs by mail to become a large and successful streaming service, enabled by Cloud and AI-based capabilities. From these and many other case studies, the clear question is: do we wait and watch until our industry and business model are disrupted by others, or do we renew/disrupt and radically innovate ourselves?

Notes

1 Lorenz, M., Gerbert, P., Waldner, M., Engel, P., Harnisch, M., & Justus, J. (2015). Industry 4.0: The future of productivity and growth in manufacturing industries. BCG.

2 www.ericsson.com/en/blog/2020/7/how-to-improve-roi-for-industry-4-0-use-cases

3 Moula. (n.d.). About us. https://moula.com.au/about-us

4 SEEK Limited H1 22 Results Presentation.

5 Australian Financial Review (2021, 1 June). How Macquarie blitzed the mortgage market. www.afr.com/chanticleer/how-macquarie-blitzed-the-mortgage-market-20210601-p57wyq

6 Australian Financial Review (2022, 15 March). Bank compensation costs could hit $10B. www.afr.com/companies/financial-services/bank-compensation-costs-could-hit-10b-20190513-p51mt6

7 On 29 May 2020, National Cabinet agreed to the cessation of the Council of Australian Governments (COAG). Please see federation.gov.au for updates on the new federal architecture, including the National Cabinet and the National Federation Reform Council.

8 IAG. (2020). IAG predictive total loss announcement. www.iag.com.au/sites/default/files/Documents/Announcements/IAG-predictive-total-loss-301120.pdf

9 Fifth Quadrant. (2021). Responsible AI Index. www.fifthquadrant.com.au/2021-responsible-ai-index

10 Chris Dolman. (2021). Practicalities and oppportunities of ethical AI. www.datadrivenanalytics.com.au/podcast/e66-chris-dolman-practicalities-and-opportunities-

11 Yarriambiack Shire Council. (n.d). Your Council. Retrieved November 4, 2021, from https://yarriambiack.vic.gov.au/council/

12 Yarriambiack Shire Council. (n.d). Discover Yarriambiack. Retrieved November 4, 2021, from https://yarriambiack.vic.gov.au/tourism/our-region/

13 Thank you to Jo McCallum and Cori Stewart for their contributions to this case study.

14 https://armhub.com.au/

15 Thank you to Jo McCallum and Cori Stewart for their contributions to this case study.

16 Christensen, C. M., Raynor, M. E., & McDonald, R. (2020). What is disruptive innovation? *Harvard Business Review*, https://hbr.org/2015/12/what-is-disruptive-innovation

17 Christensen, C. M., Raynor, M. E., & McDonald, R. (2020). What is disruptive innovation? *Harvard Business Review*, https://hbr.org/2015/12/what-is-disruptive-innovation

4
INTERNATIONAL LEADING PRACTICE[1]

Introduction: 'World's best practice' in AI-/Cloud-enabled transformation

Internationally, incumbent companies that demonstrate leading Cloud and AI adoption practices tend to share common characteristics despite the variety of industries, geographies and cultures in which they are grounded.

The enterprises we feature as case studies in this chapter were undoubtedly alive to the possibilities of the new digital toolkit earlier than others in their industry cohort. However, though early Cloud and AI adoption was a feature of the enterprises we studied, we did not feel that early engagement with new technologies was in itself the primary differentiator for these entities. We noted instead that our exemplars uniformly:

- Innovated their business models both *boldly* and *serially*, as first movers in their industries and in their commitment to iterating strategy based on their experiences.
- Adopted digital technologies in pursuit of *higher-order strategic goals* central to the evolution of the enterprise, rather than as point solutions to discrete business challenges.
- Strongly and competently led both the *technology implementations* and the *business-connectedness* of those, in order to win the benefits in business terms.
- Focussed on their *human resource* as well as the *technical developments*, to get both of these transformed into the desired state for their new business model deployment.

The Cloud/AI inflection points in the case studies here represent a continuous arc of innovation within each organisation, each increment being consistent with

DOI: 10.4324/9781003255529-4

the last and grounded in the entity's prior experience. At the time they were taken, however, these decisions would have seemed something of a leap into the unknown.

Each decision represents a conscious choice of paths. Clearly, there are many ways to proceed with Cloud and AI, and some will be much more successful than others. Given the substantial investment in time, cost, capability and forgone opportunities, each of our case study organisations demonstrated confidence both in their ability to predict the contribution of these new technologies to their future success, and in their own ability to unlock this contribution for the benefit of their firms. Such investments were made in the light of uncertainty, but with the sense of opportunity in hand, as well as the consequences and threat of inaction, and of losing ground to competitors.

These international case studies are of well-established and generally large businesses, being Rolls Royce, Samsung, DBS Bank, Bank of America and Netflix. Being generally large, and highly successful companies, these businesses provide much food for thought as to why and how they used either or both of AI or Cloud to transform their businesses, including to quite a large extent, not just their services and processes, but their business models. This includes how they work internally, and how and what they interface their stakeholders with, and offer their 'wares' to their customers.

It can be argued that for large and successful companies, there is much inertia, even active resistance to change inherent in their cultures, yet these companies are fine examples of incumbent firms whose leaders refused to allow themselves to become victims of their own successes. While these companies have many differences across them, such as industry, technological sophistication and business strategy, they also have much in common, especially the 'proactive innovation desire' and a refusal to accept the status quo. They were all prepared to venture into new territory – necessary when one innovates – with the confidence and knowledge that comes with sensibly bringing customer requirements and a visionary value proposition together with the asset capabilities that AI and Cloud technologies have enabled.

Rolls Royce (UK): 'Flight-as-a service'

Background: an illustrious aviation heritage

Rolls Royce Holdings Plc is a UK headquartered entity which designs, manufactures, supplies and maintains powerplants for aviation, marine and industrial applications (the luxury car manufacturer of the same name was spun off as Rolls Royce Motors in the 1970s and the companies are not associated). Rolls Royce's engines are notable in the history of aviation. They propelled the first successful crossing of the Atlantic Ocean in 1919. After achieving success in the air races of the 1930s, Rolls Royce Merlin engines powered the WWII Spitfire and Mustang fighters that signalled a peak of piston-engine development.

Rolls Royce then turned its attention to pioneering the development of jet engines, setting a world air speed record as early as 1945. Later Rolls Royce engines fired up the gorgeous Concorde, and the iconic RB211 turbofan lofted the Boeing 747 – the 'Queen of the Skies' – for the many decades that aircraft crossed the globe.

Rolls Royce has successfully weathered turbulent conditions over the century of its existence, including two world wars, the dawn of the jet age, the oil crisis of the 1970s, ownership changes, market consolidation, and intense competition by the remaining jet engine manufacturers. In 1971, it was crippled by the research and development (R&D) costs and delivery delays of the aforementioned RB211 unit, coming close to bankruptcy and requiring government intervention to survive.

'Power by the Hour': inventing servitisation

In the early 1960s, the jet engine buyer market was starting to expand as the business aviation sector emerged and the prospect of mass air travel crystallised. This new base of potential customers did not possess the financial resources or engineering expertise of the 'flag carrier' national airlines that represented the majority of civilian aviation operators in that era.

In response to the needs of this new customer segment, Rolls Royce launched an offering that would, a quarter of a century later, come to be known as 'servitisation'.[2] This term describes the process of turning a product into a value-added service. As an alternative to buying and maintaining an engine, the company proposed to operators of the new Hawker-Siddeley HS125 corporate jet the option of paying a fixed price per flying hour that included both the supply of the engine and its maintenance.

This offering, snappily trademarked as 'Power by the Hour', proved attractive to fleet operators seeking more predictable operating costs, better cost variabilisation, reduced capital outlay, and the transfer of operational and performance risk back to the OEM (original equipment manufacturer). Customers thought it provided an incentive for Rolls Royce to focus on reliability, because they no longer paid for break-fix and maintenance-interval servicing. Instead, they paid for outcomes that were easy to measure and for guarantees of availability. For the manufacturer, too, the upside was substantial. As a business model, 'Power by the Hour' allowed Rolls Royce to capture the value of its engineering and maintenance capability, and provided a secure, long-tail stream of revenue from engines, which might previously have been maintained by other companies.

Today extended and re-branded, the programme counts over 85 enrolled customers and, pre-pandemic, was delivering in excess of 14 million flying hours annually. Somewhere in the world, a Rolls Royce powered aircraft was taking off or landing every 16 seconds. 'Power by the Hour' has been adopted in some form by all Rolls Royce's competitors and has also become a preferred basis for contracting for civil and defence buyers. It is currently the subject of an EU study into circular economy business models and asset value maximisation.

This servitisation model has also proven influential outside the aviation world, especially in capital intensive, variable utilisation contexts. Examples include EMC (now a division of DELL) which in the late 1990s contracted computer storage based on capacity utilisation and Hitachi's more recent 'Trains as a Service', which is invoiced based on miles travelled and stock availability.

Arguably, the ground-breaking servitisation theory behind Rolls Royce's 'Power by the Hour' model also laid the groundwork for all 'as-a-service' platform offerings that underpin much of the digital economy today. Rolls Royce was no newcomer to innovation in business models when new technologies such AI came to the fore, this century. Note that a deep dive into innovation, using the example of the Doblin innovation framework, is covered in Chapter 6.

Fuelled by analytics

Data acquisition and analysis were from the outset, critical to the commercial viability of Rolls Royce's 'as-a-service' model. The data insights that keep an engine operating contribute both to higher revenues for the company and to more satisfied customers. These insights also inform a span of in-house decisions from design choices, through inventory control, and on to operations planning.

In the 1990s, data analysis required the stored telemetry from engines to be downloaded after each flight. Advances in Internet of Things (IoT) devices means that engine health could be monitored in real time. Modern jet engines generate terabytes of information every flight cycle, and in-flight data-capture and analysis requires both bandwidth and computing power. Rolls Royce tackled these transmission and interpretation challenges in 2016 by cementing partnerships with aviation specialist SITA together with Microsoft's Azure Cloud platform, IOT, and data-mining capabilities.

With these foundational capabilities in place, Rolls Royce launched the Derby-based Aircraft Availability Centre the following year. This facility continuously monitors the 70 trillion datapoints generated annually by its customers all over the world. The data is analysed in the Cloud by AI tools that generate user-friendly interpretations to be mined for insight by both data experts and aircraft engineers. From the centre, descriptive and predictive analytics can flag when and how an engine is performing poorly and the monitoring team can ensure that spares and engineering teams are available quickly to meet the aircraft at the point of need. These technical capabilities give effect to the servitisation business model.

Rolls Royce then started to look beyond its initial goal of optimising engine wear and efficiency parameters for individual operators. The company understood that the massive dataset generated by the Aircraft Availability Centre was an even more valuable asset when aggregated. It realised that it could mine data across routes, destinations, fleets, aircraft configurations and over time to see patterns that would help customers optimise overall flight profiles.

Rolls Royce claimed this broad advisory service could reduce operating costs by millions, citing that increasing fuel efficiency by just 1% would create savings of USD0.25M for each aircraft. Industry sources broadly agree that the big data approach has the potential to deliver customer benefits at scale. A mere two-minute reduction in 'operator controllable' flight delays (the kinds of delays Rolls Royce is drilling into) would, they say, save US airlines USD16M annually. To do this analysis effectively and efficiently, humans need help from artificial intelligence.

The Intelligent Engine

In early 2018, Rolls Royce articulated its belief that AI and data analytics sat the heart of its future business and design philosophy. The company published its 'Intelligent Engine' vision for the company's future:

> The Intelligent Engine vision is based on a belief that the worlds of product and service have become so closely connected that they are now insepar-able, thanks to rapid advancements in digital capability. By the end of this year Rolls-Royce will be set to receive more than 70 trillion data points from its in-service fleet each year. Harnessing the power of this data is cen-tral to delivering the Intelligent Engine and developing an engine which is connected, contextually aware and comprehending.
>
> *Rolls Royce, 2018*[3]

The firm imagines the Intelligent Engine as connected to every other engine in the fleet, and to the manufacturer's and operator's infrastructure. Such an engine would be 'aware' of its location and experiences, including weather conditions and pilot inputs. Ultimately, an Intelligent Engine would use machine learning and other AI technologies to learn and understand about its operations and environment, and would act on that understanding to optimise, diagnose and self-repair. From a tech-nical perspective, these use cases are archetypical examples of supervised learning models and digital twins (covered in Chapter 7), which quantify the relationships between this vast array of data points, and the target business outcome (e.g. engine uptime, total maintenance cost).

The company's leadership visualises this future as three interlocking circles of product, service, and digital, which it is seeking to progressively – and eventually completely – overlap to drive new value for customers.

AI now at Rolls Royce

AI and other digital technologies that complement or extend AI are already well embedded across many business lines in Rolls Royce, including design, manufac-turing and aftersales processes. Speaking in 2018, Paul Stein, the firm's Head of Research and Technology commented that AI was pinpointing the optimum design balance between 'cost, manufacturability and performance, and overall systems performance'.

In common with other advanced manufacturers, AI is used extensively in Rolls Royce's production environments. AI is deployed both within the production line and to check production outputs. In its Sunderland (UK) facility, the company uses AI to enable machine tools to self-correct their wear patterns. In Singapore, AI is used to scrutinise turbine blades for tiny flaws, automating a previously manual inspection task to deliver scale efficiency and to better utilise the expertise of the human inspectors.

'Digital twins' of working engines highlight another facet of how this balance is being achieved. Digital twins are complete virtual simulations of a working engine. They allow scenarios to be tested faster than real-time, and can have predictive as well as diagnostic power:

> In design, we use AI to learn from our past engine design and our past simulation data. If we have a new engine design in mind, AI can help us to predict performance.
>
> *Terence Hung, Chief of Computational Engineering*

AI and the complementary technology of VR have been deployed to improve collaboration between design teams. Marius Swoboda, Head of Design Systems Engineering, knew that the human brain struggles to interpret 3D data in 2D plans, leading engineers to misperceive up to 40% of a design's fine detail. He turned to VR to address this challenge and created a CAVE (Computational Automatic Virtual Reality!) that renders full-scale models of an engine and its dependent systems from CAD data onto curved screens. These representations enable design teams of up to ten participants to work holistically in the same space:

> An engine has a lot of oil, electricity, and air pipes, plus wiring and other elements. In the past, every department did their wiring and the routing independently from each other. Today, we can come together to discuss interface problems, and literally walk around the designs.

AI and VR have also been combined to create remote maintenance training environments for the civil and military maintenance personnel who service Rolls Royce products. These virtual environments can partly or wholly replace traditional hands-on, in-person attendance, thus reducing the downtime for personnel and equipment. Rolls Royce says the programme also creates a more consistent learning experience and reduces the risk of instructor induced training errors. The programme uses VR to connect learners to their study in new and self-guided ways and does not simply replicate traditional training. In VR, learners can drill down to explore the smallest engine component and zoom out to appreciate entire subsystems. They can also practice hangar-scale maintenance operations, like removing an engine from a wing, that are very difficult to train in an operational context.

The rollout of the virtual programme was accelerated in the COVID-19 pandemic to overcome barriers to face-to-face training.

Surfacing new opportunity and ethically governing AI

The firm's leadership has been clear that AI adoption is critical to the future business:

We know it is going to change most of what we do – how we design, manu-facture and support our products and how we run our business. And we know it's certainly going to impact our customers. But beyond that we don't really know – and that's exciting.

Paul Stein, 2018

It was this sense of engagement with the future that prompted Rolls Royce to establish its global network of data innovation accelerators to generate future com-petitive advantage. 'This is about new thinking, new ways, new ideas and new value in terms of Rolls Royce and our customers […] in our new digital strategy, data innovation is the very heartbeat of it, the cutting edge', said Neil Crockett, Rolls Royce's Chief Digital Officer, at the 2017 launch.

Operating in cross-disciplinary 'cells', the sweeping mission of R2 Data Labs is to partner with business lines with Rolls Royce to develop new applications for data analytics, ML, and industrial AI in design, and to consider potential new business models springing from this work. Each lab is also tasked with establishing an ecosystem to tap the idea generation capabilities of academia, start-ups and OEMs in their geography. Lastly, the labs have a remit to reach out to governments and venture capitalists with the intention of securing investment and co-funding opportunities.

Early collaborations between the business lines and R2 Data Labs led Rolls Royce to identify the need for an AI governance framework. For Lee Glazier, Head of Service Integrity, this framework was a natural extension of the product safety culture that is deeply rooted in the aviation industry.

The framework was launched in late 2020. It was claimed to be the first AI ethics framework developed for an industrial context and was named 'Aletheia' after the Greek goddess of truth. It has been open-sourced as a contribution to the growing field of AI data ethics – so you can judge it for yourself! In his pro-logue to its publication, Chief Executive Warren East explained his reasoning for this decision:

> As we emerge from the global Coronavirus pandemic, the need to free up human creativity to find new routes forward has never been greater. Making full and ethical use of our AI tools will contribute to the growth, wealth and health of our world. For these reasons, Rolls-Royce is making The Aletheia Framework™ freely available to all that might benefit from it.

Meeting the pandemic challenge with AI

The world aviation market collapsed in the face of COVID-19. Power by the hour contracts do not generate revenue when airlines aren't flying, and Rolls Royce reported a pre-tax loss of GBP 4B in 2020. It shuttered six manufacturing facilities, reduced hours in others, and cut 7,000 of 19,000 jobs in its civil avi-ation division.

In these difficult circumstances, Rolls Royce turned to the AI and data innovation capabilities it had already established through R2 Data Labs. This has resulted in a number of initiatives being launched or commercialised, most notably:

- Yocova: Standing for 'you + collaboration = Value', Yocova is a data marketplace and collaboration hub for the aviation industry https://public.yocova.com
- The Emergent Alliance: This collaboration between 50 industry and technology entities offers downloadable tools such as AI chatbots and dashboards to help develop insights and practical responses to the pandemic https://emerg entalliance.org

The company is also continuing its commitment to the governance of digital environments through a research partnership with Carnegie Mellon and Purdue Universities. With them, it is developing AI-based intrusion detection technologies.

For Rolls Royce, understanding the power of AI and data innovation started with a desire to better understand and manage engine environments. Today, facing into the future of the pandemic, this understanding may represent a way forward in an environment where the engines are silenced.

Samsung (South Korea): insight and efficiency with AI

'This is a time of real crisis. Global companies are crumbling. We don't know what will happen to Samsung either', Samsung's visionary chairman Lee Kun-Hee was quoted as saying after his return to the company in 2008. 'Within 10 years, all Samsung products may disappear. Now, we have to start anew. Let's move on, with eyes set straight ahead'.

This was clearly a statement of proactive leadership from the top of this company.

Background: change and reset

In 2020, Forbes calculated Samsung to be the eighth most valuable brand in the world. That same year, Interbrand rated Samsung as number 5 in its Best Global Brands research. Samsung rose from the ashes of occupation and war and has since weathered both product and personal scandals to attain these plaudits.

Samsung was founded as a wholesale grocer in 1938, and from its earliest years demonstrated an appetite for diversification and growth. Interests as diverse as textiles, fertilisers and sugar, and banking and insurance companies were acquired through the 1950s and 60s. This growth was fuelled by government policies aimed at reducing the post-Korean War reliance on foreign aid and investment. The government supported businesses that it hoped would develop domestic capabilities in heavy industry, manufacturing, and R&D, and these policies created the highly diversified conglomerates (including Samsung) known as 'chaebols'.

In early 1969, Samsung entered the electronics market. Daringly, given the country's longstanding tense relationships with Japan, it took a chance on cooperating with Japanese businesses to improve its market standing and production capabilities. A number of joint ventures were born from the alliances and these entities manufactured domestic electronics and white goods such as TVs, washing machines and fridges. These items were produced in high volumes and were considered to be of low quality. A 1988 foray into the mobile phone sector that Samsung now commands (with 18.8% of the market) was initially marked by poor sales and indifferent quality.

New products and new technologies

The group's chairman, Lee Kun-Hee, a son of the original founder, had become deeply concerned about the future of the company in the years since his 1987 ascension to the role. In 1993, he gathered top executives at a Samsung plant in Germany to lay out his 'New Management Initiative', in which he famously exhorted them to 'change everything except your wife and kids'.

Then, in 1995, and to the shock of the 2,000 employees assembled as witnesses (and his own board of directors), Lee Kun-Hee smashed up, burned, and finally bulldozed quantities of his own company's product. He was reportedly humiliated that the Samsung mobile phones he had offered as seasonal gifts to employees were defective.

Lee Kun-Hee had decided to pull back from retail products in order to learn how to build their components to the level of quality that would eventually allow Samsung Electronics to successfully reenter the market. The subsidiary had already been rebuilding a bankrupt chipmaker acquired in 1974 and was by this time a market leader in chip manufacture.

In 1996, Lee Kun-Hee declared that 'an enterprise's most vital assets lie in its design and other creative capabilities' and, consistent with his focus on change, set about reinventing Samsung's culture, systems and processes around innovation and design. He clarified: 'Samsung's future hinges on new businesses, new products and new technologies. We should make our corporate culture more open, flexible and innovative.'

Entrepreneurial in-house IT

Surprisingly, one of the principal beneficiaries of the emphasis on new products and technologies proved to be Samsung's own internal IT department. Created in 1985, Samsung Data Systems initially offered systems integration and IT outsourcing expertise to manage the technology base of other group entities. Renamed Samsung SDS in the late 90s, it also started to establish presences in the parent group's overseas markets. By 2020, Samsung SDS was established in 41 countries and had over 23,000 employees.

In 2018, Samsung SDS announced its intention of becoming a 'data driven digital transformation leader'. Well before then, however, it had channelled R&D efforts intensively into emerging technologies including AI, IoT, AR/VR, blockchain and cyber. Between 2016 and 2017, the company launched many of its foundational AI-enabled products, including the Brightics AI data analytics platform whose functionality underpins many of the company's digital offerings. The platform ingests, processes, analyses and visually displays data from multiple systems and IoT device feeds.

Thanks to the span of the chaebol's business interests, Samsung SDS had been able to refine the platform with internal customers across a swathe of industry sectors including healthcare, logistics, manufacturing and healthcare before its public launch. Its intended customer base was however more ambitious, as their CEO declared at the launch:

> Thirty years of knowhow and analysis capacity are all included in Brightics AI, the AI-based analysis platform, which will lead the 4th Industrial Generation of IT innovation. We will lead local and overseas companies' interest in big data analysis into a good performance.
>
> *Hong Won-Pyo, CEO, 2017*

The AI-enabled workplace

Brightics AI has been put to work in Samsung's 32 factories worldwide as part of the 'Intelligent Factory' offering, where it is said by the company to collect 45TB of data daily from a million sensors. The platform collates this data into a single view with site level drilldown so that the activities and performance of each site can be centrally coordinated and compared. This data also generates 'digital twins' of physical assets that can highlight equipment performance and predict failure modes. Onsite technicians can then be sent to the malfunctioning unit, where they use AR overlays to identify, diagnose and interact with the faulty machine.

A single modern production line, says Samsung, streams information to the Intelligent Factory every second from around 2,000 pieces of sensor-enabled equipment. Production lines, however, are far from the only assets monitored by the platform. Sensor-rich environments enable AI analysis of heat, vibration, noise levels and other potential workplace risks such the location of mobile logistics drones. This data is used to deliver predictive facility maintenance and to improve employee safety.

Optimally, these data rich environments are conceived on the Brightics platform at the inception of a manufacturing plant project. At the design and build phase, AI is used to standardise datasets – like CAD files – between vendors and to suggest optimal routings for pipes and other installations based on a site's topology. Samsung estimates that this analysis can generate labour and construction cost savings of around 30–50% of a traditional project.

Samsung then set about reinterpreting today's data-saturated white-collar workplaces with the 'Intelligent Office'. Their response was a natural language chat-enabled, 'virtual personal assistant' – think Siri for work. Users can ask their 'assistant' to retrieve and present data such as sales figures for a given time period and geography, and then receive outputs as graphs or spreadsheets. More traditional technologies, such as optical character recognition, are given an AI tweak courtesy of a pre-processing module that uses machine learning to improve accuracy. The market response was positive, with technology analyst Gartner rating Samsung's vision and ability to execute into their 'Magic Quadrant' for Robotic Process Automation.

The Brightics platform is also used at shopping mall and individual retail outlet level, to analyse and predict customer behaviour. It meshes weather forecasts, holiday calendars, transport data, the movement of people through the retail space and other data to improve sales forecasting by 30%. Somewhat worryingly from a privacy perspective, its promotional videos show how personalised shopping recommendations are made through facial scanning and classification of gender and other physiological traits – though customer optionality is offered in markets like the US.

AI-enabled managed services

So far, we have considered pure-play technology offerings. In several sectors Samsung SDS also offers managed services that combine human expertise with advanced AI deployments.

The genesis of 4PL Cello reflects the conglomerate's manufacturing interests. Cello provides outsourced supply chain management and logistics with an emphasis on the value-adding contribution of 'Industry 4.0 technologies'. These enhancements include AI-based network optimisation and delivery prediction, sensor-based environmental monitoring, and supply chain assurance built on blockchain. More innovatively, customers can create a digital twin of their warehouse and use it to visualise, either onscreen or in VR, the movement of inventory through the space.

Such explosive and continued growth in systems, use-cases, and data has increased the 'attack surface' of organisations, being the places where cyber activity can be directed. Samsung SDS call the cybersecurity space 'a battle for survival for your company'. As a Managed Services Security Provider or MSSP, the company operates several global Security Operations Centres that deploy AI to monitor customers' overall security postures as well as to hunt, detect and analyse cyber threats. In 2020, the platform, which combines big data analytics capability with AI-based automation, claimed to scrutinise 40TB of security data each day, including 17B pieces of raw data relating to over 400,000 PCs and 3,000 websites.

Profit through technology innovation

Samsung SDS helps maintain its chaebol's advantage through delivering advanced technology solutions into the core operations of other Samsung subsidiaries. In addition, the firm has developed a business model which permits it to refine its innovations in-house before taking them to market, sometimes using these sister organisations as distribution channels.

These strategies are developing strong external revenue flows. In 2017, external customers represented only 11% of sales income for Samsung SDS. In 2018, this grew to 14%. In 2019, Samsung SDS flagged total revenues of USD9.3B, 17% of which from other than Samsung group companies. The company that started life as an in-house IT function had netted almost USD1.6B in revenues from its third-party customer base.

On reflection, it is useful to consider where Samsung is today, relative to where it would have been had it been an AI and Cloud laggard, rather than the proactive innovator that it is. While this question is a hypothetical and hence cannot be answered by fact, we believe that there is no question that Samsung's competitive position in many industries, its revenue and profits streams, and its productivity would be far below todays' actuality, had it not, as a business philosophy, chosen to embrace and drive hard on such new technology implementations as AI and Cloud.

DBS bank

When Singapore based DBS bank considered its future in and around 2010, it realised that it needed to think and behave much more like a technology company and less like a bank, especially a traditional bank. Its CEO stated in 2014[4] that:

> whether we know it or not, the digital revolution has put banks under siege. With Internet 2.0 and mobility, the game has been redefined. Banks in Asia are on a burning platform of competition from mobile and Internet companies. If we don't embrace digital – and quickly – there is a real danger that our lunch will be eaten. It is only a matter of time before the disruption that the retail and telecom industries have experienced befalls banking. Monumental change is just around the corner and Bill Gates will be proven right when he said that people need banking, but not banks.
>
> *Piyush Gupta, CEO, DBS*

Sia et al.[5] point to the strategic nature and pervasiveness of the DBS transformation as containing the following components: '(1) cultivate digital leadership among senior executives, (2) build agile and scalable digital operations, (3) design new digitally enabled customer experiences and (4) incubate and accelerate emerging digital innovations'. Moving to the Cloud gave advantages of speed, cost reduction, and scalability including to new markets to DBS, yet Cloud was a contributor and certainly not the whole of the strategy. Strong leadership, proactively pursuing a new 'strategic future path' was the key starting point and foundation; everything else followed and was built on that.

DBS went through a multiyear, technology enabled transformation that was phased: the first phase was getting the relationships right between the business part of the bank and the bankers, with the technologists. In many organisations, certainly including banks, there has been a traditional gap in mindset, priorities and actions between the career bankers and the internal technology service providers, sometimes a chasm! DBS started by reorganising to achieve close alignment of technology with banking operations, restructuring divisions to suit. A new division was formed, called Technology and Operations,[6] replacing the separate functions, and with the seniority and clout to have retail and business banks and bankers reporting into it. This represented a significant elevation of DBS' stated desire to achieve technological leadership and alignment as a key to its overall business strategy.

Lean management was used to pursue operational improvement in order to achieve high levels of process standards, prior to moving forward with advanced IT and automation. The lesson they learned is that automating ineffective processes still leaves one with ineffective processes! DBS improved core processes first, then disrupted its own organisation, then moved forward with Cloud-based digitalisation.

DBS followed its digital-ready reorganisation with a second phase of creating ambidexterity, meaning the ability to simultaneously exploit its market through running its existing businesses effectively but also to explore and innovate well. Multiple study tours led to a deeper understanding of leading-edge practices and technology possibilities. The aspiration at DBS was to become a technology leader. Interestingly, technology developed was insourced to achieve competitive advantage, with a 1,000 person DBS development organisation created in India.

DBS then went fully into the Cloud, partnering with AWS, and moving into agile API developments aggressively. DBS offered over 150 APIs across a wide range of financial services, by end of 2017.

DBS also attended to its culture, moving 26,000 people in its workforce from more traditional banking cultures to a nimble and agile technology-oriented set of values and processes. Much training was certainly involved, and a new cultural imprint was rolled out. For example, experimentation and risk taking were addressed and encouraged, which runs counter to decades of conservatism in banking tradition.

At the customer interfaces, emphasis was on going fully digital, removing all paper, marketing through electronic channels only, and digitising the customer's process, enhancing speed and service levels for the customer. Partners such as retailers were set up, for example for retail customers to obtain cash.

AI was used, for example in chatbots, very successfully in markets such as India. Once DBS had its technology orientation in place, it was able to diversify for its customers, offering transaction and other services in car sales, electricity sales and other markets, leveraging its Cloud and technology capabilities and its customer base. Further, there was now a sound business rationale for international expansion. DBS had built competitive advantage to bring to new markets.

Organisations approaching digitalisation face key decisions such as whether to build a new and somewhat or highly separate digital platform, capability and organisation from its traditional one, or to undertake a usually massive and challenging conversion of the traditional old into the digital new. DBS chose deliberately to convert, without exception, every part of itself, through transformation. Every unit digitised.

A balanced scorecard was used to measure and track such conversion, measuring in detail, for each business unit, details in the categories of digital value creation, customer digital joy, as well as more traditional parameters.

DBS goes platform based

Moving from banking with technology as a support, to true alignment of the technology and banking capabilities required a further DBS transformation. People and technologies were highly integrated into these platforms. There was a complete elimination of the traditional separation of technological capability from banking work. This included all functions, now platforms, from front office to back office, without exception. For each platform, from consumer services to core processing, joint CEO and CTOs were in place working together with joint KPIs, and all incentives were realigned to the new strategy, with the additional fusion of start-up mentality being brought in to induce the exploration part of innovation work. DBS executives state that DBS wishes to act as a start-up, even though it is a significantly scaled incumbent. Funding of technology projects was transformed into funding of platforms, fusing the technical and the business mindsets and measures, and hence the digitised banking work.

All this transformation and movement into the digital world required a great deal of human capability development, and DBS made large investments in training and development, at scale. For example, 3,000 DBS employees undertook training into AI and ML development and implementation.

Cloud's role at DBS

DBS has moved key functions such as payments and mobile banking fully into the Cloud. It has launched Cloud-based functionality in Indonesia, India, and a number of other countries, with 'Cloud speed'. It has found efficiency and innovation effectiveness from running its internal IT functions on the Cloud. DBS finds that Cloud services such as through its AWS partnership is more effective in providing security solutions than if these were further insourced. Mobile applications and data/analytics services on the Cloud gives DBS a speed advantage. DBS has gone strongly into the public Cloud, and achieved significant cost reductions, as well as speed and service advantages.[7]

David Gledhill, DBS Group CIO has stated:

> By being a leader in adopting Cloud technologies, DBS can deliver more customer value through our ability to experiment and scale quickly. Our teams are able to iterate and deliver products to our customers at a much faster rate, while adhering to the highest standards of security and resiliency.

With the new Cloud data centre, we are able to significantly increase our energy efficiency as well as drastically reduce our carbon footprint.

DBS, n.d.[8]

DBS has also simultaneously enhanced its sustainability and overall innovation-oriented reputation and reduced its energy use, winning numerous international banking awards, such as World's Best Digital Bank from Euromoney, and Safest Bank in Asia.

By 2020, 97% of DBS applications were Cloud ready, up from 28% in 2016. Agility in dealing with COVID-19 was vastly superior as a result of the ambidexterity and agility that DBS achieved. DBS conceives of its journey as 'never over' and looks to a future of incorporating 5G, IoT, blockchain, and privacy engineering,[9] to take it forward on the Cloud.

These new capabilities provide DBS with competitive advantage and a sound logic of how it can add value when expanding into other markets. DBS has recently acquired banking businesses in India and China, the world's two most populous countries, and the upside of such strategies are clearly based on the Cloud and digitalisation capabilities it has developed. With record profits declared in 2020 despite the COVID-19 pandemic, DBS has used its technological and business transformation to create a long-term strategic advantage.

This set of achievements at DBS was certainly not accomplished without a great deal of hard work and significant investment. Yet the DBS organisational transformation demonstrates that when done well, such efforts bring tremendous benefits. There is much to admire and learn from DBS for financial service companies in Australasia and indeed globally. As with the other international best practice cases, it can be insightful to consider where DBS would be today had it not embarked and persisted on its transformation journey: no matter which stakeholder's perspective is taken, we believe it would be only a pale shadow of its current actual self if it had been a laggard as against the industry leader that it has become.

Bank of America

Floating on the (IBM public) Cloud

When Bank of America (BoA) decided to move its data and transactions to the Cloud, it teamed up with IBM and moved increasingly to its public Cloud, as announced in the *Wall Street Journal* in November 2019.[10] In 2011, with a stock price below $6, BoA created a long-term strategy to remake itself, essentially to go digital and into the Cloud, aiming to provide modern and better services and lower the BoA cost to income ratio, especially including the cost burden of building, running and maintaining its own data centres and servers. By 2019, BoA had 37 million active digital customers and had cut its data centres and server volumes by two thirds. This was a big modernisation and transformative remake of services and operations.

BoA in 2021 served some 66 million clients in the USA, from 4,500 retail centres and 17,000 ATMs, with 41 million of its customers using digital channels, including 32 million on mobile phones. The recent growth of its digital customer base, and hence its overall growth rate has been very significant. Over the most recent decade the stock price has risen by a factor of over seven. As a company with a 240-year history, its challenge has been managing the 'explore' and 'exploit' parts of ambidexterity through being highly proactive in digital and Cloud development in recent years, while still serving customers well as it migrates with them to the 'new world' of digital.

BoA's digital and Cloud investments and its advanced technological developments were certainly not a pure play, but rather were a significant part of a full remake of its offerings. This is because BoA is a long-standing incumbent, with many customers being digital ready and able, and many others who want high touch branches and business centres. In 2018, BoA announced a planned 500 new financial centres,[11] offering a mix and client choice of high touch and high tech:

> Our high-tech and high-touch approach means our team is able to help clients with their financial needs throughout their lifetimes and deliver extra-ordinary client care at all times, no matter how they choose to do their banking, said Dean Athanasia, co-head of consumer and small business at Bank of America.

Another 2,000 financial centres were being renovated, and 5,400 verified professional staff were added in these centres in and after 2018.

The digital and Cloud solutions were aimed at lower costs and agile mobile service provision but were accompanied by over 6,000 client-facing support officers, aimed at helping clients. Online client financial education services were also introduced. Wealth management was conducted through its Merrill Lynch arm, at high volume, also using a mix of technological solutions and human advisory expertise resources.

Digital solutions were increasingly being developed and offered to clients such as 'Erica' who automatically helps clients with transactional requirements. A new Cloud-based mobile app for mortgage creation speeds up the process, allowing clients to track process, upload documents and improve the service experience. A new car shopping application similarly grew rapidly in its popularity, being an end-to-end loan platform. A new digital application was created for BoA's three million small business customers.

BoA's decade of transformation has been a primarily digital integration and transformation, according to industry observers,[12] with a reported 184 patents being granted to BoA, as a metric of its innovation efforts. In 2020, mobile users grew 15%, and Erica users grew 50%. Agility is key in this very dynamic world of digital banking, with the bank reporting 800 mobile app enhancements in the first eight months of 2020. Erica has 15 million active users, at a rate of 12 million interactions per month. Of its ten billion annual transactions, 97% are now digital or automated, and 'digital first always' is the mantra, with a modernised branch network used to back up such services for those who need it. This is indeed a true and very full transformation for what was a traditional incumbent, branch oriented, full-service bank.

> High tech for us is about bringing together banking, investing and borrowing and all of the needs that you have as an individual – whether it's about learning about those things, planning, taking action or monitoring those things – anytime, anywhere.
>
> *David Tyrie, BoA Head of Digital, Financial Center Strategy*
> *and Advanced Client Solutions*

'Where high tech and high touch come together', says Aditya Bhasin (CIO and Head of Consumer, Small Business and Wealth Management Technology), BoA provides for seamless integration of technology-based service and a hand off within the application to a human served touch if needed, or a referral to a service centre/ branch. 'High tech that can seamlessly hand off to high touch and fully integrate with high touch is where we believe there is competitive advantage', states Bhasin.

Erica is increasingly personalising its AI powered services, such as providing alerts that a clients spending is higher than usual or providing an alert that will likely be of interest to the client, such as a refund into the account. Education is available for clients on a range of topics, for example creating a budget.

As transactions have moved to the BoA Cloud, the role of branches has changed. As opposed to transaction processing sites, they have become more highly value-added advisory and consultation centres, which required physical redesign of these facilities. Significant investment was required in this series of bold transformations, and a significant return on such investments was achieved.

Innovation at BoA

Innovation is considered part of all employees' jobs at BoA. It also practices open innovation with over 5,000 innovation partners internationally. One of its innovations is to use AI via its Erica interface to give clients a forecast of their future account balance. This is an example of a valuable additional customer service on top of more transactional services that could not have been created without the new technological capabilities. 'We're a technology company, wrapped around a great bank, and that's going to be the future of what we do', CEO Moynihan insists, 'and that's because our customers demand it'.[13] With the fierce competition from other tech companies such as Apple and Google, many fintechs, and the other large incumbent (JPMorganChase, Citigroup, Wells Fargo) banks, BoA sees digital leadership as the way to go.

BoA has invested billions of dollars in the recent decade on blockchain, Big Data, Artificial Intelligence, security such as encryption, Cloud, and biometrics. Things have not always been so rosy at BoA, as only a decade ago it suffered greatly in the 2009–10 recession, and was supported coming out of it by Warren Buffet, whose firm now owns 9% of the company. Investments have been and continue to be vast in high tech and simultaneously high-touch services. BoA sees its journey and strategy as not a digital initiative, or programme, but a whole digital transformation and indeed a revolution. IBM has developed its 'confidential Cloud computing' concepts where data is encrypted and secured to the highest standards, when being stored or used. Clients such as healthcare businesses, Daimler (Mercedes Benz) and BoA have moved quickly to it with IBM as partner, and many other large players such as Apple, Google and Alibaba are developing in the same direction.[14]

Moorhead, in *Forbes*[15] magazine, wrote that 20% of IT workloads are in the Cloud and the other 80% are not as yet. He points out that banking is a particularly challenging sector to move to the Cloud because of the tight regulatory environment, the need for very tight security due to its asset intensity and liquidity (as bank robber Willie Sutton is quoted as having said, 'that's where the money is'), and the need for speedy service and agility. In examining BoA's partnership with IBM in its public Cloud, Moorhead suggests that 'banks need to transform the experience just like consumer demands and technology has transformed media, shopping, and transportation industries.' BoA realises that there will be significant comparative advantage to the bank that gets Cloud transformation right, and it is putting its faith and its USD2.3 trillion in assets behind this strategy. The opportunity cost, of not doing so, and then becoming a laggard in this regard, while competitors transform themselves, is high. IBM's public Cloud has the potential to give BoA a shift in the 'efficient frontier', of moving forward on cost and speed/agility, through technology focussed services, albeit with a human touch behind it.

Ultimately, it's been all about value creation for BoA's customers, and hence competitive advantage for BoA. The direct savings have been stated by BoA's CEO as $2B per year, since a saving of 25–30% can be gained from a third-party arrangement such as this one with the (IBM) Cloud.

Netflix

Entertainment on the Cloud

Founded in 1997 as a sales and rental DVD business, Netflix moved to streaming its entertainment from its own servers, then migrated to the Cloud, and as of 2021 has grown to achieve:

- US$25B in revenue and US$2.7B in net income. This is not a profitless growth story, far from it.
- Over 210 million subscribers, globally except in China, North Korea, Syria and Crimea.
- World's largest entertainment media company by market capitalisation.
- 12,000 employees.

- One of the world's most trusted brands, and S&P 500's highest performing stock for investors during the decade beginning 2010.

In recent years, the company has become a major producer of content, including numerous award-winning productions. This is a true transformation: that unquestionably is very successful, and it was enabled by Cloud and AI, without which it could not have proceeded.

Netflix journeys to the Cloud

Having begun as a DVD distribution business, then initially hosting its own server farms as a streaming service, Netflix saw the opportunity arising for rapid expansion. The capex costs of expanding its distribution server capacity were large, as subscriber numbers started to accelerate, and capex was also needed to acquire and then to expand its entertainment production volumes and qualities.

Subsequently, Netflix moved from owning and insourcing its own IT and service distribution, including all the infrastructure, to an outsourced model for these non-core activities to the public Cloud. This decision had a strategic fit to it, switching out of capital-hungry server infrastructure, to benefitting from AWS's role as a specialist supplier, which brought scale, cutting-edge security, and global reach. It also provided for Netflix to become agile, in terms of moving quickly to identify and offer new services and features, that can almost instantly globalise to its worldwide customer base, thanks to the Cloud's capabilities that it employs.

The decision to move to the public Cloud was brought on partly by its internal data service failure in 2008, that led to a three-day outage. The corporate shock and reputation damage of such an outage caused a rethink of its growth strategy. Over the next few years, it moved all its IT to AWS' Cloud, including databases, billing, employee information systems, and Netflix closed its last data centre in January 2016. Netflix's explosive growth was so fast that it could not have built internal capability fast enough, so the Cloud solution was a necessary ingredient to its success. The Cloud capability, of streaming petabytes (a petabyte is 2^{50} bytes, a 15-digit number) of data was the capability that Netflix needed for its 200 million plus subscribers. Netflix was also thus freed from its internal databases that came with limitations.

Importantly, the move to the Cloud was not just a 'lift and shift' approach, but a greenfield redesign, to take advantage of new technologies. New platforms were built in the Cloud. These were a large number of relatively independent microservices that represented a substantial change from the centralised monolithic approach of the prior internal IT functionality. This served to reduce risk, increase agility, and improve services.

The move to essentially modularised service pieces allowed for faster development and deployment of new functionality, which was jointly developed by AWS and Netflix. New functionality reduced buffering for customers, a significant frustration when watching streaming video. AWS came with built-in redundancy so that customers could be switched across regional servers when local disruptions might occur. This all translates into better customer services in a growing competitive market. Multiple backups were included both within and independent of AWS.

From 2008 to 2015, subscriber numbers rose 700% for Netflix[16] as it globalised. As part of AWS, the Cloud gave flexibility to Netflix with respect to volume, with 'pay as you use' flexibility bringing efficiency of resources that an inhouse facility would not achieve. Money was saved.

Netflix moved all its functionality, including production systems for its original content production, to be Cloud based and hosted. This provided for faster, more efficient and more effective content creation. For its email functionality, the Cloud move was expressed as:

> Before we migrated to Amazon Simple Email Service, Netflix had to maintain an in-house solution for sending emails. This in-house solution carried its own operational overheads, including running dedicated servers with email delivery software and optimizing email sending practices for each Internet Service Provider. We evaluated several email delivery solutions and decided on Amazon SES because it is flexible, affordable, highly scalable, has global reach, and promises excellent deliverability.
>
> *Devika Chawla, Director, Messaging and Contact Engineering, Netflix*

Cloud functionality also brought agility during the pandemic:[17]

> Production of the fourth season of Netflix's episodic drama 'The Crown' faced unexpected challenges, as the world went into lockdown for the COVID-19 pandemic just as post-production VFX work was slated to begin. By adopting a Cloud-based workflow on AWS, Netflix's inhouse VFX team of ten artists was able to seamlessly complete more than 600 VFX shots for the season's 10-episode run in just eight months, all while working remotely.

Migration to the Cloud has clearly been a key element of Netflix' success, in terms of cost, volume and capacity build, security and reliability, and global reach.

Strategic leadership of the move to the Cloud was strongly in place: without the existence of the Cloud and its effective use within Netflix, it would not have been able to grow its subscriber base, and hence fund its content production activities as effectively as has been accomplished.

Operational risk has been reduced, due to the AWS Cloud capabilities, compared with the inhouse capability that Netflix would have necessarily needed to invest in.

The Netflix holistic shift to the Cloud provided new capabilities, of fast scale, shift of fixed costs to become flexible and variable, with state-of-the-art technology including security. In strategic terms it gave Netflix a partnership in which Netflix could focus and hence 'stick to its knitting' of creating and distributing quality content and value-added services at scale to consumers, while using AWS to provide the technical capabilities as the platform needed by Netflix to accomplish its strategic goals at a level that insourcing such distribution would not have attained.

Value adding in the Cloud: AI content recommendation services

For consumers, the sheer volume of choices available for viewing was challenging. This led to its 'recommendation engine'. This engine applied machine learning with big-data based pattern recognition to combine a subscriber's viewing and searching history with data from millions of other subscribers' consumption patterns and content data on genre etc. to efficiently solve the choice problem for consumers. This is an example of how partnering on the Cloud took advantage of the scale, agility and intellectual horsepower behind the AWS suits of services to significantly improve the Netflix offering. It is doubtful that this capability would have been developed so fast and efficiently had Netflix remained with insourcing of its IT in its streaming services.

Going forward, being fully and wholly integrated in its Cloud base clearly gives Netflix the potential to create and globally scale whatever new features and services will be its next series of innovations, on a global basis, with great efficiency, scalability and powerful value propositions to customers.

Conclusions from these international transformation successes

When AI and/or Cloud are deployed successfully, these companies – Rolls Royce, Samsung, DBS, Bank of America and Netflix – show how tremendous value can be created for stakeholders, including particularly customers, employees and shareholders.

They all 'grasped the nettle' of the challenges of transformational change, whereas lesser organisations just drift or make incremental changes. These bold companies have all set themselves up for the future, with the first benefit being their current state of competitive advantage and ensuing profitability. Yet there is a second key benefit: they have become highly dynamic, they have developed a 'transformation capability', combined with a culture of innovation and made robust through technology enablement. None of them will be staying the same for long, rather they will be continuing to evolve their business models, technology enablers and service offerings. They have used their Cloud- and AI-enabled innovations to build their own internal organisational dynamism!

Notes

1 This chapter was co-authored by Catherine Thompson.
2 Vandermerwe, S., & Rada, J. (1988). Servitization of business: Adding value by adding services. www.sciencedirect.com/science/article/abs/pii/0263237388900333
3 Rolls Royce. (2018). The Rolls-Royce Intelligent Engine – driven by data. www.rolls-royce.com/media/press-releases/2018/06-02-2018-rr-intelligentengine-driven-by-data.aspx

4 Gupta, P. (2014). Banking disrupted, DBS Bank. dbs.com/newsroom/influencer/default. page.

5 Sia, S., Soh, C., & Weill, P., (2016). How DBS Bank pursued a digital business strategy. *MIS Quarterly Executive.* https://aisel.aisnet.org/misqe/vol15/iss2/4

6 Sia, S., Weill, P., & Zhang, N., (2021). Designing a future-ready enterprise: The digital transformation of DBS Bank. *California Management Review* https://doi.org/10.1177/0008125621992583

7 Wong, W., (2021, 25 January). AFTAs 2020: Best Cloud Initiative – DBS Bank. Waters Technology. www.waterstechnology.com/awards-rankings/7732206/aftas-2020-best-Cloud-initiative-dbs-bank

8 DBS. (n.d.). First bank in Singapore to launch new Cloud-based data centre test. www.dbs.com/newsroom/First_bank_in_Singapore_to_launch_new_Cloud_based_data_centref

9 Mirasol, P., (2020, 20 July) Banks enumerate the benefits of Cloud computing. Business World. www.bworldonline.com/banks-enumerate-the-benefits-of-Cloud-computing/

10 Loten, A., (2019, 6 November). IBM, Bank of America team up on public Cloud aimed at banks. *The Wall Street Journal.* www.wsj.com/articles/ibm-bank-of-america-team-up-on-public-Cloud-aimed-at-banks-11573016461

11 Bank of America. (2018, 26 February). Bank of America accelerates high-tech, high-touch approach. https://newsroom.bankofamerica.com/press-releases/consumer-banking/bank-america-accelerates-high-tech-high-touch-approach#main-content

12 Streeter, B., (n.d.). Why BofA – not Fintechs or Amazon – should keep bankers awake at night. *The Financial Brand.* https://thefinancialbrand.com/101542/bofa-fintechs-retail-bank-branch-mobile-erica/

13 Cocheo, S., (n.d.) How Bank of America became a tech-driven powerhouse. *The Financial Brand.* https://thefinancialbrand.com/86675/bofa-brian-moynihan-erica-branch-mobile-banking-millennials-fintech/

14 Greig, J., (2020, 20 August). Bank of America, Daimler, and Apple partnering with IBM for confidential computing services. *Tech Republic.* www.techrepublic.com/article/bank-of-america-daimler-and-apple-partnering-with-ibm-for-confidential-computing-services/

15 Moorhead, P., (2019, 18 November). IBM and Bank of America are developing a financial services-ready public Cloud. *Forbes.* www.forbes.com/sites/moorinsights/2019/11/18/ibm-and-bank-of-america-are-developing-a-financial-services-ready-public-Cloud

16 Babu, K., & Prasad, N. (2020). Netflix migrates to the Cloud. ICMR case study, 920-0013-1

17 Amazon. Netflix on AWS. https://aws.amazon.com/solutions/case-studies/netflix/

5

THE BUSINESS-RELEVANT DETAILS BEHIND AI AND CLOUD TECHNOLOGY

Introduction

As highlighted in Chapter 1, the increased criticality of technology to the success of a business has led to the creation of a variety of C-suite technology roles, in fact '40% of CEOs said their CIO or tech leader will be the key driver of business strategy – more than the CFO, COO, and CMO combined'.[1]

This concentration on the CIO as the critical transformation driver runs at odds with our research on the key success factors for AI- and Cloud-enabled transformation. Our research highlights the need for these transformations to be 'business-led'. We believe that – in this technology driven world – most non-IT executives and board members would benefit from having a *de minimis* level of technology literacy to enable business leaders to constructively engage in discussions associated with technology-led transformation. We believe these discussions need to focus initially on business' end state and then work down to the technology enablers rather than work up from whatever new technologies might exist at that point in time.

By technical literacy, we mean that every executive and board member should know at least enough to effectively contribute to insights and strategic decisions concerning digital transformations, technology investments and business model considerations. The Forbes Technology Council[2] has provided some guidelines for this, and we note that they recommend knowing what coders do and what coding actually is. Executives do not need to know how to create code, but it helps if they know what is involved, know what the capabilities and performance parameters are, and can converse with technical people, so as to ask them the right questions, for example during a presentation, or in approval processes for resource allocation. This is required to break down traditional barriers between the mainstream business and the 'techies' in the business and build a bridge from the business towards those who are deeply immersed in creating the technology.

DOI: 10.4324/9781003255529-5

This educative lift of achieving technical literacy in the board and executive will foster a digital mindset in those who collectively strategise and take the company forward. It is not difficult to garner enough information to become literate in these technologies: perhaps the most efficient way is to watch one or more YouTube tutorials[3] on AI, Cloud and other technical capability elements as appropriate to the company's context. The footnote links some further learning opportunities tutorials, many of which have been viewed over a million times. They bring familiarity with terms, definitions, capabilities, and constraints.

To conclude this discussion, we note that the business transformation choices need to be informed by knowledge of what is possible, feasible and ultimately, valuable. A prerequisite for effecting this must surely be technical literacy across the board and leadership (C-suite) team.

The purpose of this technology overview is not to enable business leaders to become 'business coders', or even to give detailed technical requirements to technologists and data scientists (which may cause more confusion and frustration). Our goal is to create a logical and intuitive description of the major innovations (which we're describing as the 'building blocks' for AI and Cloud innovation), without losing technical fidelity or using abstract analogies. We also want to bring to life our claim that there is a positive interplay and multiplicative benefit when AI and Cloud technologies are considered together.

Our goal is to allow technical and non-technical people to get 'on the same page' as one-another, and to allow everyone to have an understanding of what these innovations can practically provide to them, in a structured, buzzword-free way. We will give an overview of each of these major innovations through this chapter, but first, we will cover a range of relevant trends which have influenced the way in which technology provides value to an organisation, and the way in which the technology capability has needed to evolve in recent times, to take advantage of these trends.

Working hard for the benefits

As technologies have matured, costs have decreased, and the underlying capability has increased. The predominant drivers of these costs and capabilities are computation power, and the storage and manipulation of data. These fundamentals have exponentially improved for the last 40 years. For example:

- Moore's law predicts the doubling of transistors in a CPU every 18–24 months, which has also led to a 20–30% annual reduction in the cost per transistor over time.
- Storage costs have halved roughly every 3 years, as their underlying speed has continued to increase.

These underlying cost reductions[4] are the main drivers for the transition from mainframes, eventually to the ubiquitous appearance of PCs and other mobile computing technology. Despite the enormous expansion in technology use, the underlying IT labour expense (when well managed) has dropped to a fraction of its previous costs. Facebook often cites the example of having over one million users per engineer (in 2009) as a measure if its technology efficiency.

So, the good news is, without doing anything, organisations should expect continual capacity and capability improvements in large areas of IT spend. For organisations that are already leveraging Cloud-based services, there are additional ongoing benefits, from the security, performance and capability enhancements that they provide as they periodically update their platforms. These benefits come from multi-billion-dollar investments that the providers are making into their platforms.

Unfortunately, capability doesn't automatically translate into outcomes. In particular there are a few obvious but important steps that need to be taken, to ensure that 'the promise' meets 'the reality':

- Executing new technology-enabled business models will increase the computation and storage requirements of a business. While the cost of innovation has reduced significantly over time, these new costs, and the cost of change (both upfront and ongoing), needs to be understood and thought through carefully.
- The IT operating model needs to fundamentally change to effectively manage a range of more complex third-party relationships, shift the skill set of the technology function, and appropriately govern the shifting risk environment (especially with respect to data governance, data security, and effective ongoing management of statistical models).
- More powerful computers, with more data, don't automatically give any new insights to a business, nor do they change the underlying way a business model creates value for its stakeholders. Some historical technology innovations had obvious business impacts, e.g. moving from fax to email technology. The breadth and complexity of the potential AI and Cloud technology capabilities lead to a far greater range of potential considerations than ever previously existed. Capturing this value, requires a proactive effort from business stakeholders to better understand the way these technologies can support their future needs, and from technology stakeholders, to rethink the way in which they create value for the business.

Supervised learning

Supervised learning models (often also called 'predictive models') describe a broad range of algorithms that have been in use in business and scientific areas for the last forty years. These include Generalised Linear Models (GLMs), Decision Trees, Random Forests, and a wide range of more specialised models.

All of these models have a common mathematical goal. They all use a range of variables (called 'Independent variables' because they should vary independently of each other) to predict a single outcome (call the 'dependent variable'). The relationship between the dependent variable and all of the independent variables, differs based on the type of underlying mathematical model. We won't cover the differences between those variables in this book, as in our view, that level of technical detail isn't required when making a business decision.

What all these models have in common is that they will use a given data set, fit the formulae, and predict the outcome as best it can. The machine will provide the 'most accurate' fit between the dependent variable and those independent variables, where 'most accurate' is defined by the underlying mathematical model and its definition of statistical error.

An example of how these models have made an impact in business is in the prediction of loss for insurers. Expected loss is a key (but not the only) factor in insurance pricing, and as such, a more accurate model better manages the risk exposure of the insurer and can be used to positively select the most attractive customers to the business while adversely selecting (or 'pushing away') undesirable customers onto the competition.

While these algorithms have also been adopted in a vast range of other applications, (for example predicting sales of a product or predicting volumes in a call centre) the main innovations that have made this possible have been an increase in computing power, an increase in the availability of data (both internally and from third parties), far more intuitive programming software and the ability to integrate these models with other applications.

The Cloud is not singularly responsible for the increased use of these algorithms, but it has made their deployment significantly easier, thus reducing the cost of innovation. This is one of the reasons why we see a multiplicative benefit in the innovation provided by these AI models and Cloud platforms.

Unsupervised learning

'Unsupervised learning' (often known as clustering) is focussed on finding patterns and grouping within data, without a focus on any outcome at all (as opposed to 'supervised learning'). The algorithms that underpin unsupervised learning include K-means, Principal Component Analysis, self-organising maps and various others.

Unsupervised learning is best thought of as a hypothesis test, which presumes that there are a set of meaningfully different groups within a range of given data. For example, you may assume that there are six meaningfully different types of customer in your sales data. The hypothesis would be framed as follows: 'I believe that there are six different groups in this data set which contains their ages and incomes'. The algorithm then combs through the data, developing that set of six different groups in a way that they are as different as possible, across those groups of age and income.

Given the criticality of better understanding data, and making more tailored decisions, this can provide significant benefits. Often, these algorithms are part of a process, for example a customer segmentation which categorises types of customers by their buying and product preferences, which then feeds into a supervised algorithm to provide more appropriate product recommendations.

Like any categorisation problem, unsupervised learning can suffer from the desire to develop 'one segmentation to rule them all', where a single clustering definition is used in a wide and poorly related set of contexts. While well intended, this can often result in suboptimal business outcomes.

Deep Learning, and the neural nets we never want to speak about again

It would be negligent to begin a description of Deep Learning's innovations and value, without a brief overview of the simpler Neural Net algorithms that preceded them. The intent of this background is to provide context and an appropriate level of caution for the use of Neural Nets, even though the authors of this book find tremendous value in them when used appropriately.

Neural Nets all have a logical structure that is conceptually designed around the structure of a neuron in the human brain. Neural Nets are the underlying building blocks of a range of models (both supervised and unsupervised), and they became particularly popular in the 1990s. At that time, the available computational power, together with the mathematics known at the time for fitting these models, did not allow of particularly sophisticated models. However, they still offered some significant potential for improvement over the incumbent models.

The trade-off that gets made against more traditional models (e.g. GLMs), is that a Neural Net doesn't contain any intuitive explanation for *why* the model is working in the way it does. Instead, the users of Neural Nets have to be satisfied in the understanding of how accurately the model predicts (e.g. how many times out of 1,000, a model will correctly predict the breakdown of a machine part), without understanding the reason *why* it correctly (or incorrectly) predicts that outcome.

Due to the lack of understanding of how these models work, a range of appropriate management systems are required, to address the impact of misclassifications and mispredictions. Several businesses using these models in the early 90s threw some of this caution to the wind, resulting in significant financial losses and a reluctance to use these models in mainstream business applications.

Despite these early setbacks, research in this field continued. In 2006, mathematicians developed more efficient ways to train Neural Net models, allowing them to become significantly more complex, and to develop multilayer models commonly referred to as Deep Learning models. These models were able to out-perform the existing ones and, more importantly, have been able to outperform humans in addressing many problems.

This led to the understandable excitement around the use of these models in all aspects of everyday life, which we will highlight in a set of limited overviews of the most common Deep Learning applications.

Image recognition, manipulation, and Convolutional Neural Networks (CNNs)

Image recognition and manipulation is a highly complex area of computer science. Traditional programming approaches aren't suited to the wide variety of ways in which image data is provided to a computer. For example, when reviewing and classifying images, algorithms need to control for differences in positioning, lighting, distortions and a variety of other real-world disruptions. These disruptions are hard to program for.

As such, until the advent of sophisticated CNNs, most image recognition techniques were a poor substitute for human intelligence. Now, Deep Learning CNNs provide the most accurate classification of images, well beyond human capability. As a practical example, CNNs can use the image of a person's iris, to accurately predict their gender, age and ethnicity – something that people can't do, and something researchers don't fully understand how the algorithm does either.

Practically, these developments have led to a range of novel applications, well beyond the initial test of 'what is in this image'. These models can perform facial recognition, create text from images of documents, turn satellite imagery into detailed land use information, and identify tumours in MRIs, amongst a wide variety of other classification outcomes.

These algorithms have also allowed for manipulation of data, including 'filters' to beautify or change images and video (including Deep Fakes – which generate intuitively accurate but fake videos of people). These have been used to create viral memes and underpinned the growth of new platforms like Instagram and Snapchat.

From a business perspective, the key aspect to understand is that a far wider variety of data can be practically used when making business decisions or developing new solutions to old problems. This enables a range of new innovations to be created, and in particular, the development of business models which can interact with new channels of information that were previously uneconomical or impractical.

Importantly, some of the algorithms that would have previously required a team of data scientists to develop are now available as a service. This has also dramatically reduced the cost of innovation. For example, Amazon's Rekognition Cloud service,[5] allows you to send an image or video via a simple API and will return a range of structured data. This can include novel items like whether the image contains a specific celebrity, but it can also be used for much more mundane but practically important work like confirming the use of appropriate PPE on a job site or identifying unsafe or inappropriate content, amongst other practical uses. Google offers a similar capability on their Machine Learning platform, and had open-sourced TensorFlow, a powerful set of algorithms with a similar set of applications. This is yet another aspect of how and why the impact of AI is being amplified by Cloud platforms.

Chatbots, natural language processing, and Neural Natural Language Processing

Understanding the underlying meaning and context of a sentence, let alone a paragraph or document, is clearly a challenging task, especially obvious to anyone who has spent time teaching children how to read.

Like the example of image recognition, traditional rules and procedures are not a practical or accurate way to ensure the appropriate understanding of text data. This is another area where Deep Learning through Neural Natural Language Processing (NLP) has spurred a whole wave of innovation, particularly the development of chatbots.

While this is still a developing area, a well implemented chatbot can address a range of customer enquiries far more conveniently and cheaply than a person. While previous examples of voice guided systems were clunky and forced customers to adopt the organisation's singular way of interacting, Neural NLP techniques enable a much more diverse and human-centric way of interacting.

The growing power and flexibility of simulation and digital twins

Business, financial and operational simulation techniques have existed for decades, originally focused on developing a simple, best estimate of the likely outcome, e.g. financial forecasts. These forecasts were developed at a reasonably high level of aggregation and used a coarse range of assumptions.

Over time, new algorithms were developed which were more flexible and allowed for the incorporation of new sources of data, for example consumer confidence surveys. As the breadth of inputs and assumptions in those forecasts increased, there was a corresponding increase in the accuracy of the forecasts. Subsequently, the concept of 'scenarios' came into being, whereby a *range* of forecasts were developed, using the realistic range of potential input assumptions, for example, the range of potential consumer confidence survey results for the periods in question.

The main technology innovation in simulation relates to the scale and complexity of simulations being run, which are now 'Digital Twins' of real-world systems. For example, Airservices Australia runs a simulation engine that creates:

> a digital replica of Australian airspace, including all of the aircraft and weather within the airspace. This cutting-edge digital twin can be used to more accurately predict, collaborate and respond to the changing requirements and requests, enabling highly precise predictions and effective data–driven decision-making.
>
> *Airservices Australia, 2020*[6]

In addition, advancements in data visualisation and manipulation have enabled the development of 'human in the loop' interfaces to interact with those simulations and make better real-world decisions in near real time. In the Airservices example, modelling suggests a potential 33% reduction in delays due to improved decision making.

The ability to run highly complex, digital twin simulations, has great applicability in areas where there the environment is highly variable, and there are short term and/or downstream implications to on-the-ground decision making (e.g. supply chain operations).

As a simple example, many manufacturing sites already collect real-time data through SCADA systems, which provide a rich source of detailed information around production, faults and bottlenecks. If one subset of the manufacturing site shuts down due to an unexpected fault, a simulation of the downstream impacts might look at the variety of available options for the operators and suggest a change to the daily production plan to ensure that customer orders aren't missed and that overtime labour is minimised.

While the concept of a digital twin is highly sophisticated, the barriers to developing these simulations have reduced significantly through advances in data collection and transformation, simulation software and data visualisation tooling.

Strong AI and the AI control problem

As the various AI and machine learning technologies have emerged, so have concerns about our ability to control machines. To quote Elon Musk in 2014:[7]

> We should be very careful about artificial intelligence. If I were to guess like what our biggest existential threat is, it's probably that … With artificial intelligence we are summoning the demon. In all those stories where there's the guy with the pentagram and the holy water, it's like yeah he's sure he can control the demon. Didn't work out.

These existential concerns relate to a type of AI research under the umbrella term of 'Strong AI' or 'Artificial General Intelligence' and are important to separate from all of the aforementioned AI types, which are categorised as 'Weak AI' or 'Narrow AI'. The primary demarcation between these AI techniques, is the concept of consciousness and, critically, the ability for the creators of these algorithms to 'lose control' of the technology as the algorithm begins to make its own decisions.

There is an ongoing debate about how much concern our society and government should place on Strong AI. In our view, these considerations should not factor into current planning, as the technology is both unavailable over the medium term, and still being defined. In contrast, we recommend that all organisations seriously consider the ethical aspects of Narrow AI as they develop new candidate business models.

The practical reality

It would be easy to look at the various marketing buzz around AI and 'big data', and assume that these new, magical models, will somehow trawl through large swathes of data and suddenly provide the business with gold nuggets of insight.

There is a structured, hypothesis-led approach to data analysis, which needs to be followed, to ensure that the reality of these technologies lives up to the hype. The two major model development risks we would like to highlight, are that:

1. If you torture the data enough, it will say anything you want it to. Robust statistical modelling relies on a structured process for testing and developing models (and underlying assumptions), which can be manipulated (or unintentionally omitted). It's critical for this testing and deployment process to be part of any business deployment of AI techniques. The bottom-up, hypothesis-free approach to model building is highly likely to find lots of 'insights' that don't result in reliable outcomes in the real world. This comes through the risk of statistical overfitting, where models unintentionally fit to random noise (which is a part of all data), rather than the underlying signal.

2. To accurately predict something, you need *the right data* not just *lots of data*. This is where 'big data' can become a distraction and is often one reason why these models don't live up to their hype. Moreover, correlations within a dataset do not necessarily translate to a causal relationship. Incorrectly making that assumption can lead to incorrect business decisions. While this isn't a book about model development best practices, the authors have strong views on the ways in which human insight should be incorporated into the data collection and feature development process, and how model accuracy needs to be assessed, to ensure the delivery of benefits.

These risks are not intended to act as a roadblock to better using data in an organisation. In practice, the hypothesis-led approach is also helpful in giving a structured understanding of the requirements and limitations of the existing organisation's data for a particular use case, in contrast to a more generic view of 'we need more data' or 'we need cleaner data'.

In addition, there have been significant improvements in the use of external data, either to validate or correct problematic internal data or to supplement internal data by giving a broader, more comprehensive view of the environment in which an organisation operates. For example, retailers are now able to leverage mobility data (sourced through mobile phone network operators) to understand the volume and demographics of the people within walking distance of their stores to better measure their performance and optimise their staffing.

In addition to the model development process, there is a need to methodically manage the deployment, ongoing management, and update of statistical models in a production environment.

Those disciplines are typically covered in an MLOps (Machine Learning Operations) capability, for which there are many helpful references and reports.[8] The key points to highlight from a business context, is that any model is a point in time reflection of the data on which it's been built. As such:

1. It will be susceptible to bias risks, which needs to be measured and tested using standard statistical processes and business sense checking.
2. It will need to periodically be refreshed and enhanced, as data can become out of date, statistical correlations can drift, and more relevant data becomes available.

Thinking about Cloud in the context of competitive advantage

As technology became more and more important in the past 40 years, IT departments had to be developed, to take on the enormous task of developing and running IT platforms. The traditional model of IT reflects a need to manage everything from:

*   Building and managing hardware, including networks, servers and storage. This includes the ongoing effort to fix devices on short notice, upgrade hardware as requirements change, manage an inventory of assets etc.
*   Manage the safe and secure collection, reconciliation and management of a wide range of data. In recent years, this has become increasingly complex, due to the increasing threat of cyber attacks and privacy breaches.
*   Installing, upgrading, debugging and patching systems, from the core operating system, through to a broad range of applications. In recent years, this workload has increased as end-user expectations have grown, especially as people interface with technology across multiple channels.

In contrast with traditional IT, Cloud managed services provide various versions of those capabilities through third party management of (Figure 5.1):

*   Infrastructure as a Service (IaaS), where the core technology infrastructure is provided and managed by the IaaS provider, based on a flexible set of requirements that can easily and frequently be adjusted to suit the needs of the business.
*   Platform as a Service (PaaS), which builds on IaaS by including a layer of functionality for highly configurable business applications. For example, a PaaS can include an ability to connect databases into machine learning models, which can then be deployed through flexible web interfaces.
*   Software as a Service (SaaS), which continues to build on PaaS by offering a best-practice application solution to specific problems, i.e. a pre-configured solution to a business problem.

The diagram below describes the varying responsibilities in business managed versus Cloud service supported technology.

This raises the obvious question of what capabilities should be supported by fully internal IT, versus each of the Cloud service options. The appropriate solution depends on the unique service requirements and should be assessed on a

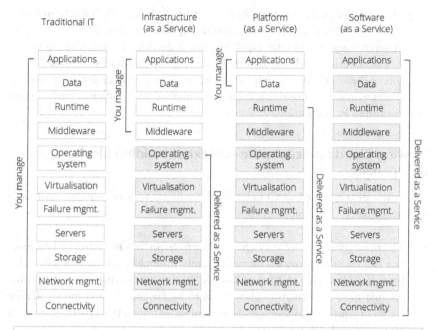

FIGURE 5.1 Comparison of as-a-service models

Source: adapted from Chou, 2018[a]

a Chou, D., (2018, 28 September). Cloud service models (IaaS, PaaS, SaaS) diagram. Dachou. https://dachou.github.io/2018/09/28/Cloud-service-models.html

case-by-case basis. An oversimplified but helpful approach for conceptualising these decisions, is that:

- In SaaS solutions, you're essentially getting the same service that everyone else is. In some functional areas, the adoption of a relatively rigid, best-practice based system, could be great. For example, HR processes are complex and expensive to develop and manage with homegrown solutions. In addition, they are rarely a source of competitive advantage. This is where SaaS providers (e.g. Workday's HCM suite) can offer a significant advantage by providing best practice solutions for managing payroll, training, leave and people administration etc.
- For PaaS solutions, you are able to leverage capability from third parties, but the configuration and tailoring of that solution is up to you as the designer. That ability to tailor is a critical element of developing a practical competitive

differentiation and is the primary reason why we believe PaaS solutions have a broad, sector-wide ability to differentiate organisations at scale.

- In some cases, the unique capability being developed cannot be supported by PaaS offerings and may require IT to take ownership of some or all elements of the stack. For example, an organisation may wish to deploy specialised processes and algorithms that can't be configured with sufficient performance in existing PaaS solutions.

Viewing Cloud services in the context of building blocks of capability

Regardless of the choice of Cloud service, there are a set of implicit capabilities from third-party Cloud providers:

- The management of security updates, bug fixes, patches and other IT best practice can often be provided more efficiently through specialised, highly scaled providers like Azure, AWS and Google. It's not to say that internal IT can't provide these services, though it tends to be far cheaper and more effective for an organisation to leverage these capabilities from a third party, given their enormous scale advantages.
- Simplifying development and orchestration of solutions by leveraging the investment that Cloud services providers have made into PaaS and SaaS solutions. As above, an internal IT organisation may be able to provide similar services but will almost always have far less scale and cost-efficiency that could be gained through the major hyperscale platforms.
- The ability to 'rent' services and flexibly scale requirements, significantly reducing up-front cost and capital expenditure. This is most evident when developing new services or expanding into new geographies, as you can leverage the availability and capacity of the Cloud provider's investments, rather than making your own. This has been critical to scale applications and streaming services, or to manage seasonal variations in computing requirements.
- The ability to connect between Cloud platforms and existing systems, through the use of clearly defined APIs (Application Programming Interfaces) and microservices. The definition and impact of these, are covered in detail below.

APIs and simplifying doing business

An API (otherwise known as an Application Programming Interface), is best thought of as a standardised way of communicating between machines. The system specifies, in a standardised and openly accessible approach, what services, process or data it will provide a requestor, if that requestor follows a specific process laid out by the system. While this seems like simple, common-sense logic, APIs are a relatively recent advancement, and have become critically important in many transformations.

One simple assumption made in this book is that the reader agrees on the benefits of having 'situationally relevant' data at hand when making a business decision. For example, knowing when a customer is having an issue in the service being provided enables a customer service operator to reach out and resolve the problem. Together with this assumption is the implication that data can only be valuable when it is provided to relevant parties in a situationally relevant way, at an appropriate time.

To that end, APIs and microservices are the backbone of simplifying the flow and manipulation of data in a modern organisation, or even between organisations. APIs are seen as a reducer of business friction, with little-to-no downside. This trend has led to the increased use of APIs both within an organisation to drive efficiency, and external to the organisation, to drive growth through the creation of new products and services.

The most well publicised push to drive up the use of APIs in an organisation, is a legendary 'API mandate' email that Amazon founder Jeff Bezos allegedly sent in 2002:

1) All teams will henceforth expose their data and functionality through service interfaces.
2) Teams must communicate with each other through these interfaces.
3) There will be no other form of interprocess communication allowed: no direct linking, no direct reads of another team's data store, no shared-memory model, no back-doors whatsoever. The only communication allowed is via service interface calls over the network.
4) It doesn't matter what technology is used. HTTP, Corba, Pubsub, custom protocols – doesn't matter.
5) All service interfaces, without exception, must be designed from the ground up to be externalizable. That is to say, the team must plan and design to be able to expose the interface to developers in the outside world. No exceptions.
6) Anyone who doesn't do this will be fired.

Jeff Bezos[9]

It's important to recognise the difference between the use of APIs and the communication systems that preceded those standards. In the not-so-distant past, information sharing wasn't standardised due to the use of proprietary systems (whereby the provider often had an incentive to avoid interoperability) and the lack of commonly accepted standards for machine-to-machine interfaces.

This lack of interoperability means that a range of legacy systems will often require significant and expensive integration programs to enable now-basic, reliable connectivity between systems. In contrast, APIs typically run on common, web-based standards and can be thought of as digital contracts, as in bridges, between systems.

For example, the Australian Open Banking API standards describe the way a message can be sent to a bank (with a supporting security token and authorisation) to request the balance of a customer's account. The format and structure of that response is a clearly and consistently defined message, which the recipient can then convert into business-relevant insights. That standard doesn't change depending on which bank you're interfacing with, and the open standards being used significantly reduce the cost of these integrations when compared to prior alternatives.

Open banking is an example of a 'Centralised API ecosystem', whereby a central authority has defined the way in which interactions will occur between multiple operators, for the purpose of realising a specific objective. DBS Bank in Singapore runs a centralised API ecosystem[10] with the objective of simplifying the delivery of a broad range of customer services that would traditionally involve complex integrations with banking systems, e.g. payment processing, loyalty rewards payments. This ecosystem allows DBS Bank to maintain relevance to customers in a complex and changing environment by leveraging the investment of many other third-party operators that benefit from the simplified integration from following DBS Bank's API standards.

Alternatively, 'Sequenced API ecosystems' are an approach to define more traditional value chains, where the assumed customer journey has been broken up into stages, each with an assumed set of inputs and outputs. REA Group owned Realestate.com.au runs a sequenced API for prospective homebuyers and renters,[11] whereby third parties can integrate common processes such as listing houses, running campaigns, and following up on leads. This integration process helps REA Group reduce friction with agents, buyers and sellers, who all have to maintain accurate and timely data throughout the sales process.

As the barriers for integration are reduced, it's easy to see the way in which different strategic opportunities come about through tighter integration with third parties. For example:

- Customer service can be improved by integrating with logistics providers, for example by giving live updates on the delivery of a customer's goods
- Data from sensors and other internet-of-things (IoT) devices can be integrated into the proactive management of supply chain and operations issues
- Partnerships with third parties can more easily come together, to create new and differentiated customer propositions.

That's great, but what's the catch?

It's easy to look at this chapter and assume that if barriers to innovation are reducing, and the world is simplifying its interfaces, very little could go wrong so long as you're making significant investments in technology. Unfortunately, these innovations also create a range of challenges, including:

- *Competition will continue to increase* – As barriers to innovation drop for your organisation, they also drop for all others, therefore a standard technology-led approach is highly unlikely to yield any lasting competitive advantage.

- *Markets have become more complex* – As competitors look to innovate and provide greater value to their customers, they will often expand into adjacent services outside their traditional core. Often, this means that you will face competition from new competitors. Moreover, in the example of complex ecosystems (like the DBS Bank example), having a tech-enabled business model may become a table-stakes customer expectation. Consumers have rising digital expectations, shaped by their best experiences across many suppliers.
- *Too much choice is a bad thing* – While the cost of innovation has significantly dropped, the complexity of potential technology innovation has increased exponentially. Historically, business leaders faced waves of 'common upgrades'. Going forward, each organisation's technology strategy needs to be tailored in a way that more tightly aligns with their business strategy, their customer expectations, and their business capabilities.
- *Regulators will drive further competition* – Traditional value chains and business ecosystems, particularly those in Australia, tend to form oligopolies. One of the purposes of regulators such as the ACCC, is 'promoting the economically efficient operation of, use of, and investment in infrastructure, and identifying market failure'.[12] Put simply, the technology innovations highlighted in this chapter are a set of new tools and approaches for regulators to break up these traditional value chains and business ecosystems. Open Banking, and the broader Open Data movement, are common examples of this trend.
- *Sophistication needs to increase, to capture the opportunity* – As platforms become more sophisticated, there is a need to uplift the technical and non-technical capabilities of the organisation. For example, there may be a need to employ more data scientists to build predictive models, while also uplifting the risk management team's capability, to ensure those models are sufficiently explainable and meet evolving regulatory requirements.

There has never been a time where the technology strategy (and its successful rollout) has been more critical to an organisation's success. While experimentation is a critical capability to help navigate through the potential business model options enabled by these technologies, we strongly caution that 'experimentation is not a strategy'.

Notes

1 Khalid, K., Phillips, A., Perton, M., & Nann, E. (2020). The new CIO: Business-savvy technologist. Deloitte Insights. www2.deloitte.com/us/en/insights/focus/cio-insider-business-insights/the-new-cio.html
2 www.forbes.com/sites/forbestechcouncil/2017/03/27/11-smart-simple-ways-to-promote-tech-literacy/?sh=7b47f30f7114
3 YouTube example introductions for AI are: www.youtube.com/watch?v=-ePZ7OdY-Dw; www.youtube.com/watch?v=s0dMTAQM4cw; www.youtube.com/watch?v=cW9shEB8h5E; On Cloud: www.youtube.com/watch?v=36zducUX16w; www.youtube.com/watch?v=36zducUX16w

4 Including, we note, the increasing invested cost of data scientists and engineers.

5 AWS Rekognition, https://aws.amazon.com/rekognition/

6 Airservices Australia. (2020, 24 September). Airservices technology wins Isg Paragon award 2020. www.airservicesaustralia.com/airservices-digital-twin-technology-wins-isg-paragon-award-2020/

7 Tognotti, C., (2014). Elon Musk is Afraid of AI. *Bustle*. www.bustle.com/articles/46019-elon-musk-calls-artificial-intelligence-summoning-the-demon-and-thats-not-very-reassuring

8 Ammanath, B., Farrall, F., Kuder, D., & Mittal, N. (n.d.). MLOps: Industrialized AI scaling model development and operations with a dose of engineering and operational discipline. Deloitte. www2.deloitte.com/xe/en/insights/focus/tech-trends/2021/mlops-industrialized-ai.html

9 Api-University. (2022, 10 March). The API Mandate – Install API thinking at your company. https://api-university.com/blog/the-api-mandate/

10 DBS. (2017). Reimagining banking, DBS launches world's largest banking API developer platform. www.dbs.com/newsroom/Reimagining_banking_DBS_launches_worlds_largest_banking_API_developer_platform

11 REA Group. (n.d). REA Group Partner API overview. https://partner.realestate.com.au/documentation/api/

12 Australian Competition and Consumer Commission (ACCC). About the ACCC. www.accc.gov.au/about-us/australian-competition-consumer-commission/about-the-accc

6

INNOVATION

Introduction

A large portion of this book is focussed on the antecedent capabilities required to develop a new business model, powered by AI and Cloud technologies. In this section, we shift the focus to the innovation approach taken to develop the candidate business models. This section is not a comprehensive guide to innovation, and we recommend readers to consider other books and courses if they want to learn more, for example *Ten Types of Innovation: The Discipline of Building Breakthroughs*,[1] or Samson and Gloet,[2] for further detail on some of the themes highlighted in this chapter.

The interplay between innovation, transformation and technology enablement

While our book title includes the term transformation, when technology and new business models are involved, this clearly overlaps with the field of innovation. Innovation can be defined (adapted from the OECD definition) as 'New or enhanced products, processes, business models or organisational methods that create value for stakeholders'. Transformations can be highly or lowly innovative: this depends on just how new the changes are that are being designed, trialled, and implemented. It is also worth considering 'newness' in the context of risk and reward of the technology enablement being considered. If key elements of a transformation are brand new to the world, with perhaps unproven technology or unknown consumer demand, then risk (and hopefully reward) is reasonably expected to be higher than if a transformation is being done in a local company that is similar to what has been tried and tested multiple times in overseas markets.

DOI: 10.4324/9781003255529-6

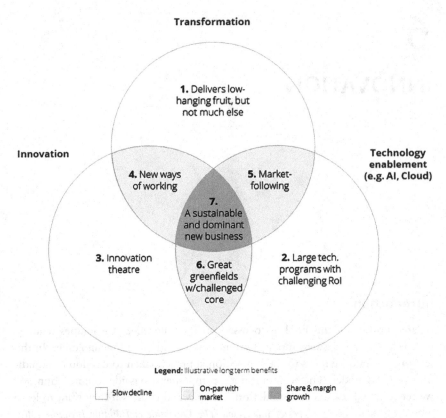

FIGURE 6.1 Interactions between innovation, transformation, technology enablement and business impact

Figure 6.1 articulates the integrated roles of innovation, transformation and technology enablement, as well as the varying impact on organisational growth and returns.

Generally speaking, there are a set of archetypes that we have identified in our research and experience:

- A slow decline of the organisation, due to the limited focus of the executive on only one of these roles:
  1. A singular focus on transformation, typically characterised by a well-intended focus on reducing waste in existing processes. These programmes tend to drive a meaningful short-term benefit, but due to their narrow design, do not address any fundamental challenges in the business model and the way value needs to be created into the future.
  2. A singular focus on overhauling technology, often by performing 'lift and shift' of existing on-premise applications and processes to the Cloud. Depending on the degree of waste in legacy platforms, this may provide

some benefit, but the economics of moving from significantly depreciated technology platforms to new platforms (without transformation of the business process itself) tend to result in low returns on investment.

3. Innovation theatre, where well-meaning and intuitively beneficial innovations are developed 'off to the side' of the business. Without an explicit path and plan to integrate these innovations into the core business, and to support their scaling with technology, these projects tend to fizzle out over time.

- The ability to keep up with customer and market expectations by effectively leveraging skills across two of the three roles:

4. Driving a 'new way of working' whereby tools and methods in innovation and transformation are both used by the organisation to reduce waste in existing processes and also to re-engineer the existing business process through a structured innovation framework.

5. Adopting a process of 'market following', where transformation works in tandem with technology enablement to quickly adopt the best technology system solutions seen in-market, following the leadership of other organisations.

6. The development of a successful 'greenfields' business, effectively separated from the core through a separate technology stack and culture of innovation. These new ventures can be quite successful, but there is the ongoing challenge of how to transform the existing business.

- Creating breakthrough benefits for the business, by appropriately using skills across innovation, transformation and technology enablement (point 7 in the diagram above). In these examples, innovation is at the scale of business model transformation and advanced digital tools are used to enable these outcomes, raising the barriers to entry for would-be competitors. Examples include Netflix and Rolls Royce (see Chapter 4) where there was clearly a strong sense of innovation in their strategies, these strategies were transformational for these businesses and their customers, and that those innovations were enabled by AI and Cloud technologies. In financial services, DBS, Bank of America and (although it was more a fast follower than the leading-edge DBS) and (Canadian) Scotiabank also qualify as having been innovative, transformative, and accomplished through technology enablement.

Prioritising innovation, transformation and technology enablement

Given the complex range of choices (each with potentially significant execution risk), the 'answer' is not always to immediately seek a highly complex, technology-enabled and innovative transformation programme. Some of these risks can be managed with internally controllable risk mitigation strategies (e.g. incremental application building, pilot testing), while others can have much larger impacts (e.g. consumer-acceptance risk) and would be expected to provide larger rewards. One does not need to be a first to market transformer, but indeed it may make sense to be neither on the leading edge and certainly not on the 'bleeding' edge of new technologies, but be a 'fast follower', as a legitimate position for transformation/innovation.

Scotiabank, headquartered in Canada, adopted such a position, beginning from behind the pack with its digital Cloud transformation yet moving towards a leadership position once a sound basis for Cloud-based modernisation was achieved. With 92,000 employees substantially in central and south Americas, Scotiabank (Bank of Nova Scotia) started later than its competitors with AI- and Cloud-based transformation. Yet between 2019 and 2022 it has moved apace, changing its organisational structure[3] and moving fast to catch up and in some ways overtake the industry average in terms of digital offerings and business model transformation.

Having built numerous AI applications efficiently, Scotiabank has taken a cutting-edge approach to open systems developments going forward. It positioned its Cloud platform as much more than a way to outsource: a way to modernise its whole organisational business model. This bank has recently won many awards and seen its stock price continue to rise significantly as it transforms, embracing 'the future' and using its new approaches to being value to new market opportunities and geographies.

This example demonstrates that a fast follower approach can be very successful, with good returns on effort and investment. Scotiabank's journey demonstrates that a careful and low-risk approach can lead to a successful catch up, but we stress that this is clearly not the same as a laggard approach! Scotiabank did not 'do nothing' or just pay lip service to the AI/Cloud opportunity. It invested well, transformed substantially, succeeded, but wasn't first as the innovator in its market. This example relates well to Australian businesses who can learn from leading edge international practices – perhaps the most efficient way to proceed in some cases is not to be the groundbreaker but to learn and follow the cutting-edge players, fast.

Just as some transformations can be highly innovative while others can be lowly innovative, some innovations can be highly transformative for the organisation and others not so or less so. For example, when one of the authors was working closely with the top leadership team at National Australia Bank[4] during its very successful decade (1990–2000), new products such as wealth management were innovated but were not transformative for the bank as the scale of impact was not relatively large. Similarly, a cultural transformation attempted during that period was, while potentially transformative, not really innovative and certainly had nothing to do with advanced or digital technologies.

The evolution of innovation

Before delving into the details of how to capture the transformative benefits of AI and Cloud technologies more effectively when developing candidate innovations, we want to highlight:

1. The business model is defined as the way in which the organisation or a functional part of the organisation creates, delivers, and captures value. At this level of abstraction the focus is on 'the what' rather than 'the how', which therefore excludes incremental improvements which are often done at the operating model level, for example switching to a lower cost provider of a service which isn't materially different to the incumbent service provider.
2. Business model innovations can be internal *or* external. For example, if the asset maintenance part of a manufacturing business shifts from scheduled maintenance to a more proactive approach powered by lead-indicators of upcoming faults and issues, we would classify that as a change in the internal business model (specifically the key activities and value proposition of that maintenance function, inside the business). An external innovation could involve supplier relationship changes or servitisation as in Rolls Royce 'Power by the Hour' (Chapter 4), wherein the innovation crosses or bridges the firm's boundaries.
3. There are many ways to define the business model. One suitable approach would be the Business Model Canvas,[5] which breaks down the business model across a range of key elements including: infrastructure (key activities, key resources, and partner network), offering (value propositions including price, efficiency, customer experience and outcome), customers (customer segments, channels, and customer relationships), and finance (cost structure and revenue streams). For this book and the associated research, we have defined Business Model Innovation as having occurred when any part of the Business Model Canvas has fundamentally changed.

There are numerous frameworks and methodologies for innovation. Over the past two decades, many organisations have moved towards a customer or Human Centred Design (HCD) approach (epitomised by the IAG case study) which focusses on 'unmet needs' in addition to the traditional focus on reducing waste and inefficiency in the incumbent business process.

The critical reason why we wanted to focus on the innovation process itself was because of the broader range of potential innovations that are possible to create, using AI- and Cloud-based technologies. When overlaying these new capabilities against a typical HCD design process model used in business, these new possibilities are both a blessing and a curse for business leaders. These design process phases are:

*   *Discover*: Understand the issue rather than merely assuming it. It involves speaking to and spending time with people who are affected by the issues.
*   *Define*: The insight gathered from the discovery phase can help to define the challenge in a different way.
*   *Develop*: Give different answers to the clearly defined problem, seeking inspiration from elsewhere and co-designing with a range of different people.
*   *Deliver*: Involves testing out different solutions at small-scale, rejecting those that will not work and improving the ones that will.

The focus on 'unmet needs' particularly comes through in the 'Discover' and 'Define' phases where there is a significant emphasis on looking outside the current ways of working and current customer needs. The flexibility and optionality inherent in these new technologies means that there are far more new potential solutions to consider (particularly in the 'Develop' phase) and there is a critical need to carefully rule in/out potential options as you enter the 'Deliver' phase.

How do these innovations practically impact the business model?

To illustrate the impact of AI and Cloud technology against specific types of innovation and potential business model options to be considered, we have highlighted the way in which some of the technology innovations covered in the previous chapter can be applied against Doblin's 10 types of innovation[6] (these were summarised in Chapter 1 and are re-listed below).

Category	Type	Overview	Example AI or Cloud innovations
Configuration	Profit model	The way in which you make money	Creation of marketplaces, platform business models, enabling niche specialisation within a value chain
	Network	Connections with others to create value	Simplifying and reducing the friction in partnerships and joint value propositions
	Structure	Alignment of your talent and assets	Enabling new organisational structures, with an increased ability to specialise in certain areas, while outsourcing others
	Process	Signature of superior methods for doing your work	Leveraging improved data and decision-making using AI-enabled automation and process controls
Offering	Product performance	Distinguishing features and functionality	Adding new capabilities to proactively provide service to a customer through AI
	Product system	Complimentary products and systems	Using Cloud and APIs to simplify partnering with third parties for added value

Category	Type	Overview	Example AI or Cloud innovations
Experience	Services	Support and enhancements that surround your offering	Leveraging customer and service data to drive improvements in customer experience and R&D spend
	Channel	How your offerings are delivered to customers and users	Offering both a multichannel experience (e.g. web, app) which is personalised to the needs of that specific customer
	Brand	Representation of your offerings and business	Taking a proactive position in the use of these technologies as part of the brand, e.g. Apple's stance on data sharing and data ownership
	Customer engagement	Distinctive interactions you foster	Leveraging customer use data, to prioritise the services enhancement and future engagements (e.g. Netflix's recommendation engine)

In practice, many new business models will adopt more than one of these types of innovation, increasing success likelihood, for example:

- When Netflix disrupted its DVD-delivery business model and developed an online streaming service, that was an example of its Profit Model (as the economics of running a web-based distribution were fundamentally different), Channel Experience (as users could use the service 'on demand') and Product Performance (as you could immediately access orders rather than wait for them to arrive in the mail).
- PEXA's mortgage settlement process innovation is an example of a new Profit Model (as a new facilitator of a traditional value chain), Network (as the creator of a new standard process for mortgage settlement), Process (due to the electronic and traceable nature of the transaction flow) and Product System (as banks and lawyers could offer a better service and faster settlements by partnering with PEXA).

Alternative approaches for innovation and venture development

A broad range of approaches have been taken for the development of new innovations and ventures, for example:

- Internal capability uplift – Where the business unit develops its own capability to design, test and deploy new innovations, typically in the core of the business.
- Accelerators – Where a dedicated multidisciplinary team accelerates the validation of new business models, or the commercialisation of a business model.
- Incubators – Where a dedicated multidisciplinary team help develop 'net new' solutions that leverage capabilities or assets from the core business.
- Corporate venture capital – Where direct investments are made into external organisations, typically with the purpose of creating partnerships across an ecosystem, for the purpose of developing new solutions.
- Crowd-sourcing – Where an organisation announces external challenges (together with incentives) to develop new solutions or challenge in-progress innovations.

Each of these approaches offers pros and cons across different parts of the innovation cycle. However, a recent report[7] highlights a range of lessons learned across innovation and venture development in Australia:

1. There is no one size fits all innovation and venture development model. The approaches need to be considered in the context of the organisation; and knowing why and how to deploy each of them selectively is key to their success.
2. The support of the CEO is key to the success of these innovations, as is the 'pull' from the broader business, who will need to see value for their functions in the innovation and venture development process.
3. Long term success requires a portfolio focus, supported by clear success metrics, stage gates and long-term commitment.

Conclusion

In summary, our view is that a structured process for developing innovations should be used to select and effectively manage the broad range of potential business model innovations that could be pursued. This statement has always been true, but the nature of the disruptive technologies covered in this book mean that there are more potential ways to innovate, there is a greater need to effectively prioritise those innovations, integrated with technology enablement and effective transformation.

Notes

1 www.amazon.com.au/Ten-Types-Innovation-Discipline-Breakthroughs-ebook/dp/B00DZLBHU8
2 Samson, D., & Gloet, M. (2015). *Innovation and Entrepreneurship*. Oxford University Press. www.oup.com.au/books/higher-education/management-and-marketing/9780190300647-innovation-and-entrepreneurship-ebook

3 Davenport, T., & Bean, R. (2021, 29 December). Catching up fast by driving value from AI. *MIT Sloan Management Review*. https://sloanreview.mit.edu/article/catching-up-fast-by-driving-value-from-ai/

4 See Argus, D., & Samson, D. (2021). *Strategic Leadership for Value Creation*. Palgrave (Springer).

5 Barquet A.P.B., Cunha V.P., Oliveira M.G., & Rozenfeld, H. (2011). Business model elements for product-service system. In: Hesselbach J., & Herrmann C. (eds). *Functional Thinking for Value Creation*. Berlin, Heidelberg: Springer. https://doi.org/10.1007/978–3–642–19689–8_58

6 Keeley, L. (2013). *Ten Types of Innovation: The Discipline of Building Breakthroughs* (1st ed.). John Wiley & Sons.

7 Monitor Deloitte (2022). *State of Ventures Report, forthcoming, May.*

7

THE BOARD, EXECUTIVE AND LEADERSHIP'S ROLE IN BMT

Introduction

We (the authors) hope that our book appeals to a broad audience. Hopefully our readers include senior leaders considering 'what's next', emerging leaders seeking to get traction with AI and Cloud business model transformation initiatives, and students seeking to understand what it takes to become an emerging leader. We also hope that at least a portion of our readers are board directors of Australian organisations. This chapter is intended to help board directors consider whether and/or how to proceed with an AI and Cloud business model transformation. Hopefully other audiences also find value in the discussion.

This chapter is structured as follows. First, we will provide an overview about how the business press and the academic community characterise the opportunities and risks associated with Cloud and AI. We will then discuss the role of the director in helping organisations navigate through these issues. As part of this discussion, we will share some findings of some contemporaneous research we are undertaking regarding director attributes and AI, and we will suggest some questions that directors may wish to contemplate. Finally, we will talk about how the broader organisation (the top management team and other leaders) can help board members to acquit their responsibilities.

Opportunity and risk

The authors have had the good fortune to speak with a number of board directors and other senior leaders of organisations on the topic of AI and Cloud. These individuals talk about some of the uncertainty caused by the business press: are AI and Cloud key to the future success of an organisation, or will they be the source of an organisation's demise?

DOI: 10.4324/9781003255529-7

	Opportunity and risk
Cloud	• Opportunity: 'Kmart (Australia) is one of the first retailers globally to migrate mainframe applications to the Cloud and has an agile Cloud platform that puts them in a great position to innovate and optimise customer experiences rapidly and at scale…' –Forbes • Risk: 'Amazon Cloud service outage in Japan disrupts brokerages, banks and airlines…' – *Japan Times*
AI	• Opportunity: '"I think [the Telstra/Quantium AI JV] great for Australia. I was reading somewhere that there are basically only four ways to grow the economy: you either grow the population, you sell resources, you innovate, or you drive productivity", he said. "And innovation and productivity is exactly what this is going to enable"'. Andy Penn, quoted in the Australian Financial Review • Risk: 'The problem with engagement algorithms is they are agnostic to content and will do whatever it takes to keep users on the platform, regardless of the rabbit hole it takes them down'. – Australian Financial Review, Facebook's disconnection problem

Our view is that there are no risk-free options, and that boards will have to make decisions which balance risks against one-another, cognisant of the fact that inaction is usually not the lowest risk option.

The academic community is also exploring both the opportunities and risk associated with AI and Cloud technologies. Whilst academics have been developing the technologies underlying artificial intelligence since the 1950s, research into the potential impact of such technologies is a relatively more recent phenomenon. Back in 1988, Leonard-Barton and Sviokla wrote an article in the Harvard Business Review discussing how to gain benefit from expert systems, an early form of AI.[1] Such articles have continued to the point that the question is no longer whether there is potential benefit, but rather how does one compete in an environment where AI is commonplace.[2]

Similarly, the risks and regulatory implications of AI are being actively explored. Whilst research has been going on for several years, Shoshana Zuboff's 2019 book *The Age of Surveillance Capitalism: The Fight for a Human Future at the New Frontier of Power* helped expose these academic discussions to a broader audience. The pace of research is accelerating, and new research groups are being formed. As one example, the University of Melbourne recently launched a dedicated Centre for Artificial Intelligence and Digital Ethics (CAIDE) to facilitate cross-disciplinary research, teaching and leadership on the ethical, regulatory and legal issues relating to AI and digital technologies. Major users of AI are also investing in understanding the risks and ethical parameters of AI. Google recently stated a goal to double its research staff studying responsible AI to 200 people. Non-profit organisations (such as the Partnership on AI, committed to responsible AI) are also exploring this issue and regulators are becoming increasingly aware of the potential harms associated with artificial intelligence. Beyond potential harms outside of organisations, academic researchers have been exploring potential harms to organisations that use AI. In 2021 a team of researchers led by Nripendra Rana[3] concluded that poorly executed (lack of governance, poor data quality, and inefficient training of key employees) AI initiatives can lead to operational inefficiency, which then contribute to negative sales growth and employees' dissatisfaction, which in turn results in a competitive disadvantage for these firms.

The academic community has also been active in exploring issues associated with Cloud technologies. There are numerous examples of studies exploring the benefits (and drivers thereof) of migration to the Cloud – Chen Chuang and Nakatani's study, identifying that businesses benefit more in enhanced scalability than in cost reduction and increased business capability, is but one example.[4] On the risk side, numerous researchers have been exploring the cybersecurity implications of Cloud computing.[5] Whilst some of the discussion in these papers can be a bit esoteric the implications are not. A 2012 study by Benaroch, Chernobai and Goldstein found that organisations that experienced an IT operational risk event resulted in a significant drop in the market value.[6] That market value exposure equally applies to events linked to Cloud providers.

How then should a board director look at business model transformation through the use of AI and/or Cloud technologies?

Directors' duties: managing risk

We start with our understanding of the role of a director. There are a number of different models of the roles of a director. One model – the Tricker model[7] – outlines the roles in terms of two sets of trade-offs: internal perspective versus external perspective, and past and present versus future orientation (occasionally known as conformance versus performance). The Tricker model also defines four substantive role categories: providing accountability, monitoring and supervising, policy making and strategy formation. Other writers[8] in the strategic management literature simplify this down to three roles: a ceremonial role, a monitoring role and a strategy role.

Leaving aside the ceremonial role, the legal and regulatory environments set expectations on the monitoring role. Please note that none of the authors are lawyers – bush or otherwise. Having said that, it should not be too controversial to state that, at least in Australia, directors' duties are developed through three sources. The Corporations Act of 2001 (Commonwealth) is the primary source of directors' duties, and the Act sets out the obligations of companies and their boards. The duties described by the Act are augmented by other fiduciary duties that have been developed through case law since the adoption of the Act. Furthermore, other directors' duties ('statutory duties') have been developed through other legal instruments. Occupational Health and Safety duties are an example of such statutory duties. Going beyond meeting legal requirements, other monitoring duties are well discussed and laid out by the Australian Stock Exchange and the Australian Institute of Company Directors.

We hope that directors will see initiatives associated with Cloud and AI. In this 'monitoring' context, we suggest a number of questions that you may wish to ask to provide comfort that the organisation is meeting its obligations:

- What is being proposed, and how does that align to our ethics and risk frameworks? (Please note that if you don't have an existing ethical framework, the Commonwealth Department of Industry, Science, Energy and Resources[9] has published 'Australia's Artificial Intelligence Ethics Framework'. Several organisations such as the World Economic Forum[10] are making their frameworks available for use by others, and other organisations such as Google[11] are publishing relevant better practice guides.)
- What are the relevant legal and regulatory requirements, and how do we ensure that we stay within these requirements? (Please note that there are distinct requirements for privacy, security, data sovereignty and anti-discrimination.) How might these requirements evolve, and how do we 'future-proof' for these evolving requirements?
- How would our initiative be perceived by our stakeholders, and are we comfortable with those perceptions? How would we need to refine/reposition our initiative in order to obtain the stakeholder perception we desire?
- What policies do we need to develop and what procedures need to be put in place to ensure that we stay within our ethical frameworks?
- How do we make it easy for our staff to 'do the right thing' and comply with these policies and procedures?
- What supporting infrastructure should we put in place/other investments we should make to help manage any negative repercussions of a possible failure of our initiative?
- How do we ensure that our decision-making and counterparty responsiveness is not unintentionally degraded as a result of our initiative?
- Similarly, how do we ensure that we are able to treat all counterparties with due process after the initiative?
- What governance and risk considerations should we have as we adopt these technologies, and how do our governance and risk management approaches need to change to reflect the risks associated with these technologies?

Directors' duties: managing opportunities

The list of issues and questions associated with managing risk might seem daunting. We think that this is the 'glass half-full' perspective.

Two decades ago, one of the authors had the pleasure of interviewing one of Australia's leading board directors. That board director said that the role of the board was twofold: to challenge then endorse the strategy, and to select the right CEO.

Some might say that in order to challenge a strategy with respect to the use of Cloud and/or AI the board needs to have an individual (or three) with directly relevant experience – the so-called Digital Non-Executive Directors (NEDs).[12] Others might say that an organisation can't commence a Cloud/AI initiative without dealing with the technical debt. We sympathise with these views – but we find them too limiting.

One of the authors has been recently researching the characteristics (individually and collectively) of a board of directors and how those characteristics influence an organisation's approach to considering data as a source of advantage. More than 40 directors were interviewed for this research, and these directors represented over 70 organisations across all 11 top-level industry sectors defined by MSCI's Global Industry Classification Standard. These organisations also represented the range of possible organisations such as large listed firms, unlisted entities, mutuals and family-controlled firms. This research indicated that whilst individual board director experience with data and organisational proximity to clean data were factors, they were minor factors relative to three mindset factors:

- Exploration mindset: the willingness and ability of an individual leader to be a change agent and 'explore possibilities and ask "what if?"' rather than stay with what has been done traditionally.
- Discomfort with the traditional sources of competitive advantage: many board and top management team members are aware of the late Clay Christensen's work on innovation and the disruption of previously successful organisations. Some individuals ask the question 'What will be our basis for competition now and in the future?' and realise that the traditional sources of competitive advantage will not be sufficient for sustained performance.
- Future focussed strategy: positioning theorists such as Michael Porter and Roger Martin suggest that organisational decision makers consider how their organisation is positioned relative to its market and its competitors. Whilst some practitioners undertake such analysis within the immediate planning horizon to ensure that immediate financial and strategic objectives are achieved, other practitioners specifically consider the far future in order to identify the decisions that need to be made in the short term.

This research gives us comfort that all organisations can consider business model transformation through the use of AI and/or Cloud technologies – not just those (rare) organisations that have Digital NEDs and limited technical debt.

We therefore suggest a few primary questions for the leaders of all organisations:

- What is our current basis of advantage, and how will that change in 'the Age of AI'?
- What should/could our future business model be? How might AI and Cloud support that?
- How do the attributes (variabilised cost, lowered cost of decisions, lowered cost of innovation) of AI and Cloud open up opportunities for the organisation?
- What might happen to this organisation if existing (and new competitors) use AI and Cloud and we do not?

- Are our existing AI and Cloud initiatives incremental, or will they allow us to refresh our business model?

We recognise that there are a number of questions associated with making such a change happen. For example, many organisations will need to get an understanding of their current situation to determine their optimal transition path. Other organisations may wish to consider supply and sustainability issues around new required capabilities. Still other organisations will need to consider data access rights and similar. However, we see these as implementation issues to be worked through rather than barriers preventing organisations from starting the journey.

How the broader leadership team can help

Whilst board directors have an overall responsibility for organisational performance through its governance role, board members (individually and collectively) can benefit from actions taken by other leaders in the organisation. These other leaders include not only the CEO and top management team, but also those further down the organisational hierarchy.

Our research and our professional experience indicate that there are four specific actions that these other leaders could/should take:

- *Prepare the ground:* The degree to which a board drives strategy versus challenges strategy is a decision for that board. Whichever path they choose, it is important to remember that board members are generally non-executive and part-time – rarely do they have the luxury of time to deeply consider issues in the same way that a full-time leader might consider issues in their area of responsibility and expertise. Boards (and the associated decision-making process) would benefit from individual leaders allocating a portion of their time to undertake the thinking associated with the opportunities and risks associated with AI and Cloud technologies. This thinking could cover a range of topics, including but not limited to:
  - a refresher of the key means of competitive advantage in the area in focus
  - an understanding of the current and probable future capabilities of the technologies relevant to the area in focus, and how those current and probable future capabilities influence the existing means of competitive advantage
  - a perspective of current competitor initiatives
  - a perspective of possible disruptors or 'new to field' competitors that might change the competitive landscape, and finally
  - a perspective upon what a 'well capitalised, blank slate' competitor might build to compete in the area of focus.

It is important that these leaders use the mechanisms available to efficiently and effectively communicate the relevant insights of this thinking to the decision-making chain (including the board).

- *Take a 'Future Focussed View'*:Throughout this book, the authors have mentioned the danger of organisations delaying thinking through future business model transformation due to progress and effort devoted to proof-point style innovation on a legacy business model. We believe that it is equally important for individual leaders – when developing their perspective on potential actions – to consider not just what needs to be done for the area in question for the current horizon, but to also consider where the broader organisation should be in the medium to long term as a means to prioritise investment and activity that build towards that goal.[13]

- *Avoid the 'New to Organisation' risk fallacy*: In the late 20th century, Professor Paul Slovic noted 'novelty' as one of the ten factors that influence how humans perceive risk.[14] Professor Slovic's insight was that individuals spend more time considering a risk that they have not encountered before, thus unintentionally causing a new situation to be perceived as more risky than a situation seen before. The authors have seen this effect numerous times within the business world and its consideration of new capabilities. It is important that leaders ensure that operational (and other) risk assessments are adjusted for this effect.

- *Actively manage the implementation, overcoming the 'Unknown Unknowns'*: Once a decision has been made, there will be a range of tactical issues to be worked through. Risk registers will need to be worked through to reflect the change in risk parameters being managed, and internal financial systems and capital planning may need to be adjusted to account for the cost variablisation associated with Cloud. A potential 'governance impact' assessment might be considered as a means to give boards comfort that the governance and control processes, procedures and thresholds are appropriate for the refreshed business model.

It is important to note that not all organisations need all leaders to undertake all of these actions. In this realm, Churchill's quote 'Perfection is the enemy of progress' rings true to us.

How risk management should evolve through these disruptions

As any new technology enters mainstream use, there is a need to revisit the ways in which the technology can be used for positive ends, and the potential risks of its misuse. AI and Cloud technologies are no exception to that.

An early example of a negative outcome from the application of machine learning was the 'redlining' within the insurance sector in the US in the 1990s as more granular credit score data became available. The intended use of this data was to better understand the correlation between risk and people's credit score. Those insights could subsequently drive a better alignment between risk and price, which would subsequently allow for a more equitable allocation of capital and incentives to the users of these products.

Unfortunately, a range of issues with the data and its application resulted in a range of negative outcomes for consumers and insurers:

- Due to the historical lack of access to financial services for minorities, low credit scores (or no credit score) were highly correlated with race. Due to the additional correlation between race and geography, the resulting higher prices gave the appearance of areas where minorities lived, being unable to access these services at a reasonable price. Mapping those areas gave the appearance of a red boundary line, in which insurers deliberately excluded the minorities that lived in those areas.
- At the time, credit scores were opaque and offered little opportunity for consumer recourse if there were any issues with the score. This lack of clarity left people without any reasonable explanation or solution when presented with these high prices (or worse yet, ineligibility due to underwriter exclusion).
- Risk is only one factor in pricing, and at the time, the prevailing view was that people with low credit should also incur higher mark-ups while discounts would be provided to people with high credit scores. In reality, these mark-ups were both unjustifiable and unprofitable, as the discounts were being given to people who were less price sensitive while mark-ups are being charged to people who are most likely to face financial vulnerability.

Today, the use of credit score data (and much broader) is a standard in the insurance sector, and insurers have delivered on the promise of more aligning risk and prices with addressable consumer behaviour. We wanted to use this example of redlining as a cautionary tale for what can happen when poorly structured, poorly thought-through applications of new technologies come to market.

The application of automated decisioning through AI technology can result in similar negative outcomes, but the negative examples we could find were all associated with poor use and a lack of robust risk management, rather than an issue with the AI technology itself.

There are a range of helpful AI ethics frameworks which we recommend all boards consider, for example Data 61's ethics framework for AI in Australia.[15] In particular, we wanted to highlight a set of considerations that we believe all organisations should (at minimum) be applying:

- *Define and measure the protected groups and negative outcomes*: Metrics need to be created, potentially with external data if required, to understand the impact of a business decision (e.g. racial bias). This may appear counter-intuitive, but without gathering and measuring this impact, it is far more likely that you will unintentionally make decisions which have profoundly negative consequences. In addition, there is a need to measure and optimise a broad range of outcomes, e.g. false positives, false negatives, statistical significance.
- *Define fairness in the context of the decision being made*: Human decisions tend to be made within a context of sensibility and values, which are part of the

organisational culture. As decisions are increasingly being made by computers, there is a need to define the boundaries of fairness. For example, is there a maximum margin you are willing to make on a sale? Is there a need to drive consistency in decision making across certain cohorts of customer?

• *Scenario test the unintended consequences*: As smart as AI technology may appear, there is no underlying consciousness or intelligence. Consequently, these algorithms can make 'smart' decisions that are completely inappropriate in the real world. As an example drawn from the social media context (the 'in vogue' example), a recommendation of content which drives engagement through enraging suggestions takes users down a highly isolating, and potentially fraudulent rabbit hole. The AI that makes these recommendations hasn't been designed in a way to differentiate between different kinds of engagement, hence why these outcomes can occur. (We note that more recently, several platforms have taken steps to mitigate these risks).

• *Focus on the root cause of the decision*: In the redlining example, the absence of credit history can be explained by a range of factors, many of which are not reflective of a person's risk factors. While a model may provide a clear finding at the surface, there is a need to focus on the root cause of the findings

Closing thoughts

AI and Cloud technologies provide one of those rare opportunities to fundamentally alter, indeed transform an organisation's basis of competitive advantage. While there are some considerations for leaders to be aware of when undertaking AI and Cloud initiatives, major impediments to implementation are thankfully rare. Whilst board members may not have recent working experience of these technologies, we believe that the timeless values of challenging the status quo and providing stewardship for the organisation's success beyond an individual's involvement remain.

Notes

1 Leonard-Barton, D., & Sviokla, J. (1988, March). Putting expert systems to work. *Harvard Business Review*. https://hbr.org/1988/03/putting-expert-systems-to-work

2 Iansiti, M., & Lakhani, K. (2020, February). Competing in the age of AI: how machine intelligence changes the rules of business. *Harvard Business Review*. https://hbr.org/2020/01/competing-in-the-age-of-ai

3 Rana, N., Chatterjee, S., Dwivedi, Y., & Akter, S. (2021, 1 August). Understanding dark side of artificial intelligence (AI) integrated business analytics: assessing firm's operational inefficiency and competitiveness. *European Journal of Information Systems*. https://doi.org/10.1080/0960085X.2021.1955628

4 Chen, T., Chuang, T., & Nakatani, K. (2016). The perceived business benefit of Cloud computing: an exploratory study. *Journal of International Technology & Information Management*, 25(4), 101–121. 21p.

5 Myeonggil. C. (2019, 1–3 August). The security risks of Cloud computing. 2019 IEEE International Conference on Computational Science and Engineering (CSE) and IEEE International Conference on Embedded and Ubiquitous Computing (EUC), pp. 330–330. doi: 10.1109/CSE/EUC.2019.00069

6 Benaroch, M., Chernobai, A., & Goldstein, J. (2012, December). An internal control perspective on the market value consequences of IT operational risk events. *International Journal of Accounting Information Systems*, 13(4), 357–381. https://doi.org/10.1016/j.acc inf.2012.03.001

7 Tricker, R. (2019). *Corporate Governance: Principles, Policies, Practices*. Oxford University Press. ISBN 978-0-19-870275-7

8 Ruigrok, W., Peck, S. I., & Keller, H. (2006). Board characteristics and involvement in strategic decision making: evidence from Swiss companies. *Journal of Management Studies*, 43(5), 1201–1226. https://doi.org/10.1111/j.1467-6486.2006.00634.x

9 Department of Industry, Science, Energy and Resources. (n.d.). *Australia's Artificial Intelligence Ethics Framework*. www.industry.gov.au/data-and-publications/australias-art ificial-intelligence-ethics-framework

10 World Economic Forum. (n.d.). *AI Ethics Framework*. www.weforum.org/projects/ai-eth ics-framework

11 Google. (n.d.). Responsible AI practices. https://ai.google/responsibilities/responsible-ai-practices/

12 Hambrick, D. C., & Mason, P. A. (1984). Upper echelons: the organization as a reflection of its top managers. *Academy of Management Review*, 9(2), 193–206.

13 Deloitte. (2019). Strategic planning: why you should zoom out and zoom in. www2.deloitte.com/us/en/pages/finance/articles/strategic-insights-zoom-out-zoom-in.html

14 Slovic, P. (1987). Perception of risk. *Science*, 236(4799), 280–285.

15 Dawson D., Schleiger E., Horton J., McLaughlin J., Robinson C., Quezada G., Scowcroft J., & Hajkowicz S. (2019). *Artificial Intelligence: Australia's Ethics Framework*. Data61 CSIRO. Australia.

8

WHAT'S NEXT FOR AI- AND CLOUD-ENABLED INNOVATION IN THE AUSTRALIAN BUSINESS ENVIRONMENT

In addition to the intuitive expectation that Cloud-based technologies will offer major opportunities for business and economic benefits, various quantitative studies have also demonstrated these likely benefits. Most recently, a Deloitte Access Economics report[1] across eight focus markets finds:

- The adoption of Cloud services is forecast to contribute a further $US160 billion to the Asia Pacific economy from 2020 to 2024.
- Public Cloud expenditure will grow at 28% per annum, from $US32.1 billion in 2019 to $US116 billion in 2024, delivering significant productivity (and economic) benefits.
- Industries that comprise 50% of the Asia Pacific economies are facing the most significant levels of disruption that could benefit from greater Cloud adoption.
- Only 10% of businesses across the region believe they have a high level of Cloud-readiness, while 46% are hesitant, or totally unprepared.
- 62% of businesses across the region expect their level of Cloud adoption to grow in three years' time (although just under 30% expect adoption to remain unchanged).

Across a range of emerging technologies (e.g. AI, IoT, AR/VR), a survey within the study highlighted AI as the technology which is expected to be used most on these new platforms.

According to the report authors 'the growing adoption of Cloud services, their ever-increasing sophistication, and the forecasted take-up of Cloud-based applications, suggests that the productivity benefits of Cloud will only increase'.[2]

With that being said, the most significant reason for the authors of this book to dedicate our time and effort into this research and publication was our fear that Australian organisations will miss out on this opportunity.

DOI: 10.4324/9781003255529-8

While Australia's track record of economic growth is a standout across many OECD nations, there are a range of concerning trends underneath the surface. For example, when excluding mining related investments, the private sector has continually made smaller investments into the future. In other words, the data would suggest that there is less and attractive opportunity for future investment in the private sector over time. This trend is particularly concerning, given the significant and ongoing reduction in the cost of capital over the past 10 years. This relates to the worrying lack of 'complexity' in Australia's economy as measured by the Economic Complexity Index,[3] that currently ranks Australia at 87th nation, wedged between Uganda and Burkina Faso. For a longitudinal comparison's sake, according to Harvard's index[4] measures, since 1995, Australia's 'economic complexity' has fallen in national rank from 55th to 86th, while China has risen from 46th to 16th, and Vietnam has risen from 107th to 56th. This indicates important factors about the quality and nature of 'value adding' that occurs in Australia's economy, related indeed to technological development and deployment.

There are a range of possible explanations for these trends, some of which would be extremely concerning for the future of Australia's economic prosperity. For example, is it possible that there simply aren't enough long-term opportunities for innovation?

We believe the most likely explanation, is a risk-aversion or disproportionately high risk-adjusted rate of return, particularly for large scale, technology-enabled transformations. Reserve Bank Chief Economist Luci Ellis says that:

> the AI/machine learning revolution is the first time that an apparent general-purpose technology is actually harder to use, and requires a higher – and rarer – set of skills to operate, than the technologies it seeks to replace. This is not just an issue of having enough people with PhD-level skills in designing the algorithms.

Ellis, 2018[5]

What if we did nothing?

The underlying principles that drive economic and competitive advantage don't change, however the underlying technology and supporting innovations do. By implication, business leaders should view the 'do nothing' option as one in which the organisation is going backwards in relative terms, as competition continues to evolve. One simple and effective way to assess the competitiveness of an organisation, is across the Value Disciplines framework,[6] which defines three critical dimensions of competitive performance: Customer Intimacy, Product Leadership and Operational Excellence.

To illustrate the extent of the disruption we expect, and the risk of the 'do nothing' option, we have listed a limited view of the impacts across these dimensions below:

- *Customer intimacy*: This reflects the organisation's ability to understand and support a customer's needs, in the way they want to be served. AI and Cloud technology has enabled people to be served in consistent ways across multiple channels (e.g. enhanced in-person support, digital self-service, voice and others), and provides a way for organisations to structure much more consistent and holistic approaches to understanding current and future customer needs through internal and third party data.
- *Product leadership*: This reflects the way in which products and services are innovated, to provide better value to customers. As highlighted in the innovation chapter in this book, AI and Cloud technologies are fundamental to a range of types of innovation, for example: enabling connectivity across an ecosystem to provide new services, creating unique and differentiated services.
- *Operational excellence*: This reflects the ability for an organisation to be productive and efficient in its operations. While this book has tended to focus on revenue and margin enhancing transformations, there are many applications of AI and Cloud technology to drive increased efficiency and operational excellence, e.g. proactive maintenance of large and complex assets.

To illustrate the risk of not continually innovating and leveraging these technologies, just imagine what would have happened to an organisation like Netflix had they not disrupted their own mail-based business model through the use of video streaming and recommendation engines. Rather than being the leader in their sector, they too would have gone the way of Blockbuster. Likewise (albeit at a smaller scale), had an organisation like Canningvale (see Chapter 3) not developed a direct-to-consumer channel, it is reasonable to assume that they would have grown more and more distant from the end-consumer and faded away as an organisation.

Is this just a passing fad?

In this context, we wanted to go beyond our current state understanding of the state of how AI and Cloud technology has disrupted business thus far and consider how this impact may change over the coming ten years. Will these technologies be a fad, like the wave of 3D televisions, or will business leaders look back at this period and regret that they didn't act earlier when they were faced with better options to transform their organisations?

The Adapted Gartner Hype Cycle (Figure 8.1) has been a helpful way of thinking through the phases of maturity and adoption for new technologies. While it's an imprecise science, it highlights the need to consider 'where we are at' in terms of adoption, and most importantly, the emotional and performance-related biases that may be holding back an appropriate business investment in new, technology-enabled capabilities. AI and Cloud are now clearly past the hype section of the Figure 8.1 adapted cycle, and they defy the plateau effect when used as transformation agents, according to our case study company participants. This overcoming

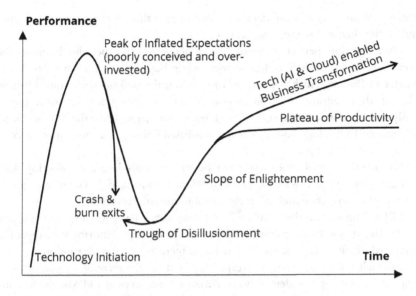

FIGURE 8.1 Adapted Gartner Hype Cycle

of the plateau is built on correctly aggregating innovation, business transformation, and AI/ Cloud enablement as shown in Figure 6.1.

At each point in the cycle, it's easy to develop biases around the relative opportunity and risks associated with a new technology, and as such, we find this to be a helpful way of 'separating the hype from the true opportunity'. We note that the original Gartner[7] hype-cycle acknowledges a plateau, meaning a flattening, that both our Australian and global case study companies overcame, through their continued transformation accomplishments. Our adapted framework considers actual performance (rather than Gartner's 'expectations') as the key parameter on the vertical axis.

Some of the fundamental disruptors are accelerating

Advancements in these technologies has enabled massive business disruption in markets across the world, but it is worth exploring whether these disruptors are receding, stable or accelerating, the latter being our viewpoint. We base this view from the changes on a supply side (increased talent and platform capability) and the demand side (customer expectations, globalised competition and regulatory change).

One of the authors of this article, began his career in a start-up. At that time in Australia, the idea of investing in five years of a double-degree education to work for a 'business' based in a house in Port Melbourne was considered by many of his friends as being a poor life choice. While Melbourne is still far from Silicon Valley (both physically and culturally), the cachet of being a 'techie' and the supporting start-up community in Australia means that finding this talent is orders of magnitude easier than it was, even five years ago.

Over that time period, universities have begun to offer specialised courses for previously niche fields like data science, while business schools have developed Master of Business Analytics courses focussed on the holistic application of these ideas in the 'mainstream' of business skill training. Institutions that were previously only accessible to the elite through multi-year degrees, like the Massachusetts Institute of Technology, began offering web-based training at a much more accessible entry point and price.

Outside the formal education sector, people can self-educate and develop skills through online platforms like Kaggle (a machine learning and data science community) or the many thousands of freely available YouTube tutorials.

SEEK estimate that there will be 27.7% more data science jobs over the next five years.[8] Together with the continued improvement in these platforms, we expect the increased supply of capable talent to drive an increased pace of disruption.

In parallel, we also expect the capability of these the technology platforms to improve, as the hyper-scalers (Google, Amazon Web Services and Microsoft) continue to grow and compete with one another through differentiation. Each of these organisations has a simple business model, in that they have significant investments in R&D and data centres and drive revenue primarily through the increased use of storage and computation on their platforms. This means that their future success is highly dependent on making their platform offer more capabilities than their competitors (e.g. improved AI tooling, more simplified integration between technologies), rather than racing to the bottom on a highly commoditised infrastructure cost comparison. Many analysts[9] expect this to also result in the introduction of more 'vertical Clouds', which offer functionality tailored for specific sectors and their use cases and regulatory requirements. The implication of all this is that the cost of innovation should continue to drop, as the time to develop and scale new business models on these platforms continues to shorten.

While technology platforms have improved, so have the variety of business support services which an organisation can access, to provide a reduced cost of innovation. These include but aren't limited to end-to-end supply chain capability (offshore and in-market), business process outsourcing and customer servicing.

Altogether, these factors make up a range of 'supply drivers' of continued disruption. From a 'demand perspective', it's hard to imagine a scenario where competition and expectations don't continue to increase.

The drivers of these can be framed in a number of ways, for example:

1. *Customer expectations only increase over time*: Consumers have become accustomed to a level of service and capability in the internet era, which previously wasn't possible. When buying a product or service, customers now have a far greater set of options, often accompanied by detailed reviews and tips on how to get the most out of the prospective purchase. The proportion of 'internet natives' will only increase over time, while the COVID pandemic has acted as a catalyst

to rapidly drive adoption of digital technologies. There is no going back to the olden days.

2. *Globalised competition opens up more markets*: Put simply, there is less and less rationale for organisations to limit themselves to competing within their 'home borders'. This is particularly the case for asset light businesses, given the low cost of entry to new markets. What makes us believe that this driver will accelerate over the coming years is the improved access and reduced cost for a variety of data about markets in which you currently don't operate.

3. *Regulatory change is moving in the direction of increased competition*: Open Banking is only a subset of the broader Open Data movement and is deliberately intended to drive competition and portability of user data. The removal of these 'moats' will act as a catalyst for a new generation of start-ups and service enhancements, enabled by AI and Cloud technology. While there is an increased focus on privacy and the protection of user data (like GDPR in the European Union), we believe many organisations will invest beyond compliance to build new capabilities that will support their future growth.

Most uncertainties present opportunities, not threats

There are many areas of uncertainty which will significantly shape the future of global competition and the business models that will make up the successful organisations of the future. It is not difficult to generate a range of possible scenarios:

- A technologically divided world, in which Chinese and Western companies are unable to access one-another's markets. (The 'cancelling' of Russia and decoupling of Russia from the broader financial markets in response to the Ukrainian invasion is a prelude to such a scenario).
- A fundamental change in consumer expectations or regulatory requirements, which limit the use of advertising-based business models or business models whereby personal data is openly collected and sold to third parties.
- The extended (or ending) dominance of the FAANGs (Facebook, Amazon, Apple, Netflix, Google).
- The potential opening or closing of governments and public services to external service provision.

These uncertainties are material and will have an outsized impact in certain sectors (e.g. media). This is a reason for increased investment of management time and capital into strategic planning, not an excuse to pause and 'wait it out'.

Notes

1 Deloitte Access Economics. (n.d). The Cloud imperative, the unmissable opportunity for Asia Pacific. www2.deloitte.com/au/en/pages/technology/articles/Cloud-driven-transfo rmation.html

2 Deloitte Access Economics. (n.d). *The Cloud imperative, the unmissable opportunity for Asia Pacific.* www2.deloitte.com/au/en/pages/technology/articles/Cloud-driven-transformation.html

3 https://en.wikipedia.org/wiki/Economic_Complexity_Index;

4 https://atlas.cid.harvard.edu/rankings

5 rba.gov.au/speeches/2021/sp-ag-2021–11–18.html

6 Treacy, M., & Wiersema, F. (1995). *The Discipline of Market Leaders: Choose Your Customers, Narrow Your Focus, Dominate Your Market.* Addison-Wesley.

7 www.gartner.com/en/documents/3887767/understanding-gartner-s-hype-cycles

8 SEEK. (n.d). *Data Scientist.* www.seek.com.au/career-advice/role/data-scientist

9 Virtana, K. (2021, 28 March). *Industry Clouds could be the next big thing.* Venture Beat. https://venturebeat.com/2021/03/28/industry-Clouds-could-be-the-next-big-thing/

9

SO WHAT SHOULD I DO NOW?

We hope that this book has served both as an illustration of the opportunity for incumbent organisations to transform their business models as well as an inspiration for action. Because the magnitude of these shifts can seem insurmountable, we want to highlight the first steps that we would take to catalyse the transformation process.

Genuinely assess whether your business model will thrive in the future

The disruption across sectors and markets over the past 15 years has been extensive, fundamentally shifting the valuation of many organisations. The biggest winners have been the organisations that can run a platform-based model, which incurs minimal additional cost as new customers come on board, or those with a network-based model, which created a more enduring competitive advantage through a data or intellectual property advantage. Those who have been most disrupted have had expensive distribution models which relied on barriers to entry that no longer exist.

In this context, we believe the first critical step is to assess whether your existing business model will maintain a sufficient competitive advantage to endure into the future. When reviewing your own business model's future suitability, a basic re-questioning of Porter's Five Forces[1] can reveal significant risk and create the burning platform required to change: How will competition in the industry change? How might a potential new entrant gain share? How will the power of suppliers or consumers change? How could substitutes drive competition? Clarity on the specific changes in the competitive environment and market forces, is a critical starting point to drive change in the organisation.

DOI: 10.4324/9781003255529-9

Create new business model options and align on the preferred future choices

Given the evolving and less constrained technology landscape, businesses have a much broader range of business model options which they can economically design and implement. There are various strategy development frameworks available to boards and executives, but in our experience the key for a successful strategy development process is to follow a strategy process which makes a *comprehensive and integrated* set of choices across the organisation's future aspirations, chosen markets ('where to play') and competitive differentiators ('how to win'), capabilities and supporting management systems.

The book *Playing to Win: How Strategy Really Works*[2] provides excellent insights into why each of these choices is a critical part of an organisation's strategy and on the strategy development process itself. Articulated more simply, the successful future strategy needs to be more than a set of high-level feel-good statements – it must make specific, hard choices that impact the day-to-day workings of the organisation.

Take a broader lens to your innovation approach

Twenty years ago, few people could have accurately predicted which products and services would be provided by our leading organisations, let alone the ways in which we now consume these services. To that end, nothing has changed.

Looking forward, the candidates for business model innovations are numerous, and increasingly involve collaboration with third parties and complex ecosystems.

As described in Chapter 6, the most sustainable and high impact transformations create value by combining transformation with innovation and technology enablement. While many organisations have functional silos that can execute on one or two of these priorities, we believe that there is a general need to uplift the focus on innovation (without descending into 'innovation theatre') within most organisations.

Objectively self-assess your ability to transform

As competitive intensity increases and the underlying drivers of innovation become more complex, the skills and capabilities required to manage a business model transformation require more of the organisation. The capability framework referenced in Chapter 2 (Figure 2.1), is designed in a way that should enable self-assessment and self-reflection, on whether your organisation is well set up with the range of skills and capabilities required to successfully navigate through all stages of these transformations. The authors of this book have decades of experience across consulting, academia and industry. In our experience, many organisations will be quite effective in two or three of the required capabilities. Unfortunately, few are 'born ready' for this challenging new age across all required skills. Being clear about where these gaps are, and what needs to be done to close those gaps, is critical to the success of these transformations.

Raise the prioritisation and shared responsibility for technology-enabled innovation

When writing this book, we took great care to focus on 'technology enabled' rather than 'technology driven' transformation. Our research, and our own experiences, have highlighted the risks and challenges of leaving the technology function with the responsibility to transform the entire organisation. Whilst we are not opposed to having the appointed leader of these initiatives be from a technology function, we strongly believe that there is a need for the whole organisation to understand the way in which they want to change their business model, and what they can do to better shape and guide that transformation.

In particular, we want to highlight the importance of the different roles played across the organisation:

- *For Boards and C-Suite members:* We suggest you thoroughly assess a range of potential strategies and ensure that the selected strategy is the one which is best suited to the future operating environment. This assessment includes the support that will be required once the strategy is selected, up-lifting capabilities and risk management, investing in new skills, and supporting the experimentation and evolution of the business model through its up and downs.
- *For the top-management team:* We suggest you need to consider how to drive change in the ways of working, not just make an ask of the technology function. This includes shifting the mentality, skill sets and operating rhythms that are expected in this changing environment.
- *For the core of the business:* We suggest you invest in up-lifting and reskilling team members so that they are able to support the organisation in its new business model. This will undoubtably require major changes in operating models to break down silos and investment in digital technologies to empower staff to make better decisions more efficiently, as well as a broad change in investments in training and developing staff over the trajectory of their careers.

Last but not least

The fundamental purpose of this book and its supporting research is to provide confidence and guide the revitalisation of Australian businesses through the fore-seeable future. Our hope is that we're able to inspire business leaders to go beyond thinking, and to take action in the real world.

To that end, we plan on revisiting this study in the coming years, and hope that we can add to our insights and case studies with many more success stories. We have established a web forum (www.bizmodeltransformation.com) to capture these stories and promote the discussions. We would love to hear more from our readers and welcome any feedback or questions you might have.

Notes

1 Porter, M. (1998). *Competitive Strategy: Techniques for Analyzing Industries and Competitors.* New York: Free Press.
2 Lafley, A., & Martin, R. (2013). *Playing to Win: Introduction, How Strategy Really Works.* Harvard Business Review Press.

APPENDICES

Appendix 1: Diagnostic questions for antecedent capabilities

In considering whether your business transformation can benefit from AI and/or Cloud, the following diagnostic can be a starting point in considering your 'organisational readiness'.

APPENDIX 1: TABLE A1 Antecedent capabilities (internal behaviours)

Antecedent capability	Inhibitor	Moderate benefit	Significant benefit
Proactive leadership	Board/top management team does not support the initiative	Top management provides resources and permission, but is not actively involved	Proactive, bold and committed leadership seeking a pivot of business model and shaping a culture of change acceptance and innovation
Innovation culture	Significant organisational culture and structural barriers to innovation	Innovation is valued by senior members of the firm	Commitment to embracing a culture of innovation within the organisation that supports employees to drive, embrace and amplify the change required to adopt new business models and ways of working
Exploration and Exploitation	Excessive focus on either exploration (find out the possible) or exploitation (making current numbers) inhibits an organisation's ability to envisage and deliver business model transformation	Some organisational recognition (outside of the scope of this specific initiative) of the importance of conducting both exploration activity and exploitation activity	The ability and willingness to strike an appropriate balance between exploration of (and investment in) new value pools with the exploitation of core value pools through existing assets, products and services
Risk tolerance	Change is inhibited due to career risk concerns for failure	Explicit risk tolerance positions are developed and communicated, and individuals work within those risk tolerances	Organisational willingness and supporting infrastructure (processes, governance) to accept increased but appropriate risk associated with major transformations – 'nothing ventured, nothing gained'

APPENDIX 1: TABLE A2 Antecedent capabilities (internal capabilities)

Antecedent capability	Inhibitor	Moderate benefit	Significant benefit
Strategic Process Strength	Initiative inhibited by cumbersome, inflexible or chaotic decision-making process	A clear process for making and executing decisions exists, and the initiative was executed within this process	The presence of effective, rapid and responsive decision-making mechanisms that enable the development, realisation and refinement of strategic pivots and major transformations
Foundational Data and IS	Legacy data/IS platforms and processes prevent material changes to business model – stuck with high-cost incremental improvement	Legacy data/IS platforms able to support significant changes to business model OR acceptance that data/IS platforms and processes will need to change	Data availability, information architecture and systems readiness that enables the rapid design and deployment of innovative technologies without impediments or burdens associated with legacy IT landscape, OR A willingness to leapfrog to an entirely new platform
Market & Customer Sensing	Limited focus on sensing current and future customer needs and market directions	Effective market and customer sensing mechanisms that allow organisations to identify, assess and respond to current and emerging needs across the ecosystem	Effective market and customer sensing mechanisms that allow organisations to identify, assess and respond to current and emerging needs across the ecosystem

APPENDIX 1: TABLE A3 Antecedent capabilities (external capabilities)

Antecedent capability	Inhibitor	Moderate benefit	Significant benefit
Opportunity/ Threat Drivers	Limited visibility or belief that there will be any material change to an organisation's ability to sustain their current competitive advantage into the future	Some general awareness that technology and other disruptions might influence an organisation's basis of competitive advantage	Leadership considers that discrete market disruptions are likely to impact the organisation's ability to sustain their current competitive advantage into the future and is focussed on getting ahead of those disruptions
Industry Dynamism	Monopolistic or 'mandated provider' models that reinforce continuation of today's practices	A low level of competitive intensity within an organisation's wider industry and a low pace at which new services and products are displacing traditional/ legacy revenue streams	A high level of competitive intensity within an organisation's wider industry and a rapid pace at which new services and products are displacing traditional legacy revenue streams

Appendix 2: Further references, definitions and background research

Business models

There has been considerable research conducted on Business Model Innovation (BMI), it's impact on organisations and success factors associated with implementation. While there are many definitions of BMI in prior research, we use the definition by Snihur and Zott[1] that refers to BMI as 'the introduction of a business model that is novel (in terms of its content, structure, or governance) to the product market space in which the venture competes'. They write that firms can innovate their business models by introducing novel elements in each of these core elements. It should also be noted there are several definitions of a business model itself. Teece[2] describes business models as the architecture that defines how an organisation delivers value to customers and generates profits. In their work to understand Cloud-enabled BMI and transformation, Muhic and Bengtsson[3] note that there are various motivations and triggers to BMI. In many cases, firms decide to adapt new technology such as Cloud in chasing common benefits such as lower cost, scalability and standardisation of processes.

AI and impact on BMI

AI technology is seen as an increasingly pervasive technology that organisations will need to adopt to keep up with competitors. A recent survey by Deloitte[4] revealed that a majority of AI adopters believe that it will substantially transform their organisation and industry over the next three years. The report finds that this acceleration of adoption might be driven by the proliferation of data science and machine learning platforms, greater computing power and improved algorithms, and that organisations are, in general, able to access these technologies easier than before, and create value using them.

Similarly, in a report by ESI Thought Lab,[5] over 60% of executives indicated their belief that AI was crucial for the future of their businesses due to its ability to create cost efficiencies, drive faster business growth and transform customer and employee experiences. The COVID-19 pandemic has further accelerated AI adoption due to the sudden spike in online use across every industry, and firms' requirements to process and analyse data quickly.

However, the current wave of adoption has seen organisations focussed primarily on utilising AI for improving existing business models rather than creating new ones. The Deloitte survey mentioned above also reached this conclusion and found that this was likely due to the heavy emphasis on efficiency-related benefits in current AI business use cases. More research is required on how businesses can use AI to truly transform entire business models or create new ones.

AI or Cloud impacts on business transformation

As can be inferred by the significant literature on business model innovation, there are a number of ways that an organisation can undertake BMI. AI and Cloud are just two means that leaders can adopt as drivers of their transformation, but a number of other technologies or other means could also be chosen. Teece found that while it is difficult to invent an entirely new business model in a highly competitive market, organisations that do so are periodically enabled by technological progress. [6] Consider iTunes. For example, they write that the internet enabled a significant wave of innovation, not just to industries shifting online but creation of entirely new models through network effects, such as peer to peer and other marketplaces. EBay, Twitter and Facebook are examples.

Cloud computing and impact on BMI

Cloud computing technology has been a significant driver of transformation for many years now, Akter et al.[7] write that as business across the work focus on lowering infrastructure costs, finding new revenue streams and digitising their operations, Cloud technology is a key enabler for these changes. In particular, Cloud computing has proven to be a strong enabler for BMI in new ventures. Alrokayan[8] found that Cloud computing not only enables a level of agility in value creation that supports faster adaptation of market needs using agile approaches, but also helps organisations make better decisions due to improved ability to collect data and measure performance.

Newcomers versus incumbents: who explores and who exploits?

It is important to note that this factor is quite different for newcomers than incumbents. As newcomers do not have existing certainties to exploit, their initial choices are geared towards exploring new opportunities and are heavily influenced by their founders. This is seen in work by Snihur and Zott,[9] who looked at early-stage companies to understand what characteristics founders have, which lead to higher instances of BMI and their goal of exploring opportunities. They argue that founders' behaviour, thinking style and decision-making patterns help shape their organisation's BMI. Founders are seen to perform cross-industry scans to search for inspiration to design novel business models, engage in active analysis of industry players, leverage their ownership and expertise to influence BMI, and help facilitate the implementation of exploration through centralised decision making leading to more novel solutions.

Other factors that influence a firm's ability to explore new opportunities such as BMT include personnel turnover and environmental turbulence. March[10] found that having a modest level of personnel turnover actually helps increase exploration without reducing organisational knowledge due to the gains from diversity of experience, and that increasing environmental turbulence in the market makes it difficult for exploration to occur within short periods of time.

Christensen et al.[11] also refer to this balance when discussing disruptive innovation. They find that managers use disruption theory to help make a strategic choice between a sustaining path or a disruptive one. When faced with a new entrant, incumbents must accelerate their own innovations to either offer even better products or services or acquire the entrant in order to defend their business.

Exploring and exploiting

Deloitte[12] surveyed a number of adopters of AI who ranked managing AI-related risks as their top challenge for initiatives, alongside data management and AI integration challenges. The survey found that only four in ten adopters believed their organisations were 'fully prepared' to address these risks. These were potential strategic, operational and ethical risks associated with adopting AI. Being adequately prepared to manage these types of risks is therefore a crucial antecedent to BMT. The same study also found that cybersecurity, AI failures, misuse of personal data and regulatory uncertainty are also key risks that organisations face when adopting AI. If organisations are less able or prepared to manage these risks, it may affect the likelihood of significantly transforming their business model using these technologies. Just over half of the participants in the Deloitte study also indicated that these emerging risks and negative public perceptions of AI has led to slowing down of AI adoption by their organisations. This also brings to light that there are various types of risks associated with BMT, and organisations should take a nuanced approach as to which risks may be acceptable versus not. For example, the aforementioned report by ESI Thought Lab[13] found that while over 60% of insurance firms know of the importance of AI for efficiencies in underwriting and administrative processes, the regulatory uncertainty, cybersecurity risks and ethical concerns have collectively forced the industry to progress more cautiously.

Some risk naturally accompanies significant disruption or innovation of business models. Lee et al.[14] found that if there is a culture of conservatism that solely focusses attention on exploiting rather than exploring, it is unlikely to lead to innovation. They argue that BMI requires leaders to allow a culture of taking risks and enable exposure to new ideas. On the other hand, business history is littered with cases of firms that burned too much cash seeking an innovation edge, and that never achieved a return on investment. This antecedent factor can be summarised as getting the balance right between too little and too much risk taking.

Strategic process strength

An important enabler of BMT is the quality and maturity of decision-making processes and strategy development strength within organisations. Miller,[15] when examining the organisational traits between successful and unsuccessful firms, found that strategy-making in successful firms was accompanied by use of controls, scanning, delegation and a lack of impedance from bureaucracy. Successful firms were also more adaptive, innovative, and analytical in strategy development, and more conscious of the environments in which they operated. O'Reilly and Tushman[16] further expanded on the importance of strategic process strength when discussing drivers of organisational ambidexterity and categorised them into three components: sensing, seizing and reconfiguring. First, they found that organisations with ambidexterity employ a range of processes to sense opportunities and threats and devote resources to keep up to date on technological innovations and competitive intelligence. This is also embedded in the culture of the organisation to encourage a culture of debate and commitment from senior leaders to encourage long-term thinking and exploration. Once opportunities are identified, they found that processes have to be in place to assemble complementary assets and allocate appropriate resources at the right time so as to seize and execute opportunities without falling into decision traps that many organisations face. Lastly, O'Reilly and Tushman point out that long-term success and competitive advantage requires that leaders continuously push the boundaries and make tough decisions to move investment away from mature, declining services to emerging growth opportunities. They argue that it is not the decision separating exploratory and exploitative structures within the organisation but rather the processes by which these two areas are integrated that enable organisations to achieve this long term, sustainable competitive advantage and therefore, we add, enable them to confidently take on BMT.

Market/customer focus

Christensen et al.[17] wrote that a firm's ability and proclivity to change is directly impacted by its current customers who provide revenue today and therefore, help the firm survive. As such, incumbents focus on the needs of existing customers and work on innovating for them to ensure they are retained. However, their research also found that when incumbents become solely or overly focussed on existing customers, their internal processes become too rigid to pivot towards disruptive innovation. Leaders must, therefore, place an acute focus on the customer, both current and future, with the aim of undertaking BMI that will enhance future and new sources for revenue streams and certainly go beyond just reducing costs.

In their study of coping strategies for uncertainty in BMI, Schneckenberg et al.[18] also note that customer centricity plays an integral role in aligning the firm's value proposition to customer needs and behaviours, leading to a greater likelihood of higher profits. Their research indicated that technological changes inherent in Cloud solutions enable organisations to flex their business models to address previously unknown customer problems. They suggest there are three components of customer centricity to support decision making of BMI: identification of unknown customer needs, understanding how customers use products or services, and a thorough emphasis on customer-facing business processes. For BMI, an acute understanding of the customer combined with new technology can be a powerful frame for future, new value propositions.

Data and IS readiness

This systems readiness enables organisations to undertake BMI without starting from scratch. Reim et al.[19] found that it is not just data but the right types of data and digital processes that are a prerequisite to implementing AI. They point out that rapid changes in business models require agility to scale up and down, with that adaptability coming from a foundational or minimum set of information system capabilities.

In addition to the foundational system capabilities, innovations in Cloud- and AI-based technology also require an up-lift in the skills of the technology team themselves. Wamba-Taguimdje et al.[20] note that multiple elements must be in place for success of AI in an organisation including data management, having the right domain knowledge and technologies. They found that information systems leadership can play a strong role in facilitating transformation as they must make the right decisions that enable the above capability elements to be in place, whether it be through internal capabilities or from external suppliers. The information system infrastructure must also be flexible to scale as demand changes. In a nutshell, an antecedent, perhaps best considered as a prerequisite of effective Cloud- or AI-based transformation, must be to be well organised at the more mundane levels of IS capability and maturity.

Notes

1 Snihur, Y., & Zott, C. (2020). The genesis and metamorphosis of novelty imprints: How business model innovation emerges in young ventures. *Academy of Management Journal*, 63(2), 554–583. https://doi.org/10.5465/amj.2017.0706
2 Teece, D. J. (2018). Business models and dynamic capabilities. *Long Range Planning*, 51(1), 40–49. https://doi.org/10.1016/j.lrp.2017.06.007
3 Muhic, M., & Bengtsson, L. (2019). Dynamic capabilities triggered by Cloud sourcing: A stage-based model of business model innovation. *Review of Managerial Science*. https://doi.org/10.1007/s11846-019-00372-1
4 Deloitte. (2020). Thriving in the era of persuasive AI. www2.deloitte.com/content/dam/Deloitte/cn/Documents/about-deloitte/deloitte-cn-dtt-thriving-in-the-era-of-persuasive-ai-en-200819.pdf
5 ESI Thought Lab. (2020). *Driving ROI through AI* (p. 71). https://econsultsolutions.com/wp-content/uploads/2020/09/ESITL_Driving-ROI-through-AI_FINAL_September-2020.pdf
6 Teece, D. J. (2018). Business models and dynamic capabilities. *Long Range Planning*, 51(1), 40–49. https://doi.org/10.1016/j.lrp.2017.06.007
7 Akter, S., Michael, K., Uddin, M. R., McCarthy, G., & Rahman, M. (2020). Transforming business using digital innovations: The application of AI, blockchain, cloud and data analytics. *Annals of Operations Research*. https://doi.org/10.1007/s10479-020-03620-w

8 Alrokayan, M. (2017). *Understanding how Cloud computing enables business model innovation in start-up companies* [Melbourne]. http://hdl.handle.net/11343/216075

9 Snihur, Y., & Zott, C. (2020). The genesis and metamorphosis of novelty imprints: How business model innovation emerges in young ventures. *Academy of Management Journal*, 63(2): 554–583. https://doi.org/10.5465/amj.2017.0706

10 March, J. G. (1991). Exploration and exploitation in organizational learning. *Organization Science*, 2(1), 71–87.

11 Christensen, C. M., Raynor, M., & McDonald, R. (2015). What is disruptive innovation? *Harvard Business Review*, 93(12), 44–53.

12 Deloitte. (2020). Thriving in the era of persuasive AI. www2.deloitte.com/content/dam/Deloitte/cn/Documents/about-deloitte/deloitte-cn-dtt-thriving-in-the-era-of-persuasive-ai-en-200819.pdf

13 ESI Thought Lab. (2020). *Driving ROI through AI* (p. 71). https://econsultsolutions.com/wp-content/uploads/2020/09/ESITL_Driving-ROI-through-AI_FINAL_September-2020.pdf

14 Lee, J., Suh, T., Roy, D., & Baucus, M. (2019). Emerging technology and business model innovation: The case of artificial intelligence. *Journal of Open Innovation: Technology, Market, and Complexity*, 5(3), 44. https://doi.org/10.3390/joitmc5030044

15 Miller, D. (1975). Towards a contingency theory of strategy formulation. *Academy of Management Proceedings*, 64–66.

16 O'Reilly, C. A., & Tushman, M. L. (2008). Ambidexterity as a dynamic capability: Resolving the innovator's dilemma. *Research in Organizational Behavior*, 28, 185–206. https://doi.org/10.1016/j.riob.2008.06.002

17 Christensen, C. M., Raynor, M., & McDonald, R. (2015). What is disruptive innovation? *Harvard Business Review*, 93(12), 44–53.

18 Schneckenberg, D., Velamuri, V. K., Comberg, C., & Spieth, P. (2017). Business model innovation and decision making: Uncovering mechanisms for coping with uncertainty. *R&D Management*, 47(3), 404–419. https://doi.org/10.1111/radm.12205

19 Reim, W., Åström, J., & Eriksson, O. (2020). Implementation of Artificial Intelligence (AI): A roadmap for business model innovation. *AI*, 1(2), 180–191. https://doi.org/10.3390/ai1020011

20 Wamba-Taguimdje, S.-L., Fosso Wamba, S., Kala Kamdjoug, J. R., & Tchatchouang Wanko, C. E. (2020). Influence of artificial intelligence (AI) on firm performance: The business value of AI-based transformation projects. *Business Process Management Journal*, 26(7), 1893–1924. https://doi.org/10.1108/BPMJ-10–2019–0411

Other sources of interest

Augier, M., & Teece, D. J. (2009). Dynamic capabilities and the role of managers in business strategy and economic performance. *Organization Science*, 20(2): 410–421. https://doi.org/10.1287/orsc.1090.0424

Carr, N. M. (2003). IT doesn't matter. *Harvard Business Review*, (May): 41–49.

Kim, S. K., & Min, S. (2015). Business model innovation performance: When does adding a new business model benefit an incumbent?: Business model innovation performance. *Strategic Entrepreneurship Journal*, 9(1): 34–57. https://doi.org/10.1002/sej.1193

Montealegre, R., Iyengar, K., & Sweeney, J. (2019). Understanding ambidexterity: Managing contradictory tensions between exploration and exploitation in the evolution of digital infrastructure. *Journal of the Association for Information Systems*, 20(5): 647–680. https://doi.org/10.17705/1jais.00547

Saebi, T., Lien, L., & Foss, N. J. (2017). What drives business model adaptation? The impact of opportunities, threats and strategic orientation. *Long Range Planning, 50*(5): 567–581. https://doi.org/10,1016/j.lrp.2016.06.006

Tallon, P. P., Queiroz, M., Coltman, T., & Sharma, R. (2019). Information technology and the search for organizational agility: A systematic review with future research possibilities. *The Journal of Strategic Information Systems, 28*(2): 218–237. https://doi.org/10.1016/j.jsis.2018.12.002

Vandermerwe, S. & Rada, J. (1988). Servitization of business: Adding value by adding services: www.sciencedirect.com/science/article/abs/pii/0263237388900333

INDEX

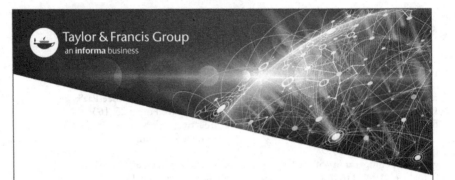

Printed in the United States
by Baker & Taylor Publisher Services

Printed in the United States
by Baker & Taylor Publisher Services